Ready, Set, READ

Building a Love of Letters and Literacy through Fun Phonics Activities

Janet Chambers

Zephyr Press

Chicago

Ready, Set, Read: Building a Love of Letters and Literacy through Fun Phonics Activities
Grades PreK–3
© 2003 by Janet Chambers

Printed in the United States of America

ISBN: 1-56976-151-5

Design and Production: Dan Miedaner
Cover: Dan Miedaner
Photographs and Illustrations: Janet Chambers
Author photograph on page 222: Doris Hollyhand

Published by:
Zephyr Press
814 North Franklin Street
Chicago, Illinois 60610
(800) 232-2187
www.zephyrpress.com

≋ Zephyr Press is a registered trademark of Chicago Review Press, Inc.

Library of Congress Cataloging-in-Publication Data

Chambers, Janet, 1959-
    Ready, set, read : building a love of letters and literacy through fun phonics activities /
Janet Chambers.
        p. cm.
    Includes bibliographical references (p.) and index.
    ISBN 1-56976-151-5 (alk. Paper)
    1. Reading (Early childhood) 2. Reading—Phonetic method. I. Title.

LB1139.5.R43 C53 2002
372.46'5—dc21   2002023850

Contents

Acknowledgments

With special thanks to JC, Samantha, Harrison,
my parents—the ultimate teachers—and everyone who
has actively encouraged me to take this further.

Preface

How I Came to Believe in Multisensory Education

A path of varied teaching positions and encounters during my 20 years of teaching has revealed to me the huge benefits of early multisensory education. I will share a few key events. Immediately after graduating from the University of London, I began teaching elementary-aged children in the suburbs. It was a wonderful job, but my train fares across the city were costing me just about every penny I was earning. Reluctantly, I looked for a teaching position closer to home. Although there were very few openings in the early 1980s in England, there was a vacancy for an English teacher in my area, so I rushed to apply. I soon discovered why the job was open.

The school was a huge public school, encompassing middle and upper age ranges (11 to 18 years old). The unfortunate reputation of the town in which it was located was known even in mainland Europe. I was soon facing classes of 36 adolescents from the "bottom" classes—those whose expectations of themselves were nil, who did not want to be there, and to whom a traditional book-and-paper education had become meaningless.

Everything I learned reinforced the message that we need to introduce the skills of literacy early, using a meaningful, multisensory approach.

Take, for example, the 14-year-old boys everyone (including the boys themselves) had given up on. Neither they, nor the class above, were expected to take any of their national examinations. There were glue sniffers in the group; more than once, I had to stick a boy's head out the window when he turned up with spots around his mouth, slurred speech, completely out of it. All of the boys were well known by the local police. I was merely expected to babysit.

It would have been a waste of time to put pencils and paper in their hands or give them books to read. I would have ended up with a riot caused as an avoidance strategy against something with which they could not cope. I decided to bring in newspapers, scissors, and glue and let them create ransom notes, which developed into "wanted" posters with pictures and descriptions of criminals. The boys loved it. The spellings were atrocious, but who cared? They had created something with language.

The following week we made picture words, drawing the letters to reflect the meaning of the word. I showed them examples using such words as *tall* and *cloud*. They produced words such as *blood* and *death,* but at least they were thinking, creating, and enjoying language. Above all, they were achieving—all because the work was multisensory and relevant to them. They were stimulated by a hands-on experience, just as very young children are.

Gradually I introduced reading and writing activities, keeping it all as multisensory as I could. They did not fear the work. They did not put up a destructive barrier. The art teacher realized what was happening and opened his supply closet to me to help enhance the fun and creativity. At the end of two years, most of the boys had built up a folder of work sufficient for the continual assessment needed to enter their national examination. All of the boys who took the exam passed.

A few months later, the boys had already left school and were laboring on a local building site. I was pregnant and due to leave school in a few days' time. One lunchtime those boys walked across town and into my classroom in their big muddy boots just to say thank you. They had passed an exam, achieving something they were not expected to do, and they were just beginning to appreciate the importance of that piece of paper. That lunchtime goes down as a highlight of my teaching career and a tribute to multisensory language work.

A few years later, I was offered the position of special-needs coordinator in an elementary school. I devised programs for children with special needs, taught these children individually or in groups, and advised classroom teachers and aides on how to adapt work for each child's learning difficulty. I worked closely with parents, learning about each child's background and experiences. Everything I learned reinforced the message that we need to introduce the skills of literacy early, using a meaningful, multisensory approach. To be meaningful, the approach must be relevant to the child's world. Retracing missed developmental learning steps using multisensory techniques certainly helped bridge gaps with these children.

Natalie, for example, was a tiny eight-year-old for whom reading and writing were a meaningless code that she had no chance of breaking. For two years, Natalie's teachers had been trying, unsuccessfully, to teach her to write her name. I gave her a tray of powdered soap. Using her finger in the powder, she was able to write her name correctly. Natalie needed to go back to raw feeling and retrace some of her tactile development. The pencil had been a barrier and a hindrance. Some earlier stage of development had been missed, and Natalie needed more time with multisensory language experiences before she could pick up a pencil to write.

When a child has difficulty with reading and writing, the problem can compound as she gets older, spilling out to become a bigger issue than coping with the skills of literacy alone. The further she gets behind in school, the more severe the consequences of having difficulties become. The child's attitude of resistance becomes more stubborn with the development of a negative mindset, and she develops more complex avoidance strategies as she raises the barriers of a destructive self-fulfilling prophecy. This misery could be avoided in many cases by relevant early childhood stimulation and activities that do not require the ability to work in abstract terms.

Writing can be another form of play.

In 1996, my family moved to Alabama, and soon afterward I was offered a job at Tuscaloosa Academy teaching three- and four-year-olds. We can provide children of this age with the tools for literacy early enough that it need never become a problem later on. Now there are four-year-olds in my class who can read and are well on their way to independent writing. They play a lot, and learning is fun—in their eyes just another super experience or discovery. The secret is in providing a well-planned multisensory approach appropriate to the developmental age of the child. ❦

Introduction

"Teach Me to Teach"

I have been fortunate enough to attend a variety of workshops and seminars in education. One always meets a good mix of people at these functions, people with a wide variety of experiences and qualifications. This is especially true when the workshop focuses on early childhood. There is always a mix of daycare providers, teachers, and university students. All have so much to offer and are so eager to improve. These are genuine, caring people. After all, let's face it: Nobody ever went into early childhood education for the money!

At these various workshops and seminars, I am struck by the frequency of the comment, "I wish they would teach us how to teach." I even heard this comment made recently by two graduates with double degrees in early childhood and special education. My heart went out to these women. Here they were, intelligent, ready to work, and ready to give but without the practical guidance necessary for them to use their talents to best advantage.

In many ways, one does develop one's own style of teaching with experience; but on too many occasions, the first teaching experiences can be daunting if the teacher is not equipped with some guidelines about how to work to best effect. How many good, qualified people drop out of teaching early on for that reason? How many never have the chance to build up valuable experience? And why should classes of children have to put up with teachers learning how to teach through trial and error because nobody showed them how to teach?

It is with new teachers in mind that I have written guidelines on how to introduce reading and writing in a multisensory way.

It is with these teachers in mind that I have written guidelines on how to introduce reading and writing in a multisensory way. I hope that the tried, tested, and successful methods of introducing literacy early on, as described in this book, can provide the stepping stone some of these new teachers need so that they can then go on to develop even more ideas.

Pressure? What Pressure?

Many believe that children who start on the road to reading and writing too young will get burned out. I feel sure that this is only applicable if too much pressure is placed on measured achievements too early, and if there is too much emphasis put on the secretarial skills of reading and writing. The whole message behind my method of teaching reading and writing to such young children is that it is introduced as a pressure-free, enjoyable multisensory experience. The initial aim is not to stretch children to earlier reading and writing—although this is a huge benefit in many cases—but to eliminate any developmental gaps that too often develop if the early stages of reading readiness are not covered thoroughly enough or early enough at the child's optimum learning time.

Reading and writing can be just as fun as playing in the sand.

Visitors to my classroom could never say that I am pressuring the children. They are always very busy, but they are never under pressure. Children love to be busy. The activities and ideas in this book provide lots of fun, busy experiences that have the added bonus of opening up a child's basic understanding of the written word.

The lives of my early readers and writers have been greatly enriched by their fun experiences. They are enjoying an extra freedom early in life. To be able to do what older people can do is a huge boost to self-esteem, and we all know the positive effect that feeling good about ourselves has in our lives.

All work should be based not on age, but on readiness.

All work should be based not on age, but on readiness. Children vary in their rates of progress, and there will always be times of apparent plateaus. Learning is a multiskilled process, and progress may not always be clearly visible at certain points. Some three-year-olds will be able to work happily on phonic activities, while some six-year-olds will work best on purely physical crafts and activities. Some three-year-olds will immediately show evidence that they understand the idea of the sound; others will not. As long as you offer a hands-on experience that any young child will enjoy, there is no pressure, and there is no failure. Everyone has a good time. Negative emotions such as embarrassment, uncertainty, and humiliation must play no part in the introduction of written language. Three-year-olds who do not demonstrate that they are ready to take in sound work may surprise you later. You have sown the seeds, vital seeds that can facilitate a deep and thorough comprehension of written language.

How to Use This Book

This book offers step-by-step instructions on how to introduce literacy skills to even very young children using a multisensory approach. The aim is for children to achieve a thorough comprehension of how the print on the page, and indeed words all around us, relate to spoken sounds. To be most effective, the methods utilize the types of activities children naturally employ to discover and learn, such as curious exploration.

Chapter 1: Child Development, Brain Research, and Multisensory Learning investigates how brain research and traditional child development studies support the benefits of multisensory teaching. If we take cues from how children learn naturally, then utilize that knowledge in our teaching methods, our message will be meaningful to each child. This chapter also shows that research reveals the positive results of an early start. The baseline of neural connectivity can be enhanced through early enrichment.

Chapter 2: Introducing the Alphabet provides guidelines on how to introduce the sounds of the alphabet. Teachers organize their classrooms and routines in their own ways. These tips will help you plan in order to use the multisensory activities effectively within your own schedule. For greater efficiency, this chapter also will help you find ways to make connections with particular sounds at times other than just "sound work" times, as well as ways to encourage even the busiest of parents to contribute to a child's understanding of sounds.

Chapter 3: Multisensory Alphabet Activities shows you how to introduce each sound in a novel group-discovery session through a series of activities for each letter of the alphabet. The activities utilize novelty, discovery, and physical involvement appropriate to the learning world of the young child. A variety of multisensory activities and follow-up tasks, including craft and movement sessions for every letter, are detailed in this chapter.

Chapter 4: Parallel Extension Activities describes activities that you can try throughout the year, at the same time as you introduce the sounds to the children using the chapter 3 activities. Although the bulk of this book focuses on learning the sounds of letters, this chapter introduces learning through sight-recognition, and gives children their first experiences with writing.

I highly recommend that you read through chapters 1 and 2 before starting on the activities in chapters

3 and 4. Chapter 1 will give you background on why the multisensory approach works, and chapter 2 provides valuable advice on each component of the activities in chapters 3 and 4. Finally, chapter 4 activities are best if done in parallel to the chapter 3 activities, rather than after the children have completed the activities in chapter 3, so it's a good idea to read through this last chapter before deciding how you wish to proceed with the rest of the activities in the book. Above all, this book is meant to be used flexibly, so you can adapt the activities to your own schedule, classroom setup, methods, and, above all, the individual children in your class. ❦

The big feely phonic letters in chapter 3 help make learning seem like play.

1

Child Development, Brain Research, and Multisensory Learning

Why Use a Multisensory Approach?

If friends show you photographs they took on their vacation, you show polite interest. If they show you photographs of a place you have actually been to, you probably will have genuine interest. Reference points aid our recall of something we understand. If we look through our own photographs, they conjure up a moment, a feeling, an experience. Each photograph can bring to mind people, places, sounds, sights, smells, tastes, emotions, and other memories. The photograph is a trigger, a starting point, to retrieve a real experience.

Teachers are faced with many opportunities and challenging responsibilities. Our primary job is to provide education in the form of meaningful experi-ences. If our teaching does not mean something to our students, we are wasting both our time and theirs. We cannot rely on books and flat images to provide the kinds of hands-on experiences that will spur our students' growth.

Experts in brain theory believe that emotional experiences stimulate the brain, and this in turn helps us to retrieve stored information efficiently. If the emotional experiences are positive, learning will be a happy experience (Jensen 1998). We all know that if we feel good about something, we'll want to do it again. Our young children are natural scientists; they thrive on pleasurable hands-on discoveries. A well-prepared multisensory approach in the classroom can provide such positive, stimulating learning experiences.

We can help children gain confidence to take new steps in learning.

I will take this one step further. Multisensory methods can be used to teach even very young children how to read and write. If we do this properly, we can prevent a huge amount of fear from building up in association with the written word.

After years of teaching older students, I now teach three-, four-, and five-year-old children in a prekindergarten class. Generally people are respectful and polite when they learn that I am a teacher. Then comes the question, "What age do you teach?" I have been horrified to discover that when I reveal the age of my students, the questioner's reaction changes to one of dismissal; some have even exclaimed to me, "Oh, not a real teacher!" The general perception of teachers of very young children is that we are mere babysitters; my day must be spent crawling around on the floor, just playing.

It is true that my day is full of happiness, and a good deal of it is spent crawling around on the floor, but I work just as hard as when I taught older students, and in fact, I spend more time now on preparation because I cover a wider variety of activities during the school day—and three-year-olds are not that great at waiting! A three-year-old may take 15 seconds to paint a story, whereas an older child may stay absorbed for 15 minutes writing an account.

Far from being dismissed, teachers of preschoolers should be hailed as the scene setters. This young and tender age is when it is all happening. We are helping to develop an incredible potential. A three-year-old is receptive, generally uncontaminated with negative emotions, eager and ready to learn. Just consider how much a baby has to master in the first two years of life. The rate at which he makes progress in physical skills, language, and relationships is astounding. If we continued to discover and learn at that rate, we could all make meaningful conversation with the likes of Einstein, even on an off day!

Our primary job is to provide education in the form of meaningful experiences.

A newborn has more than a trillion neural connections in the brain. At its peak, the embryo is generating brain cells at a rate of 250,000 each minute, or 15 million each hour. Soon after birth, the brain starts to prune away unneeded cells and billions of unused connections. How do we grow cells rather than lose cells? The same way we would grow anything—we feed those cells. The food the brain likes best is challenging sensory stimulation (Jensen 1998). We, as teachers of the young, need to ensure that the nutrition we provide is packed with a wide range of wholesome goodness: lots of positive multisensory adventures.

Child Development Studies

Let's take a brief look at child development studies, using Jean Piaget's theory about the stages of growth (Williams 1969). Piaget noted that each phase of development has its roots in the previous phase, and children move through the phases consecutively; they cannot jump from phase 1 to phase 5. This explains the source of the problems of many special-needs children. A piece of their developmental comprehension is lacking, which adversely affects everything that comes after. If early educators provide a plethora of experiences to enhance a child's understanding at every stage, taking a multisensory approach, we will be more likely to cover the needs of our children. The phases of development, as described by Piaget, are detailed in the chart at right.

The critical stage for us, phase 2, is the optimum time to introduce the code of written language. Children may not yet be able to physically reproduce what they can comprehend, but we can plant the seeds and tend the garden during this time when the mind is beginning to organize. In this preconceptual stage, two- to four-year-olds are gathering information about

Piaget's Phases of Development

Phase 1: Sensory Motor	From birth to about 2 years	The child is mainly concerned with sensations conveyed through the nervous system as well as with developing motor activities. The primary developmental task is to learn to coordinate actions (motor activities) and perceptions of self and world (sensory activities) into a whole.
Phase 2: Preconceptual	From about 2 years to 4 years	During this egocentric phase, the child is concerned with herself. Through play she is gathering information about her environment and how it affects her. This is also the time when language is developing very quickly. Thus, it is an opportune time to provide children with multisensory experiences related to the development of phonics and literacy.
Phase 3: Intuitive	From about 4 years to 7 years	Here we see the beginnings of reasoning. Children use *animism* frequently at this stage, giving everything a life of its own. If a child trips over a rug, he calls it a "naughty rug."
Phase 4: Concrete	From about 7 years to 12 years	During this phase, children are involved in concrete operations. Although they are capable of operational thought, they do not directly perceive the logic of a situation. Educators should not fall into the trap of assuming they can get away with two-dimensional teaching at this time. Children at this age still need multisensory experiences to truly learn.
Phase 5: Formal	From about 12 years on	This final phase involves formal operations. The mind is sophisticated enough to work with abstract principles. There is less need during this phase for multisensory teaching.

their environment to be used at a later stage; older children who are still in this phase of development are also gathering information for the next. Some children have limited experiences, and they cannot build on what is not there. We must provide experiences for them—memorable, hands-on experiences.

Brain Research

How do we learn? In essence, the brain rewires itself with each new stimulation, experience, and behavior. Each stimulus is sorted and processed on several levels. When a new task is initiated, many areas of the brain are activated. As we learn a task better, we use less of our brains for that task.

As the brain receives new information, impulses flow from the cell body down the axon. Most axons are about one centimeter long. The longest, in the spinal cord, are about one meter. Each axon branches repeatedly to pass information to other cells. Information is passed through the synaptic gap between the axon and the dendrites of the next cell. When the cell body sends an electrical discharge outward to the axon, it stimulates the release of stored chemicals into the synaptic gap.

As we repeat a learning experience, the neural pathways become more and more efficient as a fatty coating called *myelin* is added to the axons. This process is called *myelination*. The thicker the axon, the faster it conducts electricity and information. Myelination also reduces interference from other nearby reactions.

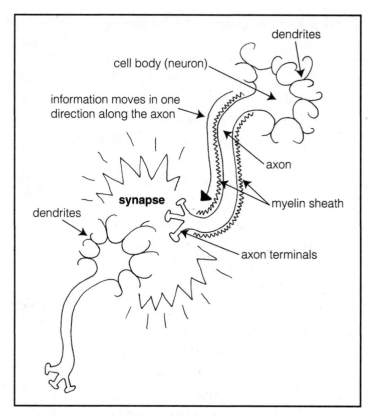

Learning takes place at the synapse.

When the environment is enriched, dendrites grow out and extend from the cell body (Jensen 1998).

The world is the brain's food: smells, sounds, sights, tastes, and touch all help to develop countless neural connections. In the classroom, we can help to forge and strengthen these neural connections by using positive emotional strategies, repetition, cross-training, and other learning techniques. The more senses we can involve, the more likely the learning will go into long-term memory (Jensen 1998).

For optimal learning, we will want to create an environment of *flow* (Csikszentmihalyi 1990). *Flow* is the term Csikszentmihalyi used to describe a state of absorption in which the body and mind are in harmony, we feel no self-consciousness, and the activity we are engaged in is motivating, meaningful, and satisfying. Athletes sometimes describe this state as being in the zone. The activity is challenging, but not so challenging that we are unable to meet the demand. To promote the possibility of flow for children, we need to eliminate or reduce stress and threat and maximize students' opportunities to experience deep concentration, enjoyment, success, and satisfaction.

Multisensory Teaching

So, why do we want to use a multisensory approach with phonics, reading, and writing instead of just letting children play in a multisensory environment? If we can introduce sounds and words in a meaningful, fun, relevant way, assisting children's ability to use written language, we can free our students' creative processes sooner rather than later.

Young children have fantastic stories to tell, and many are desperate to write them down. They need the secretarial skills of reading and writing, and the sooner they get them under their belts, the earlier they will be liberated in expressing their creative thoughts. We can eradicate or prevent related self-doubt, confusion, and fear by giving children these skills.

We don't want to miss the optimum time to learn. Once children feel in control of written language, they will want to extend their activities. They may not become novelists or poets, but they will surely want to surf the Internet, read the small print on a contract, or curl up with a good book. We must equip them with the independence and freedom to communicate and express themselves efficiently and effectively. We can do this using a physical multisensory approach. ❦

These children learn about "o" by pretending to be an octopus.

2

Introducing the Alphabet

Children find their own ways in to reading and writing. No single prescribed method will successfully accommodate all children. Some children rely heavily on one strategy, while others use a combination of cues. A true multisensory approach should introduce as many "ways in" as possible to cover the needs of as many children as possible.

Young children should not have to try to adapt their minds to fit our preferred method of teaching. As the providers, we teachers need to have every channel open to make sure that we are giving each receptive mind the clues that it needs for each child to learn.

Although I use a variety of strategies and language cues, my experience is that most (but not all) children respond well to phonics, at least as part of their reading skills. I will share with you how I plan my year and how I introduce the sounds. So far, I have followed a new thematic plan and a new order for introducing the sounds each year, and I will probably continue to do so, especially considering I often teach the same children more than one year in a row.

I have tried all of the ideas suggested here with excellent results. Once you see how rewarding "discovering" a sound can be, you will come up with many, many ideas of your own. You need not be limited by your resources; some of my best inspirations came from my son's toy cupboard and the contents of my pantry.

Plan Your Year Thematically

My first suggestion is to plan your year thematically, then relate the sounds to your topics throughout the year. This is what takes the most time and may not be applicable to the way you teach. I offer this as a method that has worked well for me. At the beginning of each year, I sit down and plan the whole year, week by week, using a system of themes or topics. As I teach some children for two years running, at least every other year must be totally different from the year before. Topics I have used include the following.

- Me
- Journey to the land of nursery rhymes
- People who help us (community workers)
- The five senses
- Baby animals
- Opposites
- Transportation
- Shopping
- Cold
- Seasonal celebrations around the world
- Stories of three

Each theme may last from three weeks to two months. During that time, each child's work is collected in a book that she helps to make. The book consolidates the separate ideas that relate to the main theme, and it is a wonderful keepsake of which children will be proud. Before their work goes into the books, the children are delighted to see their creations mounted and displayed (a great confidence booster), and parents are usually thrilled that this precious time has been documented and preserved.

An ambulance activity is perfect for introducing "a" during a people who help us theme.

I try to pick out one major aspect of the theme to focus on each week. For instance, during the nursery rhymes topic, we might spend one week on "Twinkle, Twinkle Little Star." I choose a sound to match the theme for that week, and I introduce one letter each week. (Chapter 3 contains activities and instructions

TiP It will help if the children can make a direct reference to a main word that includes your sound of the week. When we worked on people who help us, we visited the fire station during the week of "f" and climbed aboard an ambulance during the week of "a."

for introducing each letter.) The letter for "Twinkle, Twinkle" week could be "t" for twinkle or "s" for star.

Toward the end of the year, the connections between the sounds and the topics may become contrived. This is fine, because most of the work on what a sound is has already been covered earlier in the year; you will have laid the foundations of the concept. You will still introduce each sound in a multisensory way; the themes are just another connection to bring it all to life.

Introduce Sounds in Any Order

There is no need to introduce sounds in alphabetical order. It is difficult to find relevant material that begins with "a" to illustrate that initial sound, and vowels are not the easiest letters to begin with anyway. The alphabet song provides all the references to alphabetical order that you need. Even by the time children have their own independent word books (personal dictionaries in which they write words, as described on page 212), they sing the alphabet song to themselves to help them find the sound they need. You can therefore start with easily recognizable sounds that begin

You can have fun exaggerating the pronunciation of a letter and examining what it does to your voice as well as to your face.

familiar words related to fun and interesting objects and concepts.

I usually begin with "s." It offers many summer references, such as "sand" and "sun." It even looks like a snake! "S" is difficult for a child to reproduce accurately but is easily recognizable in any print. What an achievement when the child points out an "s" to his mom and dad! It is also great fun to say the "s" sound, especially if you're wriggling on the floor pretending to be snakes. "S" is a super stage setter for all your sound sensations.

The next two sounds are usually "t" and "m." "T" is very easy to draw with your finger, and the straight lines are a strong contrast to "s," making it easier for the children to successfully recognize and learn. The sounds are also very different—the everlasting "s" compared with the short, sharp "t." One of my brand-new three-year-olds apparently brought the house down at church after his second week at school. In a particularly quiet moment in the service, he pronounced loudly, "Look, Mom, there's a 't,'" as he pointed to the cross above the altar.

"M" has a distinctly recognizable look and sound, and again, there are many fun and relevant items in a child's life that begin with "m." I am grateful, for example, for the bold display of McDonald's golden arches that gives our children so many opportunities to identify the "m" sound, tell the world about it, and receive heaps of praise.

After these three letters, apart from the vowels, I allow the order of introduction of the letters to be guided by the themes I have planned. Try to leave the vowels for near the end of the year. By this time, you will be able to introduce consonant-vowel-consonant word building to some of the children, and the introduction of the vowels at this time works extremely well.

Always focus on the sound of the letter, not its name, and really emphasize initial consonants. Tell the children that all letters have a name, just as each child has a name, and that is what we sing in the alphabet song. I am sure we have all witnessed a child's puzzled face when an adult is trying to help her understand "see-ay-tee." This does not provide the building blocks the child needs to comprehend the word "cat," which really sounds like "kuh-ah-tuh."

When letters have more than one sound, deal with one sound at a time so that the child can really identify that sound and letter without any added complications. Once he's mastered that, it's quite easy to introduce an alternative because it is special information to the child.

See, Hear, and Touch Each Letter

I have created what I call the "feely phonic alphabet." These big "feely" letters are essential when I introduce each letter. Each feely letter relates to a word beginning with that sound. For example, the "e" is gray and has elephant features as a reminder that "e" sounds like the beginning of "elephant." The feely

The big feely phonic letter "j."

phonic alphabet is very easy to make, and I have included instructions and a pattern for each letter in chapter 3.

While introducing a letter, constantly wave your big feely letter around, especially when the children are all chanting the new sound. Make sure you emphasize that initial vowel sound, saying "e-e-e-elephant" (not "ee"). After you introduce a letter, display the big feely letter in a visible position in the room. I am amazed at how many references children make to these letters throughout the year. I'll often see a child looking around for the right letter, mumbling, "E-e-e-elephant . . . e!" The letters are a constant experience-related reference to the sounds covered.

I primarily deal with lowercase letters because my main focus is to promote the comprehension of how sounds work. Once a child has truly grasped that concept, and is working comfortably with a sight-recognition vocabulary (entire words the child can recognize by sight and write down), I will then start to introduce capital letters. Once you start to formally introduce capitals, then you have to deal with *when* to use them. Consequently, the logical time to introduce them properly is when you are working on writing an independent sentence with a child who has already mastered the basic skills. If you make a big deal of introducing them earlier, the child may see them as just an alternative and start peppering their words with them, which will lead to some undoing later on! Of course, there are capital letters on charts and so on around the room, and just as a matter of course, many of the children will notice many capitals, but presenting them purposefully is a different matter.

Incidentally, most parents tend to teach their children to write their names using capital letters—probably because the stick formations are easy to write—so they are aware that they exist but do not think to use them in their other writing because they've not been introduced in that context.

Feel How to Say the Letter

You can have fun exaggerating the pronunciation of a letter and examining what it does to your voice as well as to your face. What does your face look like when you say the sound? How do your mouth and tongue feel?

When I introduce "o," we make our magic fingers go round and round the round shape of our mouths.

I have observed several children doing this for themselves in later months when they are trying to distinguish which vowel sound they need in order to write a particular word.

Make Each Introduction a Big Event

Create a memorable event to introduce each sound. Brain research suggests that our learning avenues are open widest when we utilize novelty, discovery, and involvement. Our episodic, or natural, memory is "motivated by curiosity, novelty, and expectations. It's enhanced by intensified sensory input, such as sights, sounds, smells, taste, and touch" (Jensen 1998, 106). Ideally, therefore, every child will be physically involved in the discovery of each new sound.

The starting point for each sound is one of the most eagerly anticipated activities in my classroom. I introduce one sound each week. This is the big floor show. It takes a lot of preparation, but the immediate reaction and long-term results are well worth it. It's almost like a treasure hunt, but to keep the novelty factor and the strong interest of the children, the Big Event has to be at least slightly different each week for each sound.

As much as possible, relate your props and activities to the sound you are introducing. Set up circle time on sound day, an area and time where each child has a turn to physically find or do something beginning with that sound. Each discovery is novel and involves all children not only watching their friends but also orally joining in, thus completing the auditory loop, which is so important in comprehension.

For instance, when I introduce "b," I put in a big, black bag a collection of items beginning with "b," such as a ball, a stuffed bunny, beads, a banana, and so on. We all make "b-b-b" sounds until each child has pulled an item out of the bag. Most of the children shout the name of each "b" object as it is found.

When I introduce the sound "e," I have an egg tree on which are perched colored plastic eggs, the type that open up. Each child takes a turn choosing an egg and opening it. Inside may be an elephant (a little plastic toy) or another egg (a little chocolate one), or the egg may be empty, in which case the child takes another turn. As each one carefully opens the egg, the others are waiting with bated breath, usually making predictions about what will be inside. Encourage the children to call out as soon as they see whether it is an elephant, an egg, or empty. This provides loads of anticipation, participation, and fun. I have always maintained that teachers need training not just in education but also in dramatic arts. The more of an actor you can be to heighten the curiosity and the excitement, the better.

Make sure your Big Event activity is tight—that everything has somewhere to go. This provides a more complete picture of the sound. For instance, with "e," I have the children put the elephants at the base of the egg tree and the empty eggs in an enormous envelope. The children get to keep the chocolate eggs (with everyone getting one by the end of the activity).

These activities are the main starting point for the early introduction of the written word, and ideas for Big Events are included with each letter in chapter 3. They represent the happy experience on which one wants to base the learning of reading and writing, so the activities should be as positive and physical as possible. Involve as many senses as you can.

Drawing a "y" in yellow paint.

Feel How to Make the Letter

As soon as the children have taken part in the Big Event activity, build on the sound even further by having them trace the letter with their fingers—not just in the air, and not just over the feely letter, but actually *in* something that feels gooey, sticky, or grainy and leaves each child's formation of the letter for her to enjoy. Try to make the substance something that, again, relates to the sound. When I introduce "a," for example, we trace "a" in applesauce. The children can lick the applesauce off their fingers afterward, adding another sensory experience. This activity not only helps relate the sound to the letter symbol, but it also helps the children practice forming letters in preparation for writing. As I mention in the preface, this activity can be especially useful for children who have difficulty working with a pencil or other writing utensil. Chapter 3 includes ideas for substances you can use for each letter.

Build a Silly Sound Picture

Draw a silly picture on the chalkboard or on a dry-erase board, using only things that begin with the sound you are studying. You don't need great artistic skills; young children are not going to judge your prowess at drawing. We have had some of the biggest laughs in class when we have worked on this activity. To maintain the novelty aspect, do not do this for every letter. Use it only with sounds for which there are a lot of easily drawn objects that

When we did this activity, Gracie was a golden gorilla wearing green gloves and glasses. She had grapes on her head and a glass of gravy in her hand. She was going to the gas station to meet her friend the gray goose. Just as the picture was getting really crowded, one of my five-year-olds looked at me with a twinkle in his eye and said, "Gracie could be a giant gorilla!" He had the sophistication and understanding to know that he was introducing a different use of the "g" sound.

start with that sound, or if you haven't done this activity for a while, so it still feels novel.

I give the children a head start by looking through some colorful picture dictionaries first and then leaving them open at the relevant pages where they can see them. Remember, these children are very young, with limited experiences, and they generally find it difficult to come up with ideas out of thin air, especially if the object has to begin with a specific sound.

I usually begin by drawing an animal, and while I am drawing it, I ask the children if they can think of a name. When we study "g," I draw a gorilla. Last time we did this, we called the gorilla Gracie—a unanimous choice as we had a popular girl in the class named Gracie. Sometimes the children need some clues to get them started. Take this opportunity to direct the suggestions toward things you can comfortably draw. What color is Gracie? What is she wearing? What does she like to eat? When the children get the hang of the activity, they'll be calling out all sorts of ideas. Remember to ask the child where his suggestion should go in the picture. Our animals always seem to have lots of things piled on their heads!

Depending on the group of children you have, you could ask the children to draw in their suggestions themselves. However, small children tend to be slow, even getting up from a circle, and this activity benefits from speed and the flow of continuity and repetition. After your group session, you can help the children actively process the information by having them draw their own sound pictures.

Relate Let's Pretend Sessions to the Sound

Create Let's Pretend (make-believe) sessions around the sound the children are learning. The session could include mime and movement to words or music with or without props. We enjoy a different format each week and relate it to the sound of the week. Don't give it away that you planned it this way—be *so* surprised when you see the connection between the activity and the sound of the week. This will add to the wonder and excitement of learning.

Relating your sounds to your themes makes it easier to come up with a plethora of ideas, because you have given yourself a starting point. To highlight the novelty factor, which is all-important in the learning process, rotate different forms of activities. Some of the intense interest that opens the brain's receptiveness will be missing if you bring out the same music tape week after week.

Mime Fiction and Poetry

Sometimes miming a story or a poem works extremely well, especially if the children are familiar with the plot. One of my favorites for "b" is *Goldilocks and the Three Bears*. Each child takes on all the roles and everybody gets to express her own version of the story by miming it as you read it aloud. Nobody will say anything negative about anybody else, because everyone is busily involved at the same time. To enhance the involvement and excitement, add your own comments, such as,

"Oh, no, look at those big, scary claws over there!"

I find that taped stories for children can be a good tool to use sometimes, because then you get to join in on the miming. Other times, working with a theme and miming related activities can be effective. For instance, take "c" for "cold." Mime getting dressed up for cold weather, putting on mittens and hat and scarf, battling a cold wind, rubbing your hands together to warm up, and so on. The possibilities are endless.

Mime Nonfiction

Nonfiction picture books also make an effective starting point. If you have been studying bakers, show some suitable pictures and the children will love to pretend to sift the flour, knead the dough, be the dough rising,

Make-believe is yet another way to reinforce new sounds.

Boys and girls alike love to dress up.

13

Mime to Music

There are plenty of popular songs and tunes that tell a story in themselves. "Drip, Drip, Drop, Little April Showers," from the Disney movie *Bambi*, is an absolute gift for children to mime. You can relate the song to any number of letters as a starting point, such as "d" in "drip" and "drop," or "w" for "weather." They can be

- the gentle raindrops,

- the animals feeling the rain falling on their noses,

- the animals taking cover,

- the clouds swirling,

- the wind blowing,

- the trees bending,

- the lightning striking,

- the animals in shelter,

- the wind beginning to calm,

- the raindrops bouncing from leaf to leaf,

- the animals peeping out to see if all is safe,

- the sun opening her rays,

- the rainbow forming, and

- the animals coming out to play once more

and then be the surprised baker lifting the cloth to see how much his dough has risen (a little bit of poetic license can go a long way). They can also be the machine wrapping the bread and then the van driver delivering the bread to the stores. You could even extend the make-believe right up until the bread is actually eaten!

Mime to Music

Children love music, and studies have shown that different types of music can aid the efficiency of learning (Rauscher et al. 1993). Find some suitable music to which children can be leaves gently floating down from the tree in the fall or feathers fluttering in the air.

Remember, these children are very young. They can concentrate and apply themselves for relatively short amounts of time. Tape your musical excerpts in advance, making sure you do not spend too much time on one idea and that the children don't have to wait while you search for the next track. Keep the momentum going. Preparation is always the key in these physical activities. You want the children to be absolutely engrossed and involved in an idea because you have set the stage for positive, happy emotions and a physical experience, thereby opening the brain for the sound connection. Each letter in chapter 3 includes Let's Pretend ideas for stories, themes, and music.

Offer a Craft Relevant to the Sound

As the day and week continues, imprint the sound even further by engaging in crafts related to the sound. If you are working with a theme, even more ideas are available to you. Make references to the sound whenever possible. For example, in the week when "s" is introduced, make spotty snakes and salt dough snails (or even swirly snails, silver stars, and sparkling suns). This gives the children another physical reference to the sound. (See chapter 3 for craft ideas for each letter.) Neurobiologist Norman Weinberger has said, "Arts education facilitates language development, enhances creativity, boosts reading readiness, helps social development, general intellectual achievement, and fosters positive attitudes towards school" (Jensen 1998, 38), and my experience bears this out.

I made this!

Craft Supplies

My craft supplies fall into two categories: purchased equipment and donated "trash," otherwise known as collage or junk treasures. The old saying "One man's trash is another man's treasure" is certainly true in the classroom. Let it be known to all—teachers, parents, friends, family—that you need the following items:

- ✔ fabric scraps
- ✔ ribbon
- ✔ craft remnants
- ✔ yarn
- ✔ cardboard tubes of all sizes
- ✔ interesting reels and spools, such as the inside of a reel of ribbon or spool of thread
- ✔ small sturdy boxes (such as cosmetic or toothpaste boxes)
- ✔ drinking straws
- ✔ buttons (especially the flat-backed kind)
- ✔ beads
- ✔ mesh onion bags
- ✔ light bulb packages that have the fine corrugated cardboard
- ✔ Styrofoam scraps
- ✔ bubble wrap
- ✔ foil containers
- ✔ egg containers
- ✔ wrapping paper

Making a potpourri pot helps children learn the "p" sound.

You will soon have people offering you other unusual items to add to your collection. Keep three-dimensional sturdy junk-modeling equipment (such as cardboard tubes and egg containers) in a large plastic container with a lid. The soft items, such as the fabric, yarn, and ribbon, can be kept in a fabric draw-string bag.

When you know you have a craft coming up that will require each child to have a specific, maybe larger item, such as a shoe box or a coffee container, give the parents as much notice as you can. It always happens that some parents are able to provide several of the items needed to make up for the families who don't have access to what you need. For example, some people will bring home the coffee cans from their workplace and make up for those families who do not drink coffee. The beauty of such a classroom craft is that it is flexible, because everybody's creation will ultimately be different, and it is inexpensive. There is no need ever to be in a situation where a parent is running around trying to find a particular container for the child's craft activity. Use something else instead. If you are making drums and there are not enough coffee cans, some children can use oatmeal containers or margarine tubs.

You can purchase craft materials (that aren't donated) from an educational supply store (often called parent-teacher stores) or a discount general store, such as Wal-Mart. These are the staple pieces I like to have in my classroom at all times. The essential items are

- ✔ colored construction paper
- ✔ glue
- ✔ child-safety scissors
- ✔ tissue paper
- ✔ glitter
- ✔ washable paint (preferably liquid tempera)
- ✔ non-spill containers
- ✔ chunky paintbrushes
- ✔ sequins
- ✔ feathers
- ✔ pom-poms
- ✔ wiggle eyes
- ✔ craft sticks
- ✔ doilies
- ✔ felt

Overalls or cover-ups are a must for all children at the craft table. They should not be worried about spoiling their precious clothes or risk getting into trouble for being creative; they should just be concentrating on the task at hand. You can purchase overalls, make a simple over-the-head cover-up by cutting a head hole in plastic-coated fabric, or ask parents to send in an old shirt or something similar.

When the children come to the craft table, have the items needed, which may include a choice, in the center of the group table. Quantities of equipment are listed in this book per child because teachers will be working with classes of different sizes. The materials should not, however, be dished out individually, unless a craft specifically calls for this. They should be put in bowls and on trays in the center of the craft table to allow individual choice and expression. The aim is not to produce identical items.

Read Books That Refer to the Sound

When you choose books to read for the week, make sure to include some that contain references to the sound. If you are studying "b," read a book about Boomer, such as *Boomer Goes to School* (McGeorge 1996) or maybe just a book that includes bears. Act surprised when you suddenly realize that "Boomer" starts with "b." Show absolute joy at your discovery. Go overboard! In no time at all, the children will be seeing and hearing the "b" sound all around them. Make sure that when they do, you are completely delighted. Watch those little faces in front of you light up. You'll know that moment really means something.

In chapter 3, I offer a few suggestions for books to read for each sound, but I am well aware that we are all limited by our individual access to books. It is not difficult, however, to find some sort of reference to a sound if we look for it. There may not be books about things beginning with "x," but there are books about kisses—XXX!

Relate Activity Centers to the Sound

Make other independent activities in the room relate to the sound you are studying whenever possible. In the week of "p," make pink clay. In the week of "b," make a big deal of putting out beads to string. Whenever there is an opportunity to make a connection with the sound, make it! The children's brains will make that connection, too.

Involve the Parents

To complete the loop at home, involve the parents. I find that parents often ask, "What can I do to help?" Fortunately, they can do a lot. Perhaps most important, parents can read books with their children. Suggest that they snuggle down, cuddle up, and enjoy!

Tell parents, "Point to every word you are reading just as a matter of course—to help you, of course! This will help your child subconsciously connect the print with the words spoken. It will also help imprint the left-to-right direction of reading and writing. (Eventually, your child may want to take over or help with the pointing.) Don't try to teach or quiz during this special cozy time. Just be comfortable and relaxed. Make this a wonderful time of the day."

Tell parents to let their children see that they gain pleasure from reading. Children love to emulate adults, so even without realizing it, we can be their greatest inspiration.

Parents can also help by pointing out letters, words, and sounds in the environment. Make sure the

I used to actually climb into bed with my two children to read at bedtime. It was a twin bed, so we really were snuggled! By the time I had read each of the week's library books at least twice, I was usually the one who dropped off to sleep first, especially since the children often checked out the same books week after week. To this day, all these years later, if anyone says, "Good tea," my husband and I automatically respond, "Good butter in it!" If I had a dollar for every time I read *Mog's Lunch Box,* by Jan Pieńkowski and Helen Nicoll (1975), from which that line comes, I would be very wealthy indeed! My children both look back on those hours as a special time in their lives—and yes, they both love to read.

child is in no doubt that words and reading are great fun. Parents should not try to create a word lesson or a quiz, unless it is really light-hearted. They can interest and inspire children by commenting on the world around them: "Wow! How do they climb up to clean that big K on Kmart?" Or, "Oh, look, they've changed that billboard over there. Let's see what it says this time."

Another great help parents can provide is to react, or perhaps I should say *overreact*. Even if parents have absolutely no time to sit down and read with their children, their positive support of any tiny achievement in reading and writing is immeasurable. The parents' reaction when a child first points out a letter or a word can complete the circle. It can determine whether finding sounds in the environment is an uninteresting activity or a great thing that the child wants to do again and again. If the circle is completed properly, the child will understand that sounds and words are relevant not just in the classroom but also in the world outside school. This is a big connection to make.

On Friday, just before it is time to go home for the weekend, I review the sounds and words we have studied so far. Then I make a big deal of telling the children if they see a sound or word on a box, on a poster, or on the refrigerator, they should tell someone. I tell them that the person will be so surprised that he will fall over, and his legs will go up in the air! The wonderful thing is that many parents have come in to tell me that their children have let them know that this is the expected reaction. Moms and dads together regularly fall on the floor and wave their legs in the air in response to their child's phonetic discoveries! I am happy to report that those who play this game, reacting so beautifully, are now reacting to their five-year-olds' latest first-grade reading books.

It only takes a few seconds to give such a positive reaction, but the benefit is beyond belief. A teacher can work her socks off trying to teach a child to read, but if that home-school link is not made, the task is much more difficult. Having the entire positive network in operation makes such a difference. It's like rowing a boat with two oars instead of one. You can do it with one, but when you work together, the experience is much more rewarding. You are not asking busy parents to do anything too time-consuming—positive support and enthusiasm are the keys. 🐞

3

Multisensory Alphabet Activities

Now that we have our objective clear in our minds—to introduce phonic sounds through multisensory discovery sessions and consolidate their use and meaning all around us with other child-centered activities—we move on in this chapter to some ideas on how to actually do this for each letter. As you get started, you will realize that the activities here are merely a starting point for your own imagination and creativity.

About the Activities

Each letter includes the following sections.

1. **Activities to introduce the letter:**
   - See, Say, and Sing: a brief introduction to the letter. Activities include using a big feely phonic letter for the children to touch and look at, locating the letter in a picture dictionary, singing through the alphabet to find the letter, and practicing the sound of the letter.

Chapter 3

- The Big Event: an activity that immediately follows the preceding introduction, involving physical play that uses and emphasizes the sound of the letter

2. **More ideas for the letter:**
   - Sensational "a," "b," and so forth: an activity that has children tracing letters with their fingers in various substances to give them a tactile experience with the letter
   - Silly Pictures: an activity that has you drawing a composite picture that includes several items that start with the letter, with the children calling out ideas for items as well as for the placement of these items on the drawing
   - Let's Pretend: ideas for miming and make-believe related to the letter

3. **Crafts:** one or two crafts that focus on the letter

About the Process

I allocate one day each week for specific sound work. Each week, I introduce one new sound. On the first day, I review the sounds already covered (if any) and then introduce the new sound with See, Say, and Sing activities, intended to be a brief introduction, followed by the Big Event. Depending on time (some Big Events take more time than others!), we may either build a silly picture related to the sound, let each child trace the letter with his finger, as in the Sensational sound activities, or move directly to related crafts and pencil-and-paper work, if appropriate. (See chapter 4 for more information on writing activities.)

After the Big Event, which involves the whole class, the class is split into groups of approximately six to eight children who rotate around the room visiting all three stations. One group will go first to the craft table, which is set up in the wet area of the room (near the sink). That area will be ready with the materials for the day's craft (related to the day's sound, of course!) and should have adult supervision at all times. The second group will go first to the writing table for a sound-related project, such as purchased or teacher-prepared worksheets, which may involve tracing over the letter or coloring a picture beginning with the sound. This table is where I am stationed to offer one-on-one guidance as necessary. The third group will go to the choosing area, where they have a choice among the toys. This group can also choose to explore the extra activity center described for each sound. This center should be close to the choosing area if possible. As the children finish each activity, they move around to the next station.

I put out each of these special activities for just a week, therefore keeping their novelty. The next week, each center becomes brand new, with materials and activities related to the new sound for the week. I have 20 children in my class with one assistant and this system works beautifully.

On the other days of the week, we can make reference to the sound again through our theme work, Let's Pretend group activities, books we read, initial-consonant writing (as described on page 209), and other crafts.

Making the Most of These Activities

- Remember that although these instructions are listed in alphabetical order, you shouldn't introduce them that way. Start with "s," "t," and "m," then let your classroom topics guide the order thereafter. (See page 8 for more information on when to introduce the letters.)

- It is less confusing for the children if you work with just lowercase letters at this point. The main focus is to promote comprehension of how sounds work. Capital letters, along with their uses, can be introduced later.

- The activities in this chapter occasionally make use of candy and other food, such as nuts and applesauce. As daycare providers and teachers, you will already have information on file about any allergies among the children; however, it doesn't hurt to ask parents again, just to make sure, when you know you have a food-related activity coming up. 🍎

Sensational "g."

Introduce the vowels late in the year when some children are ready for building up consonant-vowel-consonant words. A good time to introduce "a" is when you are working on an animal-related topic. I particularly like to introduce "a" as part of our people who help us unit. It fits in very well with the ambulance, which we arrange to visit us at school. Another popular preschool and early grades theme that would work well with "a" is apples.

Activities to Introduce "a"

The activities in this section are for the first day you introduce "a" to the children. The first activity—See, Say, and Sing—involves a picture dictionary, a big feely letter "a" made out of felt, and the alphabet song all used together to involve the children in this exciting new sound. The second activity—The Big Event—will involve the children in a physical activity to help reinforce the sound of the letter. The Big Event for "a" is a game in which the children pretend to be ambulance drivers, taking animals to the hospital. *Important note: The Big Event should follow immediately after the brief introduction of See, Say, and Sing to be most effective in solidifying the new letter for the children. Gather materials and prepare for both activities before you introduce "a" to your class. (See pages 7–11 for more information on introducing a new sound.)*

Apple "a"

See, Say, and Sing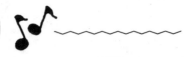

Materials

- ✔ picture dictionary
- ✔ photocopy of the "a" pattern on page 23
- ✔ 8" x 8" piece of red felt
- ✔ 3" x 3" piece of green felt
- ✔ scissors
- ✔ glue
- ✔ thin cardboard (such as a cereal box)

Preparation

1. To make the feely letter "a," photocopy and cut out the pattern on page 23 (unless you decide to make this letter freehand, without using the pattern). You may also wish to create a bigger letter by enlarging the photocopy and using larger pieces of felt.

2. Cut off the leaves and set them aside, unless you wish to cut both the letter and the leaves freehand.

3. Using the pattern as a guide (or cutting freehand), cut the "a" out of the red felt.

4. Place the leaves on the green felt and cut around them, or cut out leaves freehand.

5. Glue the green felt leaves to the red felt "a."

6. Make the letter stronger by gluing it onto cardboard and cutting around it.

Directions

1. Introduce "a" by making lots of "a-a-a" (short "a," as in "apple," not long "ay") sounds with the children, showing what it feels like to say "a."

2. Pass around the feely letter "a" so the children can see what "a" looks like and can touch the letter while they practice the "a" sound. Exaggerate the "a" sound in the word "a-a-apple." Remember to keep the big feely "a" in constant view so the children can make the connection that the activities that follow all relate to "a."

3. Tell the children that "a" has a name just like they do and discuss the difference between the name of the letter "a" and the sound of the letter "a" as in "apple." Sing through the alphabet, then discuss where "a" is hiding.

4. Sing through the alphabet again as you turn the pages of the picture dictionary. Pick out a couple of "a" pictures to show the class more words that start with the short "a" sound.

The *BIG* Event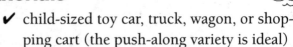

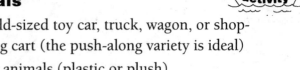

Materials

- ✔ child-sized toy car, truck, wagon, or shopping cart (the push-along variety is ideal)
- ✔ toy animals (plastic or plush)
- ✔ masking tape
- ✔ 11" x 17" (at least) paper or posterboard
- ✔ colored pens or markers

Preparation

1. Use paper or posterboard and colored pens or markers to make a simple drawing of an ambulance, which you tape to the wagon, car, truck, or shopping cart. I used a child's shopping cart and drew the ambulance on a large piece of posterboard.

2. Place the ambulance at the ambulance station, a spot you designate, where the activity will begin.

3. Put the toy animals in a pile where the children can get to them with the ambulance. Zoo or jungle animals tend to work best because the children are more likely to refer to them as animals, rather than by their actual names.

4. Designate where in the room the hospital will be, preferably away from the pile of animals so the children will have a "drive" to take their patients to the hospital. During the activity, you will be at the hospital as the resident nurse, so pick a comfortable spot and keep a roll of masking tape handy.

Directions

1. Each child takes a turn as the ambulance driver. (This could involve wearing a special hat.) The child drives the ambulance around the room, calling out, "Aa-aa, aa-aa, aa-aa" for the sound of the siren.

Taking turns driving the ambulance.

2. When the ambulance arrives at the pile of animals, the child chooses one, puts it into the ambulance, and drives off again, calling, "Aa-aa, aa-aa aa-aa," until he reaches the hospital.

3. When he gets to the hospital, he gets a bandage (really a piece of masking tape) on which the nurse (you) draws an "a." The child sticks the "a" bandage on the animal, drops the animal off at the animal pile, then returns the ambulance to the ambulance station, ready for the next child to take a turn.

As simple as this exercise is, it is still amazing to hear the children connecting the ambulance's "aa-aa" sound to the "a" sound. This is an activity the children remember always.

More Ideas for "a"

Sensational "a"

Pour a layer of applesauce into a tray (such as a cafeteria tray) and let the children take turns tracing an "a" in the applesauce with their fingers, so they can see and feel the shape. Make sure the feely letter "a" is clearly visible to all children as a model.

Tracing an "a" in the applesauce.

Silly Pictures

A silly picture composed of things that start with "a" is one more way to solidify the sound in children's minds. Use a large sheet of paper with colored pens, a dry-erase board, or chalkboard—anything that enables the children to watch you draw. Start with something that begins with the letter (such as an animal), then

ask the children for ideas. (Have the picture dictionary open at the relevant page to help, but let the children feel that you believe they really did think up the ideas on their own.)

Remember that silly pictures are most effective if they seem novel to the children. You don't have to draw for every letter but can try this activity when you haven't done it in a while or when you have a letter that lends itself to lots of ideas. (For more tips on drawing silly pictures with your class, see page 12.)

For "a," for example, you can draw acrobatic ants. Each ant needs only a couple of circular body segments and some legs. If you're feeling particularly adventurous, you could draw in a face. Make sure the children clearly know what "acrobatic" means, then ask them for suggestions. The children will be full of ideas for different acrobatic feats, such as ants standing on each other's shoulders, ants spinning in the air, or ants doing handstands! After you finish the class picture, have the children draw their own sound pictures.

TiP

Make sure that your class has apples for a snack at least one day during this week.

Let's Pretend

Involving the "a" sound in games of pretend will make the sound even more memorable and fun for the children. This activity involves acting out with the children the life cycle of an apple. It will give you the opportunity to use the "a" sound many times while the children are engaged in a fun physical activity. Use the following script, or make up your own, to help guide the children through the make-believe. Don't forget to pretend right along with them!

TIP A great companion to this Let's Pretend session is *I Am an Apple* (Marzollo 1997)

"Pretend you're in an orchard. Look around for a really juicy, rosy apple. When you have spotted one, get a ladder and climb up into the branches of the apple tree. Carefully pick the apple and put it in your pocket while you climb down from the tree. Wipe the apple to make it really shiny and then take the first delicious bite. It is so juicy that you have to wipe your mouth with your hand. Eat the rest, taking big bites and chewing the crisp apple.

"When you have finished, rub your tummy to show how much you enjoyed the apple. Look in your hand. All you have left is the core of the apple with the seeds. Rinse the seeds and shake them in your hand to help them dry. Get a shovel and dig a hole in the ground. Put the seeds in the hole, cover them with earth, patting it firmly down, then fill a watering can with water and water where you have planted.

"Now you are the seed, curled up tiny and warm in the ground. Very gradually, begin to grow your roots with your toes and feet. Then your fingers can start to be the shoots slowly growing upward. Grow your roots and shoots more and more until you need to push through the earth.

"Once you have pushed through, you can start to spread your leaves and grow up, up, up to be a beautiful apple tree.

"Now you are the child again walking under the apple tree. What do you see up in the tree? What do you do? What is left in your hand when you have finished the apple? What will you do with the seeds? What will happen then?"

Animal Activity Center

Set up an area equipped with construction paper, scissors, glue, overalls, and old magazine pages with pictures of animals. The children can practice some basic manipulative skills and produce an animal collage.

Crafts for "a"

Apple Frame

With a picture of the child inside, the apple frame conveys a great message: "You are the apple of my eye." The framed photos can also be used on a bulletin board with the title "The pick of the crop."

Materials

- ✔ photograph of each child (about 5" x 3½")
- ✔ 10" x 8" thin cardboard (such as from a cereal box) for the apple shape for each child
- ✔ 5" x 3" sheet of green construction paper for each child
- ✔ 10" x 8" sheet of red or green construction paper for each child
- ✔ a sheet of red tissue paper for each child
- ✔ glue for each child or small group
- ✔ scissors

Preparation

For young children, you will need to prepare most of this craft in advance as detailed in the following steps. For older children, you can set out the materials and have them follow these steps instead.

1. Cut out an apple shape for each child from the cardboard.

2. Cut out a second apple shape for each child, the same size and shape as the cardboard apple, from red or green construction paper.

3. Cut a hole in the center of the construction-paper apples large enough for the pictures to show through. It is helpful to have a round template, or even a lid to trace, to make the circles.

4. Mount the pictures on the cardboard apples so that each picture shows through when you place the construction-paper apple on top of the cardboard.

5. Cut a leaf out of the green construction paper to decorate each child's frame.

Directions

1. Give the children red tissue paper and have them tear off small pieces.

2. They should glue these pieces onto their top apple (the construction-paper frame) so that the pieces slightly overlap each other.

3. Show the children where to put glue (around the edge) on their top apple (the construction-paper apple) and help them place the top apple onto the bottom apple (the apple made of cardboard).

4. Have the children glue on a green leaf for the finishing touch. This is an ideal spot to write the child's name.

Trash-Bag Ants

These ants look great displayed on a red and white checked background, representing a picnic table. You can even pin up a few paper plates to complete the scene. The ants attending the picnic will certainly each be unique with the variety of individual skills involved!

Materials

- ✔ 1 square-foot piece of a black or brown plastic trash bag for each child
- ✔ fabric scraps or any suitable soft stuffing
- ✔ six chenille stems for each child
- ✔ a pair of large wiggle eyes or eyes made from white paper with black circles for each child
- ✔ transparent tape
- ✔ two small rubber bands for each child

Preparation

No preparation except to gather materials and cut the pieces of trash bag for each ant.

Directions

1. Have each child take a handful of the stuffing, wrap it in the black plastic, and seal it with the tape. It may be helpful to wrap by rolling, because it is best to have the seal on one side, which will be the underside. Younger children will probably need help with this, but let them try first; it will be a valuable manipulative exercise.

2. Next, have each child wrap two rubber bands around the trash-bag shape, making the three separate sections of the ant.

3. The children should then tape the chenille stems to the underside of the body (where the tape seam is). Keep all that tape in one place.

4. The children can shape the legs by bending the stems at the knees and at the feet.

5. Next, they stick on the eyes, using tape or by peeling off the sticky backing. They can also use half a chenille stem as front feelers. Just tape the middle of the stem on top of the ant's head and let each child structure the shape!

Bb

Try to introduce "bouncy b" (feel your lips bounce together), the delicate "pink p" (a much softer sound), and the very different "dinosaur d" quite close together to emphasize their similarities and differences. You can introduce them quite early in the year, after "s," "t," and "m," because there are so many easily found objects that have these initial consonants. Very young children can easily reproduce the circle-stick formation of the letters, even though not entirely accurately, but that doesn't matter at this stage.

The letter "b" is good to introduce if you are studying bears. I particularly enjoy matching "b" with the story of *Goldilocks and the Three Bears* when our topic is stories of three. When we are working on people who help us, I introduce "b" when studying the baker. We have even been lucky enough to have a mom come in and bake bread with groups of children.

Activities to Introduce "b"

The activities in this section are for the first day you introduce "b" to the children. The first activity—See, Say, and Sing—involves a picture dictionary, a big feely letter "b" made out of felt, and the alphabet song all used together to involve the children in this exciting new sound. The second activity—The Big Event—will involve the children in a physical activity to help reinforce the sound of the letter. The Big Event for "b" involves choosing objects that start with "b" out of a big black bag. *Important note:* The Big Event should follow immediately after the brief introduction of See, Say, and Sing activities to be most effective in solidifying the new letter for the children. Gather materials and prepare for *both* activities before you introduce "b" to your class. (See pages 7–11 for more information on introducing a new sound.)

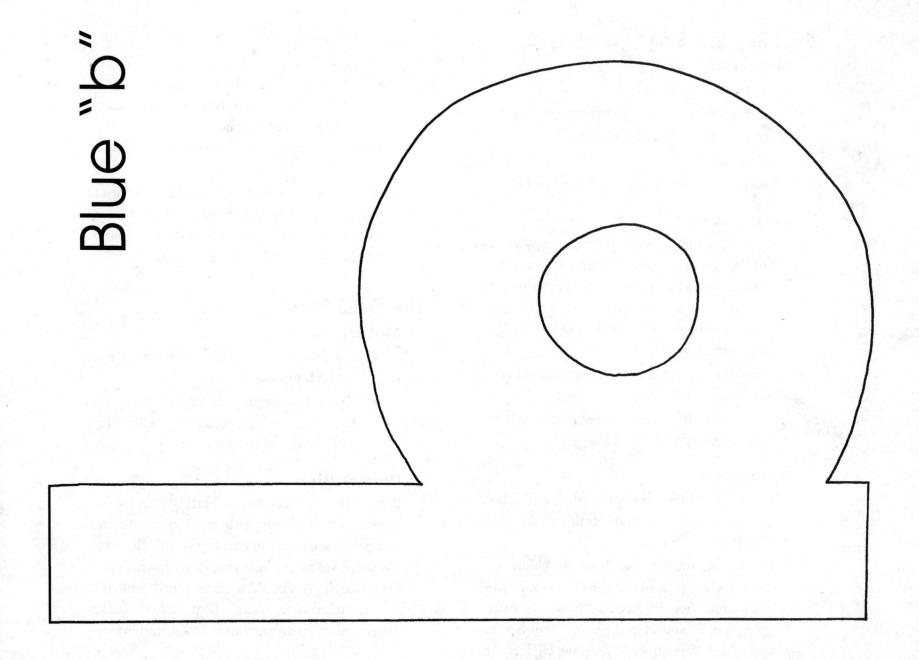

Blue "b"

See, Say, and Sing

Materials

✔ picture dictionary

✔ photocopy of the "b" pattern on page 31

✔ 8 ½" x 11" piece of blue felt

✔ scissors

✔ thin cardboard (such as a cereal box)

Preparation

1. To make the feely letter "b," photocopy and cut out the pattern on page 31 (unless you decide to make this letter freehand, without using the pattern). You may also wish to create a bigger letter by enlarging the photocopy and using a larger piece of felt.

2. Using the pattern as a guide (or cutting freehand), cut the "b" out of blue felt.

3. Make the entire letter stronger by gluing it onto thin cardboard and cutting around it.

Directions

1. Introduce "b" by making lots of "b-b-b" ("buh" not "bee") sounds with the children, showing what it feels like to say "b."

2. Pass around the big blue "b" so the children can see what "b" looks like and can touch the letter while they practice the "b" sound. Exaggerate the "b" sound in the words "b-b-big" and "b-b-blue." Remember to keep the big feely "b" in constant view so the children can make the

connection that the activities that follow all relate to "b."

3. Tell the children that "b" has a name just like they do and discuss the difference between the name of the letter "b" and the sound of the letter "b." Sing through the alphabet to find where "b" is hiding.

4. Sing through the alphabet again as you turn the pages of the picture dictionary. Pick out a couple of "b" pictures to show the class more words that start with the "b" sound.

The *BIG* Event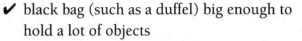

Materials

✔ black bag (such as a duffel) big enough to hold a lot of objects

✔ objects that begin with "b" to put into the black bag (enough objects for each child to pull one out of the bag)

Preparation

Prepare the big black bag by placing various objects in it that begin with "b." It is easy to find things in the classroom that begin with "b," but a few surprises from home always go down well. For example, you could use a ball, bell, stuffed bunny, stuffed bear, banana, boat, balloon, basket, battery, beads, beanbag, book, block, and brush.

Directions

1. Tell the children that there are all sorts of things in your big black bag that begin with the "b-b-b" sound.

2. Have the children come up one at a time and feel in the bag to choose something beginning with "b."

3. While the others are waiting to see what a child pulls out, have them all join in with a gentle "b-b-b" that will lead nicely into the name of the item pulled out.

TiP
To enhance the activity, you could have the children place their items in a big blue basket, a box, or even a boat!

More Ideas for "b"

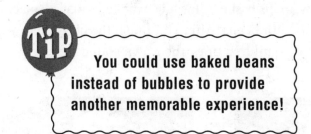

Sensational "b"

Make some thick bubbles with liquid soap in a tray (such as a cafeteria tray) and let the children take turns tracing a "b" in the bubbles with their fingers, so they can see and feel the shape. Make sure the feely letter "b" is clearly visible to all children as a model.

TiP
You could use baked beans instead of bubbles to provide another memorable experience!

Silly Pictures

A silly picture composed of things that start with "b" is one more way to solidify the sound in children's minds. Use a large sheet of paper with colored pens, a dry-erase board, or a chalkboard—anything that enables the children to watch you draw. Start with something that begins with the letter (such as an animal), then ask the children for ideas. (Have the picture dictionary open at the relevant page to help, but let the children feel that you believe they really did think up the ideas on their own.)

Remember that silly pictures are most effective if they seem novel to the children. You don't have to draw for every letter but can try this activity when you haven't done it in a while or when you have a letter that lends itself to lots of ideas. (For more tips on drawing silly pictures with your class, see page 12.)

There are so many animals, foods, and other objects that begin with "b," it will be easy to quickly build a silly picture. For example, a bunny could be in a boat wearing one boot, some beautiful beads, and a bow. In his basket is his bug, who likes to eat bananas mixed with beans. After you finish the class picture, have the children draw their own sound pictures.

The letter "b" is for "bouncing" and "ball."

Playing with a beach ball.

activity

Let's Pretend

Involving the "b" sound in games of pretend will make the sound even more memorable and fun for the children. Whether you do all or just one of the following ideas, remember to keep the session relatively short to hold the children's attention. Try to keep the novelty factor alive: For example, choose activities that are different from the Let's Pretend activities you've recently done for other letters.

If you use an audiotape, remember to prepare it in advance so you don't lose the children's attention while you get the tape ready or switch tapes. Likewise, have the bubbles or balls ready for use, or the balloons blown up, if your Let's Pretend time includes these items.

- *Goldilocks and the Three Bears* is my absolute favorite to act out. This is not a play—as you tell the story, the children mime in their own way what is happening. If you have access to an audiotape of the story, then you can join in the miming, too.

- You can use this Let's Pretend time as a general movement time also. Play some floaty music and blow bubbles or to put on some strongly rhythmic music and bounce balls.

- Bring in a bunch of blue balloons already blown up and see how long the children can keep them in the air. Later they can use them for the craft activity of making a hot air balloon.

TiP

> **You could try a Let's Pretend session in which the children pretend to bake bread. The book *Bread, Bread, Bread* (Morris 1989) would be a great companion to this session.**

Crafts for "b"

Hot Air Balloons

These look super suspended from the ceiling of the classroom, and they are a fun way to continue practicing the "b" sound as children make b-b-b-balloons. Note that this craft takes place over a few days.

Materials

- ✔ a balloon for each child
- ✔ a cup on which to rest each balloon (a plastic cup will need a weight such as a toy brick or a small rock)
- ✔ petroleum jelly
- ✔ about two double pages of newspaper for each child
- ✔ a small container of wallpaper paste
- ✔ a small milk carton for each child
- ✔ three 12" pieces of yarn for each child
- ✔ liquid tempera paint (washable)
- ✔ spray paint
- ✔ long-sleeved coveralls for each child (or have them bring in an adult's old long-sleeved shirt)
- ✔ stickers or collage items (optional)
- ✔ single hole punch
- ✔ blunt needle
- ✔ marker
- ✔ scissors or Exacto knife

TiP

One small carton of wallpaper paste goes a long way, but if it's unavailable, watered-down PVA glue works too.

Preparation

1. Cut the tops off the small milk cartons, leaving an open cube shape. Spray paint the cartons the day before class, or cover with a band of child-made weaving (see "w" on pages 181–182). These cartons are usually waxy and do not take the usual classroom paint.

2. Blow up the balloons before class, but not completely or they will be too big for the children to handle.

3. Write each child's initials on her cup.

4. Before the children begin the activity as outlined below, dress them in long-sleeved coveralls or big shirts, as this activity can be very messy. Depending on the children, you may want to start some of the following steps before class begins.

Directions

1. Have the children rest the balloons in the cups and smother the balloons with petroleum jelly. This should prevent the papier-mâché from sticking to the balloons.

2. Next, the children should tear the newspaper into strips about one inch wide.

3. Then have them dip each newspaper strip into the wallpaper paste, smoothing off the excess with their fingers. This is very messy, but the children usually love it.

4. Next, they lay the newspaper strips over the balloons, leaving a gap at the bottom where the knot of the balloon is resting in the cup.

5. The children should continue to layer the newspaper strips over the balloons until there are about two complete layers.

6. Leave the balloons to dry for a day or two. The children can spend this time decorating the spray-painted cartons with collages and stickers.

7. After the papier-mâché balloons are completely dry, the children pop or remove the real balloons, remove the cups, then paint the now solid balloon shapes with tempera.

8. You will probably need to do these last steps: Punch a hole on two opposite sides of each carton, and punch a hole on each side of the base of the balloons. Connect the balloon to the basket using the yarn.

9. Using a blunt needle, thread some yarn through the top of the balloons so they can be hung from the ceiling.

Bubble Painting

These lovely "bouquets" can be used as the front of big thank-you cards. Dark colors, such as red, blue, purple, and orange, work best because the paint becomes very diluted. Yellow hardly shows up.

Materials

- ✔ dish soap
- ✔ nontoxic liquid tempera paint
- ✔ plastic cereal bowl for each paint color
- ✔ straw for each color of paint, for each child
- ✔ five sheets of 8 ½" x 11" white paper for each child
- ✔ a sheet of green construction paper for leaves for each child
- ✔ a sheet of colored construction paper for background for each child
- ✔ glue for each child or small group
- ✔ a green crayon for each child
- ✔ scissors

Preparation

Right before class, mix a small amount of paint, dish soap, and water in one of the bowls. Use one bowl for each color.

Directions

1. Give each child a straw. Practice the difference between blowing and sucking.

2. Let the children take turns blowing gently into the bubble-paint mixture through the straw. The bubbles should grow into a dome shape above the rim of the bowl.

3. The child then takes a sheet of white paper and gently lays it over the dome of bubbles. Have him press down very gently until the paper is flat across the top of the bowl. Look at the paper and you will see that the impression of the paint and bubbles has made a flowerlike picture. Each child can make several flowers in different colors to build up enough for a bouquet. Write each child's initials or full name on the paper so you can keep track of which flowers belong to whom as they dry.

4. When the pictures are dry, you or the children cut around the bubble flowers. I usually do this the night after the activity, cutting around in a scalloped shape.

5. The next day, give each child a large piece of colored construction paper for the background, the child's pile of flowers already cut out, some green construction paper for cutting out leaves, glue, and a green crayon. Each child can design and glue onto the colored paper a bouquet with leaves, then draw in the stems with the green crayon.

Blowing bubbles for bubble painting.

Bead Activity Center

For a "b" activity center, you could set up a special area where children can thread big beads on laces. Every other day, change the beads to buttons to maintain a fresh awareness of the sound of "b" during this week.

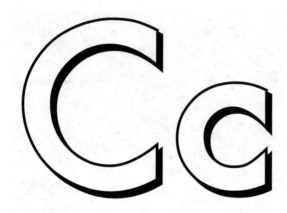

The shape of "c" is an absolute gift because it really does look like a curly caterpillar. Many teachers work on life-cycle projects that highlight the life of a caterpillar, and for this, of course, Eric Carle's *The Very Hungry Caterpillar* (1994) is a must. Other great reading for "c" includes *My Crayons Talk* (Hubbard 1996) and the popular *Clifford: The Big Red Dog* (Bridwell 1985).

As "c" is such an easy sound, you can introduce it early in the school year any time after "s," "t," and "m." During the winter, you can make good use of the many creative "cold" activities available. If your students study the five senses, you can introduce "c" when you decorate cookies as part of the sense of taste. If your students study nursery rhymes, you could introduce "c" for "clock" during "Hickory Dickory Dock."

Activities to Introduce "c"

The activities in this section are for the first day you introduce "c" to the children. The first activity—See, Say, and Sing—involves a picture dictionary, a big feely letter "c" made out of felt, and the alphabet song all used together to involve the children in this exciting new sound. The second activity—The Big Event— will involve the children in a physical activity to help reinforce the sound of the letter. The Big Event for "c" has children crawling into a cave in search of items that start with "c." *Important note:* The Big Event should follow immediately after the brief introduction of See, Say, and Sing activities to be most effective in solidifying the new letter for the children. Gather materials and prepare for *both* activities before you introduce "c" to your class. (See pages 7–11 for more information on introducing a new sound.)

Curly caterpillar "c"

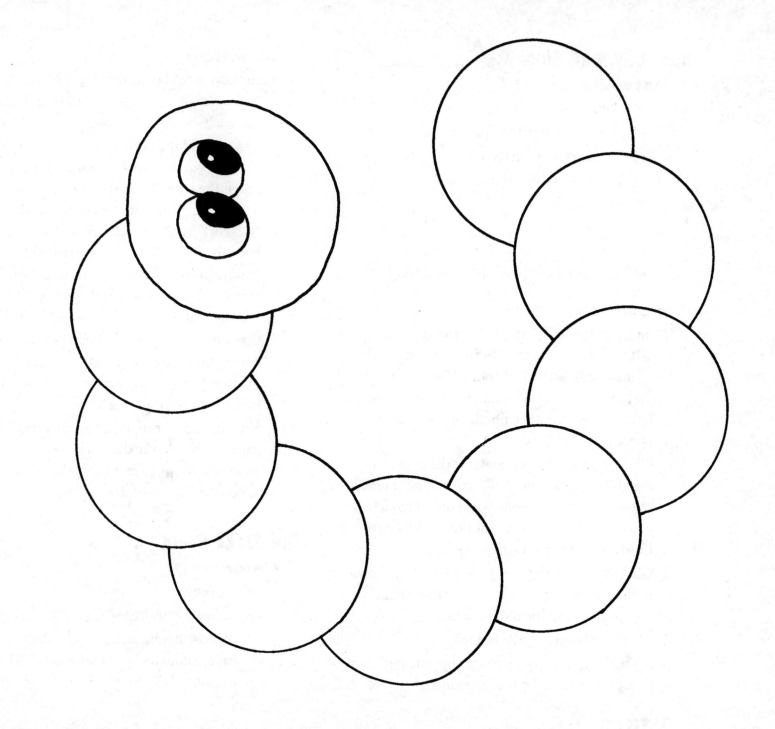

See, Say, and Sing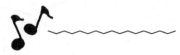

Materials

✔ picture dictionary

✔ photocopy of the "c" pattern on page 39

✔ 8" x 8" piece of green felt

✔ 3" x 3" piece of red felt

✔ wiggle eyes

✔ scissors

✔ glue

✔ thin cardboard (such as a cereal box)

Preparation

1. To make the feely letter "c," photocopy and cut out the pattern on page 39 (unless you decide to make this letter freehand, without using the pattern). You may also wish to create a bigger letter by enlarging the photocopy and using larger pieces of felt.

2. Cut out the circle that contains the eyes and use this circle as a guide for cutting eight circles out of green felt and one circle out of red felt (unless you decide to cut out each element of this feely letter freehand).

3. Glue the circles together to form a "c" as shown in the pattern, starting with the tail-end circle and ending with the red felt head.

4. Glue wiggle eyes on the red felt head.

5. Make the entire letter stronger by gluing it onto thin cardboard and cutting around it.

Directions

1. Introduce "c" by making lots of "c-c-c" (hard "c," not "see") sounds with the children, showing what it feels like to say "c."

2. Pass around the curly caterpillar "c" so the children can see what "c" looks like and can touch the letter while they practice the "c" sound. Exaggerate the "c" sound in the words "c-c-curly" and "c-c-caterpillar." Remember to keep the big feely "c" in constant view so the children can make the connection that the activities that follow all relate to "c."

3. Tell the children that "c" has a name just like they do and discuss the difference between the name of the letter "c" and the sound it makes in "caterpillar." Sing through the alphabet to find where "c" is hiding.

4. Sing through the alphabet again as you turn the pages of the picture dictionary. Pick out a couple of "c" pictures to show the class more words that start with the "c" sound.

The *BIG* Event

Materials

✔ two chairs

✔ a sheet (any size)

✔ objects that begin with "c" to put into the cave (enough objects for each child to pull one out of the cave)

Preparation

1. Prepare your cave by draping a sheet over two chairs (leaving enough space between the chairs for children to crawl through).

2. Gather several objects that begin with "c," enough for every child in your class to pull at least one object out of the cave. For example: a carrot, car, candle, cup, cone, cat, candy cane, clown, and clock. Place all of these objects in the cave.

3. Prepare a separate container or place where the children can put the objects they pull out of the cave. For example, you might have them place each object in a case, in a car, or on a big picture of a carrot!

Cave explorers search for something that begins with "c."

Directions

1. One at a time, the children take turns crawling like a caterpillar into the cave to collect an item beginning with "c."

2. While the others are waiting to see what a child pulls out, have them all join in with a gentle "c-c-c" that will lead nicely into the name of the item pulled out.

3. After each child crawls out with her "c" item, everyone should identify what the item is. Then she can crawl over and put it into another container beginning with "c."

Cave Activity Center

For a simple "c" activity center, leave the cave set up during the week. It will open up a whole new realm for role-play during choosing time.

More Ideas for "c"

Sensational "c"

Pour a layer of corn into a tray (such as a cafeteria tray)—colored corn is particularly nice. Let the children take turns tracing a curly "c" in the corn with their fingers, so they can see and feel the shape. Make sure the feely letter "c" is clearly visible to all children as a model.

TiP Try using cornflakes instead of corn for a crunchy "c."

Silly Pictures

A silly picture composed of things that start with "c" is one more way to solidify the sound in children's minds. Use a large sheet of paper with colored pens, a dry-erase board, or a chalkboard—anything that enables the children to watch you draw. Start with something that begins with the letter (such as an animal), then ask the children for ideas. (Have the picture dictionary open at the relevant page to help, but let the children feel that you believe they really did think up the ideas on their own.)

Remember that silly pictures are most effective if they seem novel to the children. You don't have to draw for every letter but can try this activity when you haven't done it in a while or when you have a letter that lends itself to lots of ideas. (For more tips on drawing silly pictures with your class, see page 12.)

For the letter "c," you could start with a caterpillar in a car, eating a carrot! After you finish the class picture, have the children draw their own sound pictures.

Let's Pretend

Involving the "c" sound in games of pretend will make the sound even more memorable and fun for the children. Whether you do all or just one of the following ideas, remember to keep the session relatively short to hold the children's attention. Try to keep the novelty factor alive: For example, choose activities that are different from the Let's Pretend activities you've recently done for other letters.

- The story of *The Very Hungry Caterpillar* (Carle 1994) is great to mime. Children just love to crawl around on the floor.

- "C" is also for "cold," and there are all sorts of miming opportunities here. The children can pretend to peep out the door and feel how cold it is outside. They can then get dressed up for the weather by putting on mittens, a big coat, a scarf, a woolly hat, and big boots. When they go outside, the cold wind is blowing them back and they have to struggle to walk against it. They try to warm themselves by rubbing their hands together and stamping their feet on the ground. At the end, they come in from the cold, take off all the extra layers of clothes, and curl up by the warm fire with their pet cat.

- *Copy Me, Copycat* (Edwards 1999) is ideal for miming.

Crafts for "c"

Caterpillars

These caterpillars look wonderful displayed on large construction-paper leaves; some could have bite marks along the edges! Note that this craft takes two days because the paint has to dry. As always, we are not looking for identical perfection. Even using just two colors, the caterpillars will all look different because of the different painting techniques, placement of the eyes, and shaping of the feelers.

Materials

- ✔ egg cartons (a row for each child)
- ✔ liquid tempera paint
- ✔ paintbrush for each child
- ✔ a pair of wiggle eyes for each child
- ✔ one chenille stem for each child
- ✔ glue for each child or small group
- ✔ scissors
- ✔ marker

Preparation

1. Cut the rows of the egg cartons apart, so that each child will get a row of at least five egg holders.

2. Pierce one end twice to create two holes for the chenille stem to go through. This will be the head.

Directions

1. Give each child a row of egg holders, a chenille stem, a paintbrush, and a pair of wiggle eyes. Groups of children can share the glue and paint. Point out which end is the head.

2. The children paint the caterpillars. Write each child's initials or full name on the underside of the caterpillars so they don't get mixed up as they dry.

3. When the caterpillars are dry (probably the next day), the children can thread the chenille stem through the holes to make the feelers by folding the stem in half and threading each end through the pierced holes from underneath. The child can curl the feelers as she wishes, then stick on the wiggle eyes—very simple, very effective.

More Crafts for "c": Caterpillar Clips

For each child, gather a clothespin, five colored half-inch pom-poms, small wiggle eyes, and glue. (You can find pom-poms at a crafts store, in an educational supply catalog, or at a general discount store.) Each child glues a line of pom-poms along the flat side of the clothespin, then glues two small wiggle eyes to the caterpillar's head. Just like that, their caterpillar is ready to keep their papers in order!

A Cold Picture

This craft is particularly effective if using "c" as part of a "cold" theme. Each child gets to mix his own paint. The process of gradually adding the Epsom salts, causing a change in the consistency, is valuable to a child.

Materials

✔ Epsom salts

✔ white liquid tempera paint

✔ a cereal-sized plastic bowl or a cup for each child

✔ a sheet of dark blue construction paper for each child

✔ winter pictures for the children to cut out, such as snow-covered trees and winter animals

✔ glue for each child or small group

✔ scissors for each child

✔ paintbrush for each child

Preparation

No preparation except to gather materials.

Directions

1. Have the children cut out a variety of cold winter pictures and make a collage on the dark blue construction-paper background.

2. When they have finished, help them mix Epsom salts with the white paint, letting them stir with the paintbrush. This gives a chunky texture to the paint to make it snowlike.

3. The children can then make their collages really cold by adding the snow-paint to their scene. Children love to apply this wonderful thick mixture to transform their picture.

TiP

Make and decorate cookies for a tasty "c" activity!

Catching Cones

This craft takes hardly any time to make, but the catching fun continues at home well after school is out. People of all ages play with the cones; for this reason, do use the toughest tape you can find.

Materials

✔ a Ping-Pong ball for each child

✔ a cardboard tube, about 6" long, for each child

✔ 2' piece of yarn for each child

✔ tape

✔ a sheet of construction paper for each child

✔ scissors

Preparation

No preparation except to gather materials.

Directions

1. Help the children make cones out of the construction paper, rolling it into a funnel and taping it closed. You may want to trim the top to make it even all around.

2. Next, they attach their cones to the cardboard tubes by putting the cone inside the top of the tube and securing with tape.

3. Then each child tapes a piece of yarn to the bottom of the tube (opposite where the cone is attached), and tapes the Ping-Pong ball to the other end of the yarn. The tube is the handle on the catching cone. The children try to catch the ball in the cone!

Playing with the catching cones is just as fun as making them.

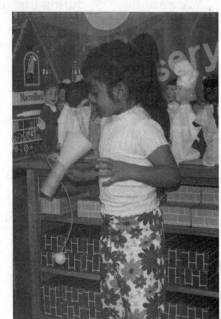

Trying to catch the ball in the cone.

Many teachers work on a dinosaur unit, so to introduce "d" during this time is ideal. If we are studying people who help us, I introduce "d" when we are finding out about the dentist or the doctor. Try to introduce "d," bouncy "b," and the delicate pink "p" close together to really emphasize their similarities and differences. They can be introduced quite early in the school year after "s," "t," and "m," because there are so many easily found objects that have these initial consonants. Very young children can easily reproduce the circle-stick formation of the letters, even though not entirely accurately, but that does not matter at this stage.

Activities to Introduce "d"

The activities in this section are for the first day you introduce "d" to the children. The first activity—See, Say, and Sing—involves a picture dictionary, a big feely letter "d" made out of felt, and the alphabet song all used together to involve the children in this exciting new sound. The second activity—The Big Event—will involve the children in a physical activity to help reinforce the sound of the letter. The Big Event for "d" is a dinosaur dig! *Important note:* The Big Event should follow immediately after the brief introduction of See, Say, and Sing activities to be most effective in solidifying the new letter for the children. Gather materials and prepare for *both* activities before you introduce "d" to your class. (See pages 7–11 for more information on introducing a new sound.)

Dinosaur "d"

See, Say, and Sing

Materials

- ✔ picture dictionary
- ✔ photocopy of the "d" pattern on page 47
- ✔ 8½" x 11" piece of green felt
- ✔ 1" x 11" piece of red felt
- ✔ scissors
- ✔ glue
- ✔ thin cardboard (such as a cereal box)

Preparation

1. To make the feely letter "d," photocopy and cut out the pattern on page 47 (unless you decide to make this letter freehand, without using the pattern). You may also wish to create a bigger letter by enlarging the photocopy and using larger pieces of felt.

2. Cut the triangle strip from the pattern and use it as a guide for cutting out a strip of triangles from the red felt (unless you decide to cut the elements of this feely letter freehand).

3. Use the "d" pattern (without the triangles) as a guide for cutting the "d" out of the green felt (or cut the "d" freehand).

4. Glue the red triangle strip to the green "d" as shown on the pattern.

5. Make the entire letter stronger by gluing it onto thin cardboard and cutting around it.

Directions

1. Introduce "d" by making lots of "d-d-d" sounds with the children, showing what it feels like to say "d," almost like a d-d-d-drill!

2. Pass around the big feely dinosaur "d" so the children can see what "d" looks like and can touch the letter while they practice the "d" sound. Exaggerate the "d" sound in the word "d-d-dinosaur." Remember to keep the big feely "d" in constant view so the children can make the connection that the activities that follow all relate to "d."

3. Tell the children that "d" has a name just like they do and discuss the difference between the name of the letter "d" and the sound it makes. Sing through the alphabet to find where "d" is hiding.

4. Sing through the alphabet again as you turn the pages of the picture dictionary. Pick out a couple of "d" pictures to show the class more words that start with the "d" sound.

5. Make the room dark, enunciating the word "dark" as you do. Children always love this. Turning off the lights for a couple of minutes creates a magical, cozy feeling.

The *BIG* Event

Materials

- ✔ large cardboard box (no higher than 12")
- ✔ toy dinosaurs (one for each child)
- ✔ Styrofoam chips/peanuts (enough to fill the box)
- ✔ feather duster
- ✔ premade plastic dinosaur landscape *or* the following materials to make one:
  - blue posterboard (as large as you wish)
  - two sheets of yellow, green, or light brown construction paper
  - colorful markers or pictures of natural items such as waterfalls, trees, mountains, and so forth
  - tape
- ✔ glue

Preparation

1. Fill the box with the dinosaur toys and Styrofoam chips. Mix everything up as much as possible.

2. Create a dinosaur landscape on which the children will place their dinosaurs after "digging." Alternatively, you could buy a ready-made landscape. I purchased a plastic sheet with a landscape already painted on it, but it is easy enough to make your own. To make one:
   - Start with a sheet of blue posterboard.
   - Using two sheets of large yellow, green, or light brown construction paper taped together, cut out a shape of an island as seen from the sky.
   - Glue this onto the blue posterboard, which has become the sea surrounding your island.
   - Now embellish your island with trees, mountains, rivers, caves, waterfalls, and plants. You can draw these with markers or use pictures cut out from magazines or vacation brochures.

Digging for dinosaurs.

Directions

1. Tell the children they are now going to dig for dinosaurs. Each child takes a turn digging in the box until he finds one dinosaur.

2. When a child has dug up a dinosaur, he should dust it off with a duster and then place the dinosaur on the dinosaur landscape.

3. As the children dig, continue to put great emphasis on the "d-d-d" sound while repeating aloud what the children are doing (*digging* for *dinosaurs, dusting* off *dinosaurs*). Keep referring to the big feely dinosaur "d."

TiP

Instead of a dinosaur, you can use a dragon to introduce the letter "d." You don't even have to change the feely letter. This could work to your advantage if you have a unit on fairy tales rather than dinosaurs.

More Ideas for "d"

Sensational "d"

Collect the dots from a hole punch and spread them out on a tray (such as a cafeteria tray). You can keep the dots forever; they take up hardly any space. Let the children take turns tracing a "d" in the dots with their fingers, so they can see and feel the shape. Make sure the feely letter "d" is clearly visible to all children as a model.

TiP

Another idea is to buy a pack of mini dog biscuits that come in the shape of little dog bones. Again, spread them out on the tray and have the children trace a "d" with their finger. Keep a tiny toy dog in the center of this activity to keep the focus on "d" for dog. This is practical only if you have a dog who will eat the biscuits afterward.

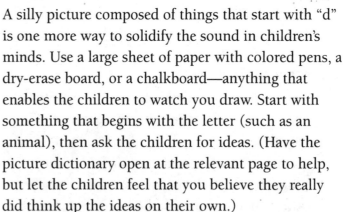

Silly Pictures

A silly picture composed of things that start with "d" is one more way to solidify the sound in children's minds. Use a large sheet of paper with colored pens, a dry-erase board, or a chalkboard—anything that enables the children to watch you draw. Start with something that begins with the letter (such as an animal), then ask the children for ideas. (Have the picture dictionary open at the relevant page to help, but let the children feel that you believe they really did think up the ideas on their own.)

Remember that silly pictures are most effective if they seem novel to the children. You don't have to draw for every letter but can try this activity when you haven't done it in a while or when you have a letter that lends itself to lots of ideas. (For more tips on drawing silly pictures with your class, see page 12.)

A dotty duck who likes to dance could be your starting point for "d." This is very easy to draw and should inspire lots of d-d-d suggestions. After you finish the class picture, have the children draw their own sound pictures.

Let's Pretend

Involving the "d" sound in games of pretend will make the sound even more memorable and fun for the children. Probably the most fun is to find something that you can do in the dark. For example: There are lots of children's poems and books that take place on a dark, scary night, which you could read as the class mimes along. I like to use the children's book *In a Dark, Dark House* (Dussling 1995). Doing the whole session in the dark will make it that much more special and meaningful. Try to do this on a different day from the day you introduced "d" and turned the lights off for the dinosaur dig. That way there will be more reinforcement of the "d" sound later in the week.

Crafts for "d"
Drum

In a year when we are studying the five senses, we make the drums when we are learning about hearing. We certainly enjoy hearing the drums we make, and there is no better sound connection than d-d-d-drum, the very sound made by the drum!

Materials

✔ a coffee can or other suitable container for each child (lids not necessary)
✔ wax paper
✔ a handful of dried corn or beans for each child
✔ rubber band for each child
✔ paper to cover the sides of each can
✔ transparent tape
✔ crayons

Preparation
1. Prepare the paper beforehand by cutting pieces in the right size to cover the sides of each child's can.
2. Cut the wax paper circles ahead of time as well, at least two inches bigger than the top of each can.

51

Directions

1. Have the children decorate their paper with crayons (or whatever you prefer) and wrap the paper around the cans, attaching it with tape.

2. Next, each child should put a handful of dried corn or beans into her container, place the wax paper on the top, smooth it down, and secure it with a rubber band. The children may need help with the band, but at least let them try first. Whenever possible, avoid taking a whole stage of the activity completely away from the children. If a child needs help, anchor one side of the band for her while she stretches the rest over the top of the can. The d-d-d-drums should now be ready to play.

Dinner Plate

It's fun to create the *Today Is Monday* (Carle 2001) dinner plate. The story features different animals eating different meals each day of the week. My children particularly enjoy this story. "Days" fits in nicely with the "d" sound, as does "dinner."

Materials

- ✔ paper plate for each child
- ✔ glue for each child or small group
- ✔ a button for each child
- ✔ 6" (at least) of green yarn for each child
- ✔ small jar of glitter

- ✔ enough construction paper to cut out one 2" fish for each child
- ✔ scissors
- ✔ a colored feather for each child
- ✔ a few small strips of spaghetti (or other kind of pasta) for each child
- ✔ a few cotton balls for each child
- ✔ seven plastic bowls (such as cereal bowls)

Preparation

1. Gather your materials. You can actually use whatever you have in your craft box as long as you have seven different pretend food items.

2. Go through the song and decide what will represent each day's food (see the example list opposite).

3. Cut fish shapes out of the construction paper (enough for each child to have at least one).

4. Cut the yarn into pieces a few inches long.

5. Set out each of the different "food" items in seven different bowls, where each child will have easy access to them.

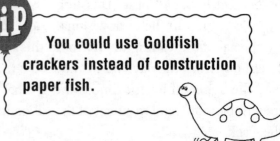

TiP

You could use Goldfish crackers instead of construction paper fish.

Directions

After singing *Today Is Monday*, the children glue their dinner servings onto their own individual paper plates. Make sure each child has a portion for each of the seven days.

Monday, string beans: yarn

Tuesday, spaghetti: dried spaghetti or pasta

Wednesday, ZOOOP (which is actually soup): glitter (something special for everybody's favorite day to sing about)

Thursday, roast beef: a button

Friday, fresh fish: the construction-paper fish

Saturday, chicken: a feather

Sunday, ice cream: cotton balls

TiP

Cookie's Week (Ward 1988) is great reading during the week of "d" because of the repeated use of "days." *Max's Dragon Shirt* (Wells 1997) is another great title: The "d" for "dragon" is very prominent in this book.

Dominoes Activity Center

Put out dominoes as a special activity. Review how to play, and use circle time to play a game in which the class plays against the teacher. The children take turns around the circle to lay one domino from a pile of dominoes. Remind the children about the various types of dominoes available, such as pictures, colors, and dots.

Spelling out "dog" with the big feely letters.

Ee

Introduce the vowels late in the year when some children are ready for building consonant-vowel-consonant words. Focus on the "e" sound as in "e-e-elephant." This will be so helpful for the children moving on to word building where the same sound of "e" is used, such as in "net" and "pen." It is very appropriate to bring out this sound in spring when there are many toy and candy eggs around.

Activities to Introduce "e"

The activities in this section are for the first day you introduce "e" to the children. The first activity—See, Say, and Sing—involves a picture dictionary, a big feely letter "e" made out of felt, and the alphabet song all used together to involve the children in this exciting new sound. The second activity—The Big Event—will involve the children in a physical activity to help reinforce the sound of the letter. The Big Event for "e" has children choosing eggs from an egg tree and opening them to reveal another egg, an elephant, or emptiness. *Important note:* The Big Event should follow immediately after the brief introduction of See, Say, and Sing activities to be most effective in solidifying the new letter for the children. Gather materials and prepare for *both* activities before you introduce "e" to your class. (See pages 7–11 for more information on introducing a new sound.)

Elephant "e"

See, Say, and Sing

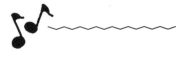

Materials

- ✔ picture dictionary
- ✔ photocopy of the "e" pattern on page 55
- ✔ 2" x 3" piece of pink felt
- ✔ 8 ½" x 11" piece of gray felt
- ✔ 2" x 2" piece of white felt
- ✔ scissors
- ✔ glue
- ✔ thin cardboard (such as a cereal box)

Preparation

1. To make the feely letter "e," photocopy and cut out the pattern on page 55 (unless you decide to make this letter freehand, without using the pattern). You may also wish to create a bigger letter by enlarging the photocopy and using larger pieces of felt.

2. Cut out the pieces of the pattern: the tusk, the inner ear, and the outer ear (unless you decide to cut the entire feely letter freehand).

3. Cut the inner ear shape out of pink felt, the tusk shape out of white felt, and the outer ear and the "e" out of gray felt, using the pattern as a guide.

4. Glue all shapes together as shown on the pattern.

5. Make the entire letter stronger by gluing it onto thin cardboard and cutting around it.

Directions

1. Introduce "e" by making lots of "e-e-e" sounds with the children (the short "e" in "elephant," not a long "ee"), showing what it feels like to say "e." The "e" for "elephant" and "egg" is particularly difficult because it sounds so much like a short "i." Think how much alike "tin" and "ten" sound when they are spoken aloud. When you introduce "e" to the class, point out that when we say short "i," we show our bottom teeth, but not when we say short "e."

2. Pass around the big feely elephant "e" so the children can see what "e" looks like and can touch the letter while they practice the "e" sound. Exaggerate the "e" sound in the word "e-e-elephant." Remember to keep the big feely "e" in constant view so the children can make the connection that the activities that follow all relate to "e."

3. Tell the children that "e" has a name just like they do and discuss the difference between the name of the letter "e" and the sound it makes in "elephant." Sing through the alphabet to find where "e" is hiding.

4. Sing through the alphabet again as you turn the pages of the picture dictionary. Pick out a couple of "e" pictures to show the class more words that start with the short "e" sound.

The *BIG* Event

Materials

✔ an egg tree (the kind used for drying painted eggs)—If you have a large class, you may need more than one tree, or you could just keep restocking the tree between turns.

✔ plastic eggs (two for each child)

✔ tiny chocolate eggs (enough for each child to have one)

✔ tiny plastic elephants, elephant erasers, or even drawings of elephants

✔ a large envelope (at least 11" x 14")

Preparation

1. Place elephants inside a third of the plastic eggs, chocolate eggs inside a third of the plastic eggs, leaving a third of the eggs empty.

2. Set up the egg tree where the children can reach the top of it easily. Place the eggs in the tree.

3. Write "eggs" on the envelope (and draw a picture of an egg on it).

Directions

1. Give each child a turn to choose one plastic egg from the tree and open it. If an elephant is inside, he can put it at the base of the tree. If a chocolate egg is inside, he can keep it. If it is an empty egg, he can put it in the envelope marked "eggs" and have another turn.

2. As each child opens an egg, have the other children say whether they think it will be e-e-empty or an e-e-elephant or an e-e-egg. In joint anticipation, we usually say in unison, "It's an e-e-e" until the egg finally opens and we can all spill out the word "elephant" or whatever it may be.

3. At the end of the activity, pass out chocolate eggs to the children who didn't choose one so that everyone gets a treat.

What's inside this egg?

Enter and Exit

A little more advanced but still great fun is the Enter and Exit game. Set up three chairs with space between them so that they make an entrance and an exit, and make signs saying "enter" and "exit." Review with the children what "enter" and "exit" mean. To enter, the child has to recognize the letter "e" (you can use the big feely "e" for this) and then receive a ticket with an "e" written on it. Everyone can make a big deal of saying, "You may enter." She enters and walks through, but to exit she has to answer a question, using a word that begins with "e." Try to make the questions as funny as possible. For instance, ask, "What is sitting on my head?" while you have a toy elephant perched on top of your head. When the child has answered the question, the class can join in with, "You may exit." The child then puts her "e" ticket in an envelope and goes to sit down.

More Ideas for "e"

Sensational "e"

Fill a tray (such as a cafeteria tray) with a layer of flour, then a layer of chocolate eggs. The chocolate eggs will roll around too much in a tray by themselves. With the layer of flour, the children will be able to see exactly where they have drawn an "e" with their fingers. The main impression to them will be that they drew an "e" in the eggs. Let the children take turns tracing an "e" in the eggs (and flour) with their fingers, so they can see and feel the shape. Make sure the feely letter "e" is clearly visible to all children as a model.

TIP

You could also try using scrambled eggs instead of chocolate ones.

Silly Pictures

A silly picture composed of things that start with "e" is one more way to solidify the sound in children's minds. Use a large sheet of paper with colored pens, a dry-erase board, or a chalkboard—anything that enables the children to watch you draw. Start with something that begins with the letter (such as an animal), then ask the children for ideas. (Have the picture dictionary open at the relevant page to help, but let the children feel that you believe they really did think up the ideas on their own.)

Remember that silly pictures are most effective if they seem novel to the children. You don't have to draw for every letter but can try this activity when you haven't done it in a while or when you have a letter that lends itself to lots of ideas. (For more tips on drawing silly pictures with your class, see page 12.)

The letter "e" may be a difficult one to draw, particularly when you're trying to stick to the short "eh" sound. Think about an elephant exercising! After you finish the class picture, have the children draw their own sound pictures.

Let's Pretend

Involving the "e" sound in games of pretend will make the sound even more memorable and fun for the children. I've had great success using an elephant for inspiration. Remember to keep the session relatively short to hold the children's attention, and try to keep the novelty factor alive: For example, choose activities that are different from the Let's Pretend activities you've recently done for other letters.

There are many books for young children about elephants. I usually use the stories about the Large family, such as *A Piece of Cake* (Murphy 1997). However, an elephant is so fascinating in its own right that a good deal of time can be spent mimicking its movements and actions. Think about the way an elephant's ears flap, how it walks, how it wallows in the cool water, swishes its trunk in the water, squirts water, reaches for food with its trunk, rubs its back against a tree, and rolls in the mud. There are many, many possibilities. When everyone is well and truly in the elephant mode, put on *Carnival of the Animals* by Saint-Saëns, or some suitable tuba music, and let your herd of elephants roam in the wild.

Crafts for "e"
Elephant's Toothbrush

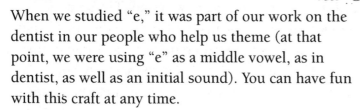

When we studied "e," it was part of our work on the dentist in our people who help us theme (at that point, we were using "e" as a middle vowel, as in dentist, as well as an initial sound). You can have fun with this craft at any time.

Materials
- ✔ a 3" x 8" strip of tough cardboard for each child
- ✔ a 2" x 3" block of florist's foam, about 1" thick, for each child
- ✔ toothpicks (as blunt as possible), at least 25 for each child
- ✔ glue
- ✔ liquid tempera paint
- ✔ ribbon
- ✔ single hole punch

Preparation

Glue the foam near the top of the cardboard. If you imagine that this is a giant toothbrush, and the foam is where the bristles will be, you will find the right position. I complete this stage the night before so the children can spend the first session just decorating the elephant's toothbrush.

Directions

1. You might want to discuss what sort of pictures the elephant would like on his toothbrush before the children begin decorating. Then have them go ahead and paint the cardboard. Write their initials somewhere on the cardboard so they can keep track of their toothbrushes as they dry.

2. When the paint is dry, the children can push the individual toothpicks into the foam. These are the bristles on the toothbrush, so the more there are, the better the brush will be. If the children work from one end first or from the center outward, they will not have to push bristles in among other bristles. This is actually a very relaxing exercise.

3. To hang the brushes, punch a hole in the end of the handle and thread a loop of ribbon through. They make a very attractive wall display.

Activities to Introduce "f"

The letter "f" lends itself to the season of fall beautifully. Not only are the leaves falling from the trees, but also fall is the season leading to Thanksgiving, when there is an abundance of "f" words and related crafts. There are the feathers on the Native American headdresses and ceremonial clothing; there is the feast itself when all the family gathers together; and there is the fruit falling from the cornucopia. For these reasons, I usually introduce "f" at this time of year.

There is an absolute plethora of great "f" material. Two favorites in my room are my feely box (described in the Big Event on page 62) and my toy farm. I bring them in only occasionally to retain the novelty factor.

The activities in this section are for the first day you introduce "f" to the children. The first activity—See, Say, and Sing—involves a picture dictionary, a big feely letter "f" made out of cardboard and feathers, and the alphabet song all used together to involve the children in this exciting new sound. The second activity—The Big Event—will involve the children in a physical activity to help reinforce the sound of the letter. The Big Event for "f" involves a feely box, a mysterious box into which children stick their hands and describe an object they feel. *Important note:* The Big Event should follow immediately after the brief introduction of See, Say, and Sing activities to be most effective in solidifying the new letter for the children. Gather materials and prepare for *both* activities before you introduce "f" to your class. (See pages 7–11 for more information on introducing a new sound.)

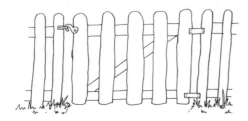

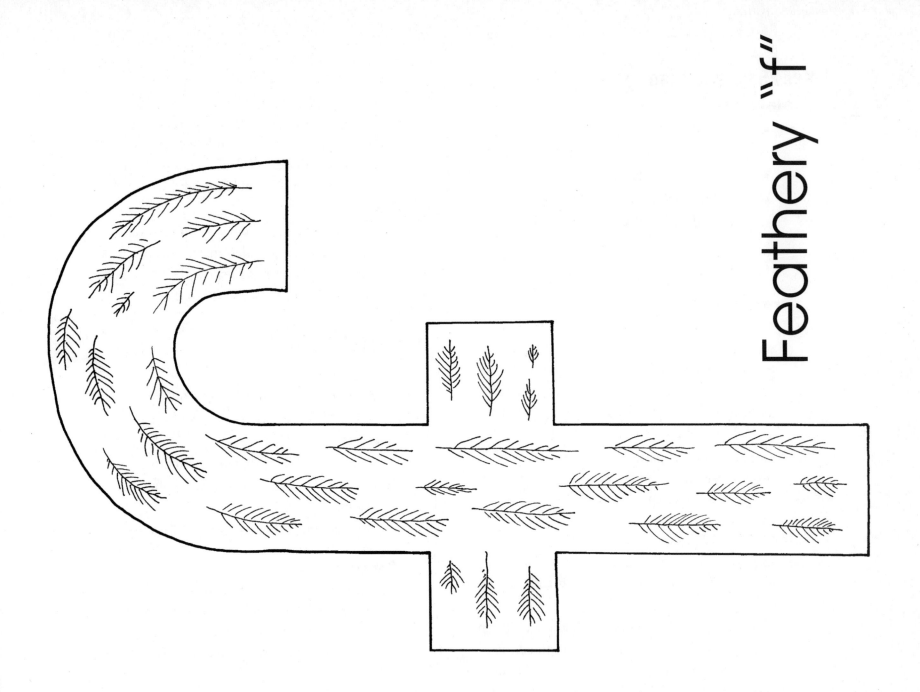

Feathery "f"

See, Say, and Sing

Materials

- ✔ picture dictionary
- ✔ photocopy of the "f" pattern on page 61
- ✔ 8 ½" x 11" thin cardboard
- ✔ feathers (available at craft stores, educational supply stores, and general discount stores)
- ✔ scissors
- ✔ glue

Preparation

1. To make the feely letter "f," photocopy and cut out the pattern on page 61 (unless you decide to make this letter freehand, without using the pattern). You may also wish to create a bigger letter by enlarging the photocopy and using a larger piece of cardboard.
2. Trace around the pattern onto the cardboard (or cut freehand) and cut out the card "f."
3. Glue the feathers all over the "f."

Directions

1. Introduce "f" by making lots of "f-f-f" sounds with the children, showing what it feels like to say "f."
2. Pass around the big feathery "f" so the children can see what "f" looks like and can touch the letter while they practice the "f" sound. Exaggerate the "f" sound in the word "f-f-feathery." Remember to keep the big "f" in constant view

so the children can make the connection that the activities that follow all relate to "f."

3. Tell the children that "f" has a name just like they do and discuss the difference between the name of the letter "f" and the sound it makes. Sing through the alphabet to find where "f" is hiding.
4. Sing through the alphabet again as you turn the pages of the picture dictionary. Pick out a couple of "f" pictures to show the class more words that start with the "f" sound.

The *BIG* Event

Materials

- ✔ large box (about 12" high and wide and up to 18" long)
- ✔ scissors
- ✔ various objects that are distinctive to the touch (such as a feather, a seashell, an apple)
- ✔ piece of cardboard (as big as you wish)

Preparation

1. Prepare the feely box by cutting a hole in the top. The hole should be big enough to allow you to reach your hand and arm into the box and pull out the largest item you plan to put in the box.

2. Gather various objects to put in the box for the children to feel. These don't have to be items that begin with "f," as the main focus should be on a variety of tactile sensations. Put them in the box before class begins.

3. Cut a footprint out of the cardboard.

Our feely box.

Directions

1. Demonstrate for the children what you'd like them to do by reaching into the feely box and describing what you feel without naming the object. For example, you might say "I f-f-feel something smooth" if you're touching an apple. Then continue to describe what you're touching, asking the children to guess what it might be. Finally, pull the object out of the box for everyone to see and put it on the big footprint.

2. Next have the children take turns reaching into the box and describing what they feel. Ask, "What can you f-f-feel?" Go on as long as the child's sophistication will allow. Many young children will just jump straight in and tell you that they feel an apple, for instance. Encourage them to describe what they feel using words such as hard, soft, smooth, pointy, and so forth, instead of guessing what the object is right away. Once a child understands that he can keep the others in suspense by giving feely clues, he will try to make the most of his turn.

3. After the child has revealed, or the audience has guessed, what he found in the box, he can pull out his object and put it on the footprint.

TiP

> You might want to fix an old elasticized wrist sleeve onto the opening so the children do not peep in, or try using a blindfold on each child as she reaches in. Young children, however, usually have no intention of peeping.

More Ideas for "f"
Sensational "f"

activity

Put a layer of flour or foam (shaving foam works well) in a tray (such as a cafeteria tray) and let the children take turns tracing an "f" with their fingers, so they can see and feel the shape. Make sure the feely letter "f" is clearly visible to all children as a model.

Silly Pictures

A silly picture composed of things that start with "f" is one more way to solidify the sound in children's minds. Use a large sheet of paper with colored pens, a dry-erase board, or a chalkboard—anything that enables the children to watch you draw. Start with something that begins with the letter (such as an animal), then ask the children for ideas. (Have the picture dictionary open at the relevant page to help, but let the children feel that you believe they really did think up the ideas on their own.)

Spelling out "fox" with the big feely letters.

Remember that silly pictures are most effective if they seem novel to the children. You don't have to draw for every letter but can try this activity when you haven't done it in a while or when you have a letter that lends itself to lots of ideas. (For more tips on drawing silly pictures with your class, see page 12.)

For "f," you could start with a fox playing football, or maybe a fish sitting on a fence. There are so many possibilities for "f," the children will give you lots of good ideas once they get started. After you finish the class picture, have the children draw their own sound pictures.

Let's Pretend

Involving the "f" sound in games of pretend will make the sound even more memorable and fun for the children. This activity involves acting out the season of fall. It will give you the opportunity to use the "f" sound many times while the children are engaged in a fun physical activity. This session has often proven so successful that we have written a class poem about fall, covering many aspects of the season, such as weather, clothing, the color of the leaves, the chores, and the playtime. Following are some ideas for pretending along a fall theme.

- Pretend you and the children are fall leaves, falling, swaying, drifting, twirling gently from the tree and landing softly on the ground without a sound.

- Pretend you and the children are getting ready to go out on a cold autumn morning. Wrap up for the cold with your hat, mittens, coat, and boots.

- Pretend you're all outside and take big steps as you crunch through the leaves.

TiP

If there are fallen leaves outside when we study "f," we go outside and crunch through them. It makes the pretending so much easier.

- With the children, pretend to rake up the fallen leaves, then jump in your big piles of fall leaves, falling down among them and making a fountain of leaves as you and the children throw them up in the air.
- *Footprints in the Sand* (Benjamin 1999) has a lot of movement and mime possibilities if you happen to be studying "f" at a time other than fall.

Crafts for "f"
Feely Farm

When choosing materials for your feely farm, remember that this involves a lot of cutting out in preparation, so choose materials that will not be too difficult to cut. For instance, if you choose sandpaper, choose a lightweight variety. If you have access to an Ellison cut-out machine, your job will be much easier. Of course, any activity to do with the farm will be much more meaningful if you can include a trip to a real farm that week.

Materials
- ✔ a variety of materials from which to cut out animal shapes, such as onion bags (netting), thin corrugated cardboard, aluminum foil, furry fabric or batting, plastic-coated fabric (such as an old plastic tablecloth), sandpaper, and bubble wrap

- ✔ a sheet of construction paper for each child
- ✔ glue for each child or small group
- ✔ colored markers or crayons

Preparation
1. The construction paper will be the farm background for each child. You might want to prepare this beforehand, drawing a farm scene with colored markers or crayons. Just a couple of fences and a basic barn work beautifully.
2. Cut out various farm animal shapes from the materials you gathered so that you have at least six for each child. Keep your shapes simple. You could cut out sheep, pigs, ducks, cows, goats, horses, chickens, or roosters.

TiP

You could also use cubes covered in construction paper instead of pieces of construction paper for the farm background if you have access to a sufficient supply of boxes (approximately six inches in all dimensions). These cubes become farm animal dice (or feely dice) that could open up many more game and activity possibilities.

Directions

1. Pass out a farm background and about six different animals to each child.

2. Each child takes one of each animal and glues it onto her farm background.

3. Under each animal, help the child write the feely word she can think of to describe that animal's particular texture. Try to encourage six different feely words. Even if the child can fill in only a couple of initial consonants, that's fine.

TiP

In the Family Tree, do not expect the child's representation of his family to be totally accurate. It is, how-ever, his tree, so if he wants to include his dog and his neighbor in preference to his brother, let him. You can always just remind the children who is in the immediate family. There will be plenty of opportunities to talk about the structure of the family. Let them enjoy their innocent interpretations.

Family Tree

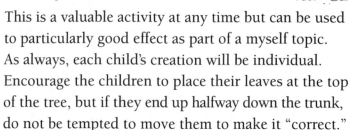

activity

This is a valuable activity at any time but can be used to particularly good effect as part of a myself topic. As always, each child's creation will be individual. Encourage the children to place their leaves at the top of the tree, but if they end up halfway down the trunk, do not be tempted to move them to make it "correct."

Materials

✔ a sheet of blue construction paper for each child

✔ a sheet of brown construction paper for each child

✔ a sheet of green construction paper for every four children

✔ a few sheets of green copy paper for each child

✔ colored pencils

✔ scissors

✔ glue for each child or small group

Preparation

1. Cut out a large supply of leaves from the green copy paper, *at least* enough so that each child will have a leaf for each member of his immediate family. It's always best to cut out more than enough because each child may define family members differently. The leaves should be about three inches long and two inches wide at the widest point.

2. Cut out a bare brown tree shape, with branches, from the construction paper, one for each child.

3. Cut a strip of green construction paper about three inches wide and long enough to fit across the width of the blue construction paper for each child. This will form the grass, but don't cut the fringe beforehand, as the children will do that with your help.

Directions

1. Have each child draw one family member on each leaf. He can name the person (or animal) with help.

2. Have the child glue the bare brown tree onto the blue construction-paper background.

3. Fold the green construction-paper strip in half lengthwise to make a crease, then unfold the paper. Have the child cut a fringe with his scissors up to the crease.

4. The child then puts glue on the unfringed half, and sticks it along the bottom of the picture. This is the grass.

5. Next, each child glues the back of each leaf to the branches of the tree. Help him glue about halfway down the back of the leaf so the leaves will flap, giving a 3-D effect to the family tree.

TIP

The Very Lonely Firefly (Carle 1999) is an "f" book with special magic! *Fall Changes* (Senisi 2001) is a simple book that is easy to work with during the week of "f."

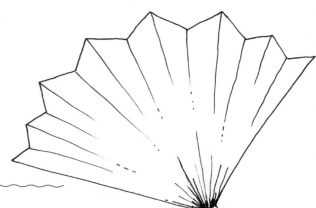

Fan Activity Center

During the week of "f," you could show the children how to make simple concertina fans they can decorate, fold, and tape at the bottom. On the activity table this week, put out paper, crayons, and tape. This is such a simple activity, but I watch the relaxed joy of my children doing this and remember my own pleasure from this basic old-fashioned childhood craft.

This is a very easy sound for the children to pick up. I usually try to introduce this one either at Halloween (lots of scary g-g-g-ghosts) or near St. Patrick's Day when there is a lot of green and glittering gold around. Groundhog Day provides another opportunity to introduce "g." Try reading *Little Groundhog's Shadow* (Craig 1998) if you introduce "g" at that time.

The main association the children seem to make is with gorillas. Small children tend to be fascinated by monkeys and gorillas. I have a plush gorilla who makes his first appearance in the classroom when "g" is introduced, and the children adore him. So my introductory session has to involve the gorilla.

Try to stay with just using "g" as in "gorilla," rather than "g" as in "giant." That way, the children can deal with one sound at a time without any added complications. Once they have mastered "g-g-gorilla" and understand generally about the sound-letter connection, it is quite easy to introduce an alternative sound later, such as "g" for "giant," as "special" information.

Activities to Introduce "g"

The activities in this section are for the first day you introduce "g" to the children. The first activity—See, Say, and Sing—involves a picture dictionary, a big feely letter "g" made out of cardboard and glitter, and the alphabet song all used together to involve the children in this exciting new sound. The second activity—The Big Event—will involve the children in a physical activity to help reinforce the sound of the letter. The Big Event for "g" has children opening the gate to the golden garden in search of "g" objects to give to the gorilla. *Important note:* The Big Event should follow immediately after the brief introduction of See, Say, and Sing activities to be most effective in solidifying the new letter for the children. Gather materials and prepare for *both* activities before you introduce "g" to your class. (See pages 7–11 for more information on introducing a new sound.)

Golden "g"

See, Say, and Sing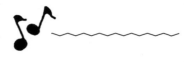

Materials

✔ picture dictionary

✔ photocopy of the "g" pattern on page 69

✔ 8 ½" x 11" thin cardboard

✔ gold glitter

✔ scissors

✔ glue

Preparation

1. To make the feely letter "g," photocopy and cut out the pattern on page 69 (unless you decide to make this letter freehand, without using the pattern). You may also wish to create a bigger letter by enlarging the photocopy and using a larger piece of cardboard.

2. Trace around the pattern onto the cardboard (or cut freehand) and cut out the card "g."

3. Glue glitter all over the "g."

Directions

1. Introduce "g" by making lots of "g-g-g" sounds with the children ("g" as in "go," not "giant"), showing what it feels like to say "g."

2. Pass around the golden glittery "g" so the children can see what "g" looks like and can touch the letter while they practice the "g" sound. Exaggerate the "g" sound in the words "g-g-golden" and "g-g-glittery." Remember to keep the big feely "g" in constant view so the

children can make the connection that the activities that follow all relate to "g."

3. Tell the children that "g" has a name just like they do and discuss the difference between the name of the letter "g" and the sound it makes in "golden." Sing through the alphabet to find where "g" is hiding.

4. Sing through the alphabet again as you turn the pages of the picture dictionary. Pick out a couple of "g" pictures to show the class more words that start with the "g" sound.

The **BIG** Event

Materials

✔ various small objects that begin with "g" (one for each child)

✔ golden fabric

✔ stuffed gorilla (or gorilla poster or drawing)

✔ two chairs

Preparation

1. Prepare the golden garden by gathering various items that begin with "g," such as gloves, toy gorillas, grapes, green beans (in a can), glue stick, and a toy goat. Place these "g" items under the golden fabric.

2. Set up your gorilla in the garden—sitting on the floor, a chair, or a table, with enough room for children to place their "g" objects on or near the gorilla.

3. Set up the chairs as the gate to the garden, leaving space between them through which the children will walk to enter and exit the garden.

Directions

1. Have the children come up one at a time, pretend to open the gate into the garden, and find an object beginning with "g" under the golden fabric. As the child is looking under the golden fabric, the other children can be making the "g-g-g" sound in anticipation of what will appear.

2. After finding a "g" object, each child gives the object to the gorilla. Tell the children they can lay the object anywhere on or near the gorilla: on his head, perhaps, or on his foot. Make the event fun and special. All the while, remember to be waving that golden "g" around, making the connection between the sound, the action, and the letter.

More Ideas for "g"
Sensational "g"

Coat a tray (such as a cafeteria tray) with a layer of gold glitter and let the children take turns tracing a "g" with their fingers, so they can see and feel the shape. Make sure the feely letter "g" is clearly visible to all children as a model.

Making a "g" in gold glitter.

Silly Pictures

A silly picture composed of things that start with "g" is one more way to solidify the sound in children's minds. Use a large sheet of paper with colored pens, a dry-erase board, or a chalkboard—anything that enables the children to watch you draw. Start with something that begins with the letter (such as an animal), then ask the children for ideas. (Have the picture dictionary open at the relevant page to help, but let the children feel that you believe they really did think up the ideas on their own.)

Remember that silly pictures are most effective if they seem novel to the children. You don't have to draw for every letter but can try this activity when you haven't done it in a while or when you have a letter that lends itself to lots of ideas. (For more tips on drawing silly pictures with your class, see page 12.)

The gorilla lends itself to fun ideas. The children usually associate monkeys and gorillas with comedy. Just asking the children what the gorilla's name could be or what color she is can be a wonderful springboard to many memorable images for them. My favorite included Gracie the golden gorilla, holding a glass of gravy, with green grapes on her head, getting gas at the gas station. After you finish the class picture, have the children draw their own sound pictures.

Let's Pretend

Involving the "g" sound in games of pretend will make the sound even more memorable and fun for the children. Whether you do all or just one of the following ideas, remember to keep the session relatively short to hold the children's attention. Try to keep the novelty factor alive: For example, choose activities that are different from the Let's Pretend activities you've recently done for other letters.

- Growing a garden is always fun to act out step by step, from sowing the seed and watering the garden to watching the big green grapevine grow and grow. The children can be both the gardeners and the grapevines. The grapevine is a particularly good plant to act out, not just because it begins with "g," but also because it grows in all sorts of directions, not just up. It twists around things as it grows, and its tendrils stretch, curl, and wrap around, just like fingers. To finish the session, before the children become too entwined with each other and the furniture, they can be the gardeners again, picking some grapes and eating them.

- Another very simple action activity that relates well to the "g" sound is a "stop-go" lollipop sign. Make a green circle with the word "go" clearly written on it, and a red circle with the word "stop." Mount them back to back at the top of a stick so that it looks like a giant lollipop. This can be used with almost any activity. The children can be stretching high, dancing, playing instruments, anything you choose while the lollipop says "go," but as soon as you turn it to the "stop" position, they must stop. When the lollipop turns to "go" again, they can start over. This is great fun, especially if you vary the "stop" pauses from very short to several seconds.

Crafts for "g"
Golden Montage

Although the children work on this for only one day, you need to allocate teacher time after school to spray paint the collages gold. The children can barely believe their eyes the next day. They have such fun trying to pick out the items they put onto the collage after it has been transformed into a golden montage.

Materials

- ✔ a piece of stiff cardboard, such as the back of a cereal box, for each child
- ✔ gold spray paint
- ✔ glue
- ✔ collage treasures such as lids, pasta shapes, onion bag netting, yarn, buttons (see page 15 for more information on collage treasures)
- ✔ 12" piece of green or golden yarn or ribbon for each child
- ✔ single hole punch
- ✔ marker

Preparation

1. Punch two holes in the top of each child's card. You will thread the yarn or ribbon through these holes later, so the picture can be hung on the wall.
2. Write each child's initials on the back of each card so that you don't lose track of which belongs to whom after you spray paint them later.

Directions

1. Demonstrate to the children how to build a collage, showing how to glue on different materials most effectively. The children can design any textured picture they wish. Some just enjoy the process of sticking down anything they like; others will create an organized design, a pattern, or a picture.
2. After school, spray paint each picture gold.
3. When the montages are completely dry, thread a piece of yarn or ribbon through the holes and tie it so the picture can be hung from the wall. The dazzling gold will be matched by the children's dazzling smiles when they see their golden works of art.

Owl Glasses

We made these glasses when we were studying the five senses. We talked about how owls can see in the dark, and we read several books about owls.

Materials

- ✔ a piece of stiff cardboard for each child (an open file folder will make two pairs of glasses)
- ✔ small colored feathers (enough to cover each pair of glasses)
- ✔ glue for each child or small group

Owl glasses.

Preparation

Cut out eyeglass shapes from the cardboard, one for each child. Remember to include "arms" to go over the ears.

Directions

The children simply decorate their glasses by sticking on the colored feathers. Show them how it is easier to layer the feathers by starting from the outside of the glasses, working in to the middle.

Pot of Gold

Just like the Golden Montage, this is another transformation craft where you apply the magic of gold spray paint after school. The children benefit from the fine manipulative activity and the visual design, and then delight at seeing their finished product. Don't be tempted to "tidy up" a child's pot. Uneven, messy pots often look extremely impressive in their own way once sprayed.

Materials

- ✔ a plastic or metal container (without a lid) for each child
- ✔ masking tape roll for each child
- ✔ gold spray paint
- ✔ pen or marker

Preparation

Write each child's initials on masking tape and stick it on the bottom of each pot, so you don't lose track of which belongs to whom after you spray paint later.

Directions

1. This is a great activity because the children do not need scissors to cut the masking tape; they can just tear it. Let the children wrap masking tape around and around their pot. They should make sure the top stays clear and that the bottom stays flat. It doesn't matter how messy it is; it will all add to the texture. They can tear short or long pieces of tape off the roll and just stick them on.

2. After school, spray the pots gold. You will be amazed at how interesting and attractive the texture of masking tape can be!

TiP

Margaret Wise Brown's *Goodnight Moon* (1991) is well loved at any time, but it is especially great with "g" because the children just want to join in! *Say Boo!* (Graham-Barber 1998), about a little ghost who cannot say "boo," is good to use with "g" because the children want to be actively involved with this story.

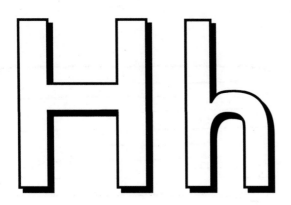

You can introduce hairy "h" very early in the year. Amazingly, the children tend to understand the h-h-hairy connection particularly easily—probably because they think hairy things are funny. In fact, "h-h-h" is just like laughing—something they love to do! The letter "h" is also very easy for the children to reproduce. As long as they can draw a stick and a rainbow, especially if they can do it all in one try, they have achieved a wonderful "h."

If we study nursery rhymes, I introduce "h" the same week as we work on "Humpty Dumpty." If we study "myself," I introduce "h" during the week we are talking about our hair.

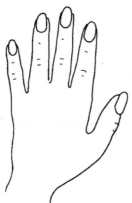

Activities to Introduce "h"

The activities in this section are for the first day you introduce "h" to the children. The first activity—See, Say, and Sing—involves a picture dictionary, a big feely letter "h" made out of cardboard and yarn, and the alphabet song all used together to involve the children in this exciting new sound. The second activity—The Big Event—will involve the children in a physical activity to help reinforce the sound of the letter. The Big Event for "h" has children choosing hats from the hat house to wear as they ride around the room on a horse. *Important note:* The Big Event should follow immediately after the brief introduction of See, Say, and Sing activities to be most effective in solidifying the new letter for the children. Gather materials and prepare for *both* activities before you introduce "h" to your class. (See pages 7–11 for more information on introducing a new sound.)

Hairy "h"

See, Say, and Sing

Materials

- ✔ picture dictionary
- ✔ photocopy of the "h" pattern on page 76
- ✔ 8½" x 11" thin cardboard
- ✔ brown yarn or doll hair (available at crafts stores or general discount stores, such as Wal-Mart)
- ✔ scissors
- ✔ glue

Preparation

1. To make the feely letter "h," photocopy and cut out the pattern on page 76 (unless you decide to make this letter freehand, without using the pattern). You may also wish to create a bigger letter by enlarging the photocopy and using a larger piece of cardboard.
2. Trace around the pattern onto the cardboard (or cut freehand) and cut out the card "h."
3. Glue brown yarn or doll hair all over the "h" to make it hairy.

Directions

1. Introduce "h" by making lots of "h-h-h" sounds with the children, showing what it feels like to say "h."
2. Pass around the hairy "h" so the children can see what "h" looks like and can touch the letter while they practice the "h" sound. Exaggerate

the "h" sound in the word "h-h-hairy." Remember to keep the big feely "h" in constant view so the children can make the connection that the activities that follow all relate to "h."

3. Tell the children that "h" has a name just like they do and discuss the difference between the name of the letter "h" and the sound it makes. Sing through the alphabet to find where "h" is hiding.
4. Sing through the alphabet again as you turn the pages of the picture dictionary. Pick out a couple of "h" pictures to show the class more words that start with the "h" sound.

The *BIG* Event

Materials

- ✔ various hats
- ✔ cardboard box (large enough to hold hats for all children in your class)
- ✔ markers
- ✔ hobbyhorse

Preparation

1. The day before you introduce "h," tell the children that the next day will be hat day. They each should bring a favorite hat to class the next day.
2. Make the cardboard box look like a house by drawing windows and a door on it.

3. Gather various hats and put them in the house. (When the children come into class, you will add the hats they bring in to the house.)

Directions

1. Put all the hats in the house.
2. Each child takes a turn to ride the horse around the room, eventually stopping at the house, where the child needs to find her hat.
3. When the child finds her hat, she should raise it in the air while everyone shouts, "Howdy!" or "Hooray!" or any other suitable "h" exclamation.
4. The child then puts on the hat and rides around once more before sitting down, complete with hat.

TiP

If you can't get your hands on a hobbyhorse, you can adapt a broomstick instead and just pretend it's a horse. A stuffed sock embellished with simple felt mane and ears and large wiggle eyes works well as the horse's head if attached securely to the end of the broomstick. You can even tie on ribbon reins.

We once received a donation of several three-foot broomsticks, enough for everybody to make a hobbyhorse. A parent who had connections with a stable arranged for us to go on a field trip to the stable. The children took their hobbyhorses with them and all galloped around the arena on their horses. Now that is a memory that always brings a smile!

More Ideas for "h"
Sensational "h"

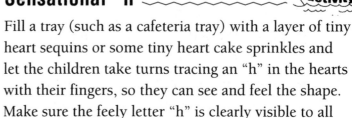

Fill a tray (such as a cafeteria tray) with a layer of tiny heart sequins or some tiny heart cake sprinkles and let the children take turns tracing an "h" in the hearts with their fingers, so they can see and feel the shape. Make sure the feely letter "h" is clearly visible to all children as a model.

TiP

There are hole punches that will punch out the shape of tiny hearts. You can use these paper hearts instead of sequins or sprinkles.

Silly Pictures

A silly picture composed of things that start with "h" is one more way to solidify the sound in children's minds. Use a large sheet of paper with colored pens, a dry-erase board, or a chalkboard—anything that enables the children to watch you draw. Start with something that begins with the letter (such as an animal), then ask the children for ideas. (Have the picture dictionary open at the relevant page to help, but let the children feel that you believe they really did think up the ideas on their own.)

Remember that silly pictures are most effective if they seem novel to the children. You don't have to draw for every letter but can try this activity when you haven't done it in a while or when you have a letter that lends itself to lots of ideas. (For more tips on drawing silly pictures with your class, see page 12.)

Children often find anything with unusually long hair amusing. A horse or a hamster, if the children are familiar with hamsters, with long hair and a hat should work well. After you finish the class picture, have the children draw their own sound pictures.

Let's Pretend

Involving the "h" sound in games of pretend will make the sound even more memorable and fun for the children. Anything with hats is always a hit. Whether you do all or just one of the following ideas, remember to keep the session relatively short to hold the children's attention. Try to keep the novelty factor alive: For example, choose activities that are different from the Let's Pretend activities you've recently done for other letters.

Try to collect in your dressing-up box an assortment of hats that go with different occupations. There are numerous possibilities depending upon what hats you can acquire. As you pull each hat out of the box, the children can mime a variety of actions to go with that particular profession.

- Cowboys and cowgirls can be preparing their horses to ride out to see their cattle. They will have to groom their horses, reach for the

saddles and wipe them down, then saddle up the horses, making sure everything is fastened tightly. Then they can climb up on their horses and ride out.

Hat day.

- Firefighters can be preparing their engines, cleaning them, and making sure all the switches are operating. Suddenly the alarm rings and they have to jump into their engines and drive to the fire. They climb up the ladder and spray water on the fire to put it out. Then they check that everybody is safe before driving back to the firehouse.

- Farmers in straw hats can be driving their tractors, sorting the hay, feeding the animals, and milking the cows.

- Construction workers in hard hats could be bricklaying, hammering, sawing, loading, unloading, and wheeling their wheelbarrows, or even driving bulldozers.

- As baseball players, they could step up to the plate, take a couple of swings at the ball, then hit the ball high, high in the air. The player runs and leads the team to victory.

- Chefs could collect ingredients, weigh and measure the food, chop, peel, pour, whisk, and stir. They check their ovens, and when the food is done, they have to make sure that the food is just right before carefully garnishing and serving it on the plate.

Crafts for "h"

Houses

There are many craft patterns for houses. This one is particularly good because the houses can be displayed as a town on a tabletop. Cover a table or board with green paper. Paint on roads and even a river. Then position the houses in the town.

Materials

- ✔ small milk carton for each child
- ✔ spray paint
- ✔ at least four different colors of paper for each house
- ✔ glue for each child or small group
- ✔ stapler
- ✔ scissors

Preparation

1. Clean the milk cartons and leave out at least overnight to dry.
2. Staple the tops closed so the cartons make the shape of houses with roofs.
3. Spray paint the milk cartons all one color. A dark color will cover the print best.
4. Cut the colored paper into small squares and rectangles (about $1/2$ inch square). These will be the windows, curtains, doors, and roof tiles for the houses.

Directions

Let the children glue the paper onto their houses to make windows, curtains, doors, and roof tiles.

TiP

You can also purchase small wooden craft tiles, which come in a variety of colors and are very effective as windows and doors.

Growing Hair

This craft has several benefits. The children exercise their fine motor skills in the cutting and sticking. They are being highly creative because every tube person will be unique. In addition to this, they get the chance to grow seeds and experience that wonder, maybe for the first time.

Materials

- ✔ a clean eggshell half for each child
- ✔ a cotton ball for each child
- ✔ one packet of cress seeds or grass seeds (available at a gardening store)
- ✔ fine markers
- ✔ 6" long cardboard tube for each child
- ✔ collage treasures such as fabric and paper scraps (See page 15 for more information on collage treasures.)
- ✔ glue for each child or small group
- ✔ scissors
- ✔ water (enough to sprinkle a few drops in each eggshell)

Preparation

No preparation necessary unless you wish to draw faces on the eggshells ahead of time.

Directions

1. The eggshell half will be the person's face. Have the children draw on the features using markers, but they don't need to draw on hair. The rounded base will be on the bottom, sitting in the top of the tube.

2. With scissors, the children cut a fringe along one edge of the tube. They fan out the fringe to help the tube stand sturdily.

3. The tube is the person's body. Using the collage treasures, the children can dress their people by sticking fabric, sequins, and whatever they like on the tubes.

4. Next, each child should put the eggshell head on top of the tube body to make the person.

5. Have each child put a cotton ball inside the eggshell head.

6. Sprinkle a few cress seeds on the cotton ball and just a few drops of water. Their people should begin growing hair very soon. Keep gently watered but not flooded!

Helicopter

My son designed this for me when he was eight years old. These helicopters were one of the most popular craft productions in my class because they had moving parts.

Materials

- ✔ a piece of 3" x 12" construction paper for each child
- ✔ two pieces of 1" x 6" construction paper for each child
- ✔ glue for each child or small group
- ✔ scissors for each child
- ✔ stapler
- ✔ two brass paper fasteners for each child
- ✔ a circle of construction paper about an inch in diameter for each child

Preparation

No preparation necessary except to cut the different sizes of construction paper as described in the materials list.

Directions

1. First, have each child glue the two strips of construction paper together in the center to make a cross. These will be the blades.

2. Next, each child cuts a fringe around the edge of the circle of construction paper with the scissors. This will be the back propeller.

3. To make the main body of the helicopter, each child should take one end of the long strip of construction paper and loop it back on itself. He should then staple about eight inches up the strip. The other end of the strip should still be free.

4. Each child then pinches that end together to make a short lengthwise fold. Inside this rests the small back propeller. He should secure it with a brass fastener through the fold and center of the propeller so it will spin around at the end of the tail.

5. The glue holding the two big blades should be dry by this time. Have each child position them on the top of the round part of the helicopter and secure them with a brass fastener so that these blades too can move around.

TiP

Use books to reinforce "h" during the week, such as *The Hat* (Brett 1997) and *Huggly Gets Dressed* (Arnold 1997). Another great title that you can use for "k" or "h" is Audrey Penn's *The Kissing Hand* (1998). This book is wonderful to read at the beginning of the school year to help with parent-child separation. It helps the children *and* the parents!

Hospital Activity Center

Most preschool rooms have a home area. If you teach preschool-age children, you can transform this into a hospital for the week you are studying "h." If you teach older children, you can create a hospital area anywhere it will fit in your classroom. Gather as many props for the week as possible, even if loaned. Put in a toy doctor's kit, a white shirt to be the doctor's coat, short strips of bandage, and dollies and Teddies with small cushions and covers for their beds. The local hospital may be kind enough to donate some disposable hats and masks. Take the opportunity to give some of the everyday home corner toys a rest for a week. They will generate fresh interest when they return.

I usually refer to "i" as "i-spot." It is short and snappy and reminds the children about the spot on the top. This has always proved helpful. This is one of those vowels best left until later on when you are working on consonant-vowel-consonant words. There is a lot more emphasis on "i" as a medial vowel rather than an initial sound. There just aren't many words out there relevant to the children that begin with "i." However, it really doesn't matter, because at this stage of the year, you will want children to hear sounds inside the words.

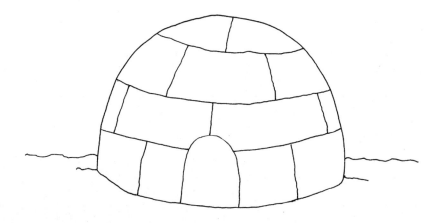

Activities to Introduce "i"

The activities in this section are for the first day you introduce "i" to the children. The first activity—See, Say, and Sing—involves a picture dictionary, a big feely letter "i" made out of cardboard and white fabric, and the alphabet song all used together to involve the children in this exciting new sound. The second activity—The Big Event—will involve the children in a physical activity to help reinforce the sound of the letter. The Big Event for "i" takes children to the chilly north where they fish for specially marked "i" fish and play instruments outside an igloo. *Important note:* The Big Event should follow immediately after the brief introduction of See, Say, and Sing activities to be most effective in solidifying the new letter for the children. Gather materials and prepare for *both* activities before you introduce "i" to your class. (See pages 7–11 for more information on introducing a new sound.)

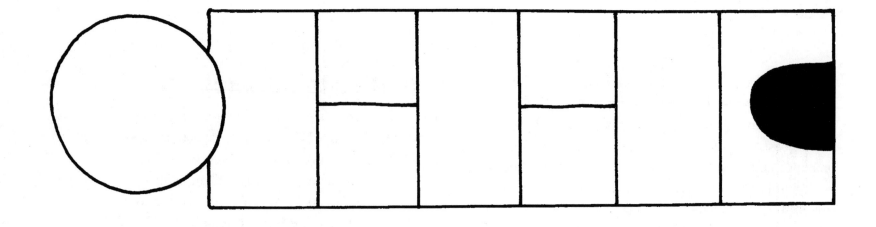

Igloo "i"

See, Say, and Sing

Materials

- ✔ picture dictionary
- ✔ photocopy of the "i" pattern on page 84
- ✔ 8½" x 11" thin cardboard
- ✔ 3" x 11" white fabric
- ✔ fine-tip permanent black marker
- ✔ scissors
- ✔ glue
- ✔ cellophane (optional)

Preparation

1. To make the feely letter "i," photocopy and cut out the pattern on page 84 (unless you decide to make this letter freehand, without using the pattern). You may also wish to create a bigger letter by enlarging the photocopy and using a larger piece of cardboard.

2. Using the pattern as a guide (or cutting freehand), cut the "i" out of the cardboard.

3. Glue the white fabric onto the "i" and cut around the shape.

4. Using the black fine-tip marker, draw on the ice-block lines and the opening at the bottom, as shown on the pattern. You can cover it with cellophane to give it more of an icy look.

Directions

1. Introduce "i" by making lots of "i-i-i" sounds with the children (short "i" as in "igloo," not long "i"), showing what it feels like to say "i."

2. Pass around the feely igloo "i" so the children can see what "i" looks like and can touch the letter while they practice the "i" sound. Exaggerate the "i" sound in the word "i-i-igloo." Remember to keep the big feely "i" in constant view so the children can make the connection that the activities that follow all relate to "i."

3. Tell the children that "i" has a name just like they do and discuss the difference between the name of the letter "i" and the sound it makes in "igloo." Sing through the alphabet to find where "i" is hiding.

4. Sing through the alphabet again as you turn the pages of the picture dictionary. Pick out a couple of "i" pictures to show the class more words that start with the "i" sound.

The *BIG* Event

Materials

- ✔ white sheet (any size)
- ✔ two chairs
- ✔ tray (as large as you can find)
- ✔ blue paper (enough sheets to cover the tray)
- ✔ cellophane (enough to cover the tray)
- ✔ five to ten sheets of construction paper

✔ marker

✔ paper clips

✔ 12" dowel (or ruler)

✔ ribbon (same length as the dowel)

✔ magnet (doughnut, horseshoe, or rectangular shapes work best)

✔ dinner plate

✔ various musical instruments

✔ parka and mittens (optional)

✔ hot glue gun (optional)

Preparation

1. First, make the igloo. This can be as simple or as complex as you like. I personally favor draping a white sheet over two chairs.

2. Next, make an ice pond. A tray covered in blue paper and then with a film of iridescent cellophane has served me well for a long time.

3. Make several construction-paper fish and write "i" on them boldly. Put a paper clip on each fish's mouth.

4. Make a rod out of a dowel and a piece of ribbon with a magnet on the end. Depending on the shape of the magnet, either tie or hot glue the ribbon to the magnet.

5. Put a dinner plate inside the igloo and a few instruments outside the igloo, such as shakers, jingle bells, triangles, drums, rhythm sticks, or whatever instruments you have handy.

Directions

1. Each child gets a turn to live in the igloo. If you have a furry hooded coat and mittens for the children to dress up in, so much the better. While living in the igloo, the child goes to the pond to get some dinner. Explain to the children that the fish are special "fi-i-ish." Have the children make the "i-i-i" sound to call the fish in their special language.

2. The child fishes for the paper-clip fish with his magnetic rod. After catching a fish, he takes it back inside the igloo and puts it on the dinner plate.

3. As a special celebration, the child can choose an instrument to play briefly before his turn is over.

More Ideas for "i"
Sensational "i"

Gather some ice cubes and have the children build an "i" on a dark-colored tray (such as a cafeteria tray). This activity will be all the more memorable if they can do this inside the igloo, which is the "i" sound this activity is meant to reinforce. Make sure the feely letter "i" is clearly visible to all children as a model.

Silly Pictures

A silly picture composed of things that start with "i" is one more way to solidify the sound in children's minds. Use a large sheet of paper with colored pens, a dry-erase board, or a chalkboard—anything that enables the children to watch you draw. Start with something that begins with the letter (such as an animal), then ask the children for ideas. (Have the picture dictionary open at the relevant page to help, but let the children feel that you believe they really did think up the ideas on their own.)

Remember that silly pictures are most effective if they seem novel to the children. You don't have to draw for every letter but can try this activity when you haven't done it in a while or when you have a letter that lends itself to lots of ideas. (For more tips on drawing silly pictures with your class, see page 12.)

The letter "i" might be difficult for this activity, but you could start with insects who play instruments. After you finish the class picture, have the children draw their own sound pictures.

Let's Pretend

Involving the "i" sound in games of pretend will make the sound even more memorable and fun for the children. Whether you do all or just one of the following ideas, remember to keep the session relatively short to hold the children's attention. Try to keep the novelty factor alive: For example, choose activities that are different from the Let's Pretend activities you've recently done for other letters.

- Miming out the story of *The Three Little Pigs* is always a hit, with an emphasis on "i" as the middle vowel in "pi-i-igs." Last year, I was lucky enough to be given three huge cartons. They were so big that I could keep them in the classroom for only a week (we needed air space!), but during free time, the story of the three pigs was enacted again and again using these boxes as the houses. Obviously, I could not use them during our class session because all the children could not fit inside one box at one time.

- Another time, I introduced "i" while studying opposites, particularly "in and out." Have the children imagine they are Alice in Wonderland going into the tiny door, Cinderella climbing into her carriage, or someone jumping into a swimming pool, crawling into a cave that is getting smaller and smaller, climbing into bed, or getting gradually into the sea for the first time, starting with her toes and ending up splashing around.

Insect Inspection Activity Center

Set up an insect inspection center. Put out some plastic insects, and if you have access to them, some real samples of insects displayed in plastic casings. Also set out plastic magnifying glasses, paper, and crayons. The children can closely inspect the insects and, if they choose to, even record what they observe.

Crafts for "i"

Igloo

I make use of an igloo yet again deliberately. This is such a difficult initial sound we need to make use of familiar reinforcement in physical activities as much as possible. The finished structures will probably resemble igloos in color alone, but as long as the children have enjoyed the construction activity, that's fine. This craft will probably take two days; one day for building, and one day for mixing and applying the chunky paint.

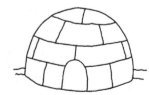

Materials

- ✔ scraps of Styrofoam packing
- ✔ glue for each child or small group
- ✔ a cardboard base for each igloo, such as the back of a cereal box
- ✔ white liquid tempera paint
- ✔ Epsom salts
- ✔ bowl or other container for mixing Epsom salts and paint
- ✔ paintbrush for each child
- ✔ marker

Preparation

No preparation required except to gather materials. You might mix the Epsom salts and paint ahead of time.

Directions

1. Have each child glue the Styrofoam pieces together to build a little igloo structure on the cardboard base. Help each child write her initials or full name on the cardboard base.

2. If you don't do this ahead of time, have each child mix the Epsom salts and white paint.

3. When their houses are dry, the children can paint over them and the bases with the thick paint mixture.

Instruments

Music plays an important role in any classroom. Children love to be able to make their own music, but budget does not always allow for every child in the group to be able to play an instrument at the same time. These instruments will ensure that you can have a class band! Depending on your resources, you could choose one instrument, or even make this into a three-day event and make all three of the instruments suggested here.

Materials

- ✔ For the shaker:
  - a container with a lid for each child (a small coffee can or a plastic bottle works well)
  - a handful of dried beans, rice, or beads for each child
  - decorations for the outside of the shaker, such as stickers and ribbons
  - masking tape to seal the container

✔ **For the harp:**
- a small open box for each child (anything from a 2" x 2" gift box with no lid to the lid of a shoe box will work)
- strong large rubber bands (allow at least 10 per child as some children will want to use more than others)

✔ **For the shiny shaker:**
- 12" piece of yarn for each child
- small silver foil containers and packaging, such as small pie holders and candy wrappers
- a few pieces of aluminum foil for each child
- as many shiny, clean foil yogurt lids as possible
- a large blunt plastic darning needle for each child

Preparation

No preparation necessary for the shaker or the harp. For the shiny shaker, thread each piece of yarn through each needle and knot it at the end, then cut the foil pieces into roughly 3" circles and squares.

Directions: Shaker

1. The children make a shaker by putting the beans, rice, or beads inside the lidded containers.

2. Next, they can seal the containers with masking tape and decorate the outside with stickers. If using a plastic bottle, tie ribbons around the neck of the bottle.

Directions: Harp

The children simply stretch their rubber bands around their boxes. They can then pluck or strum the "strings" on the open side of the box.

Directions: Shiny Shaker

1. The children can choose from a variety of shiny materials on the table and thread them one by one onto their piece of yarn.

2. When they have finished, tie each child's yarn into a complete loop.

3. The children can now hold the yarn and shake it for a different kind of sleigh bell sound.

We made these instruments!

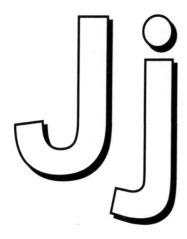

The letter "j" is not that common as an initial consonant. For that reason, it can be left until quite late in the year, but it is not difficult to learn, so if your topics dictate that "j" should make an appearance earlier in the year, that's fine, too. When we are working on nursery rhymes, we introduce "j" at the same time as "Jack and Jill." If you were making the jewelry box as a gift for Mother's Day, it would work well to introduce "j" at that time.

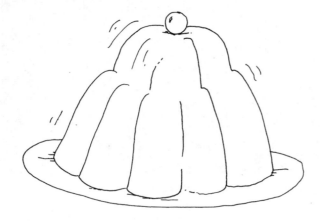

Activities to Introduce "j"

The activities in this section are for the first day you introduce "j" to the children. The first activity—See, Say, and Sing—involves a picture dictionary, a big feely letter "j" made out of cardboard and cellophane, and the alphabet song all used together to involve the children in this exciting new sound. The second activity—The Big Event—will involve the children in a physical activity to help reinforce the sound of the letter. The Big Event for "j" has children jumping into the jungle in search of jigsaw puzzle pieces. *Important note:* The Big Event should follow immediately after the brief introduction of See, Say, and Sing activities to be most effective in solidifying the new letter for the children. Gather materials and prepare for *both* activities before you introduce "j" to your class. (See pages 7–11 for more information on introducing a new sound.)

Jell-o "j"

See, Say, and Sing

Materials

- ✔ picture dictionary
- ✔ photocopy of the "j" pattern on page 91
- ✔ 8 ½" x 11" thin red cardboard (or cardboard and a red marker)
- ✔ cellophane (or clear plastic with adhesive backing)
- ✔ scissors
- ✔ clear glue (unless using plastic with adhesive backing)

Preparation

1. To make the feely letter "j," photocopy and cut out the pattern on page 91 (unless you decide to make this letter freehand, without using the pattern). You may also wish to create a bigger letter by enlarging the photocopy and using a larger piece of cardboard.

2. Trace around the pattern onto the cardboard (or cut freehand) and cut out the card "j." If you aren't using red cardboard, color in the "j" with a red marker.

3. Glue on the cellophane with clear glue, or apply the self-adhesive plastic, then trim the edges along the shape of the "j" to make it like shiny Jell-o.

Directions

1. Introduce "j" by making lots of "j-j-j" sounds with the children, showing what it feels like to say "j."

2. Pass around the Jell-o "j" so the children can see what "j" looks like and can touch the letter while they practice the "j" sound. Exaggerate the "j" sound in the word "J-J-Jell-o." Remember to keep the big feely "j" in constant view so the children can make the connection that the activities that follow all relate to "j."

3. Tell the children that "j" has a name just like they do and discuss the difference between the name of the letter "j" and the sound it makes. Sing through the alphabet to find where "j" is hiding.

4. Sing through the alphabet again as you turn the pages of the picture dictionary. Pick out a couple of "j" pictures to show the class more words that start with the "j" sound.

The *BIG* Event

Materials

- ✔ cardboard box (big enough for a child to walk into, if possible)
- ✔ several sheets of green construction paper (enough to cover the box)
- ✔ scissors
- ✔ jigsaw puzzle of a "j" object or scene
- ✔ marker
- ✔ glue

Preparation

1. Cut as many large leaves as possible out of the green construction paper and glue them onto the cardboard box to simulate a jungle.

2. Choose a jigsaw puzzle with a "j" image (such as a picture from the *Jungle Book*). On the back of each puzzle piece, write "j" boldly with the marker.

3. Put all of the puzzle pieces into the box.

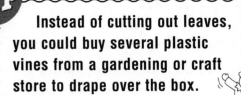

TiP

Instead of cutting out leaves, you could buy several plastic vines from a gardening or craft store to drape over the box.

Directions

1. The children take turns being a jungle explorer, jumping into the jungle, and capturing a piece of the jigsaw.

2. As each child jumps into the jungle, the rest of the class can be saying "j-j-jump." While the child is looking for a puzzle piece, the class can still be chanting "j-j-j" and then shout out "jigsaw" when she emerges with a puzzle piece.

3. The child brings the piece of jigsaw to you, and you help her piece it into the main picture.

Jigsaw Activity Center

This is the time to draw attention to jigsaw puzzles, reviewing how they work and maybe bringing out some alternatives to those already in use. We use mainly floor puzzles with large pieces in our room, so I make a point of putting a few small puzzles out on a special table for the week. They have only a few pieces each, but they make a nice change.

More Ideas for "j"

Sensational "j"

Make some Jell-o in a bright color, mash it up in a tray (such as a cafeteria tray), and let the children take turns tracing a "j" in it with their fingers, so they can see and feel the shape. Make sure the feely letter "j" is clearly visible to all children as a model.

Silly Pictures

A silly picture composed of things that start with "j" is one more way to solidify the sound in children's minds. Use a large sheet of paper with colored pens, a dry-erase board, or a chalkboard—anything that enables the children to watch you draw. Start with something that begins with the letter (such as an animal), then ask the children for ideas. (Have the picture dictionary open at the relevant page to help, but let the children feel that you believe they really did think up the ideas on their own.)

Remember that silly pictures are most effective if they seem novel to the children. You don't have to draw for every letter but can try this activity when you haven't done it in a while or when you have a letter that lends itself to lots of ideas. (For more tips on drawing silly pictures with your class, see page 12.)

Start with a jumping jellyfish or a jogging jaguar. They might be juggling jewels and jars of jam while trying on jeans and jackets. After you finish the class picture, have the children draw their own sound pictures.

Let's Pretend

Involving the "j" sound in games of pretend will make the sound even more memorable and fun for the children. Whether you do all or just one of the following ideas, remember to keep the session relatively short to hold the children's attention. Try to keep the novelty factor alive: For example, choose activities that are different from the Let's Pretend activities you've recently done for other letters.

- The idea of the jungle opens up all sorts of possibilities. *The Carnival of the Animals,* by Saint-Saëns, makes wonderful music for moving about the room pretending to be exotic animals. The children can pretend to be lost in the jungle. Where will they get water? How will they climb up to reach the fruit high on the trees? Where will they build a shelter, and how?

Do any dangerous animals come by? Do they make friends with any of the animals?

- Pretending to be jacks-in-the-box is a wonderful way of making movement fun. A clap or a bang on a tambourine can be the cue for the curled up jacks to stretch wide, reach high, and jump out like a floppy old bear or a kangaroo. You make the suggestions each time and watch the expressive differences in the children's bodies as they imitate whatever you suggest.

Crafts for "j"
Jack-in-the-Box

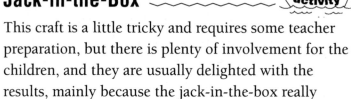

This craft is a little tricky and requires some teacher preparation, but there is plenty of involvement for the children, and they are usually delighted with the results, mainly because the jack-in-the-box really does jump out when you open the box.

Materials

- ✔ a 4" x 4" box with a lid attached on one side for each child
- ✔ magazines (for cutting out decorative pictures)
- ✔ glue for each child or small group
- ✔ two 1" x 8" strips of construction paper for each child
- ✔ a piece of thin cardboard that is longer or wider than the box by at least an inch for each child

✔ an outline picture a clown (smaller than the box) for each child to color

✔ crayons

✔ pencil

✔ scissors for each child

✔ stapler

Preparation

1. Place each box on a piece of cardboard and trace around the box onto the card, adding one inch on two opposite sides (these will form flaps on the card).

2. Cut out the shape you've traced on the pieces of cardboard and fold the flaps up.

3. Staple the two strips of construction paper at right angles to each other (to form an L shape).

4. Find a clown picture that the children can color and make photocopies so that each child will have one.

Directions

1. Have the children cut out pictures from magazines to use in decorating the outsides of their boxes.

2. The children then glue the pictures to the outsides of their boxes. Make sure they do not glue the lids shut.

3. Have the children color their clown pictures and then cut out the clowns.

4. Show the children how to alternately fold one construction-paper strip across the other, then the other strip across the first one to make an accordion pleat. The children should be able to do this alone once they get the idea.

5. These last few steps are for you: When the paper has been folded into the accordion, staple the end to secure. Then staple one end of the accordion pleat onto the center of the piece of thin cardboard for each child.

6. Glue or staple each child's clown onto the free end of the accordion.

7. Next, put glue on the outside of the flaps on the card and insert the card, with the extra flaps bent downward, into the top of the open box. It should sit just inside the top of the box. Make sure everything is dry before you attempt to close the jack inside his box. When you close him in his box, squash the accordion down so that when you open the box, he will spring right up.

Making jewelry boxes.

Jewelry Boxes

These jewelry boxes are a favorite with moms, particularly for Mother's Day, which is why I usually precut the pretty pictures in heart shapes. If the children find some other pictures they would like to cut out themselves in their own way, that is fine. Moms usually keep these boxes for a long time.

Materials

✔ shoebox for each child

✔ pictures cut from garden catalogs and magazines in heart shapes

✔ wrapping paper cut into heart shapes

✔ decoupage glue and a brush for each child

✔ spray paint in a dark color

✔ cover-up for each child's clothing

Preparation

1. Spray paint the shoeboxes in advance. A dark color works well because the flowers in the magazine pictures show up against the darkness.

2. Cut the pictures and wrapping paper into heart shapes (unless you want the children to cut out the pictures independently).

Directions

Decoupage glue is a glue and a varnish in one. It is great for the children because it dries clear, so it doesn't matter that they are not accurate when brushing it on, but effective cover-ups for the children's clothes are essential. Let the children glue their pretty pictures on the shoeboxes in whatever design they choose, just as long as the lid is worked on separately so that it does not stick to the main box.

Jungle Jim.

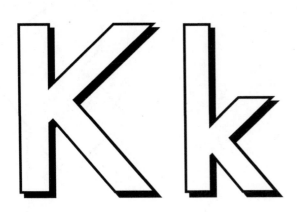

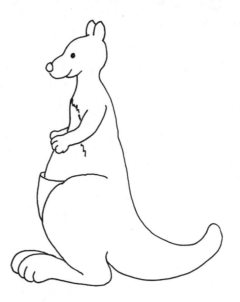

There are not many commonly used words in the child's world that call upon "k" as an initial consonant. It is also surprisingly difficult for the children to even attempt to reproduce. For this reason, I usually leave its introduction until late in the year. By that time, the children will be comfortable with how "c" works and will be quite happy to know that some words start with "curly c" and some words start with "kicking k." I am not too worried about spelling accuracy at this age, just that they are getting the idea of how the sounds work. When we are studying stories of three, I usually introduce "k" for the *Three Little Kittens*. During the week, I will read Lorianne Siomades's *Three Little Kittens* (2000), a visual account of the classic rhyme. When we last worked on opposites, I introduced "k" for "kite" when we were working on high (in the sky) and low.

Activities to Introduce "k"

The activities in this section are for the first day you introduce "k" to the children. The first activity—See, Say, and Sing—involves a picture dictionary, a big feely letter "k" made out of felt, and the alphabet song all used together to involve the children in this exciting new sound. The second activity—The Big Event—will involve the children in a physical activity to help reinforce the sound of the letter. The Big Event for "k" brings children into the kitchen, where they are kings in search of chocolate Kisses to feed to three hungry kittens. *Important note:* The Big Event should follow immediately after the brief introduction of See, Say, and Sing activities to be most effective in solidifying the new letter for the children. Gather materials and prepare for *both* activities before you introduce "k" to your class. (See pages 7–11 for more information on introducing a new sound.)

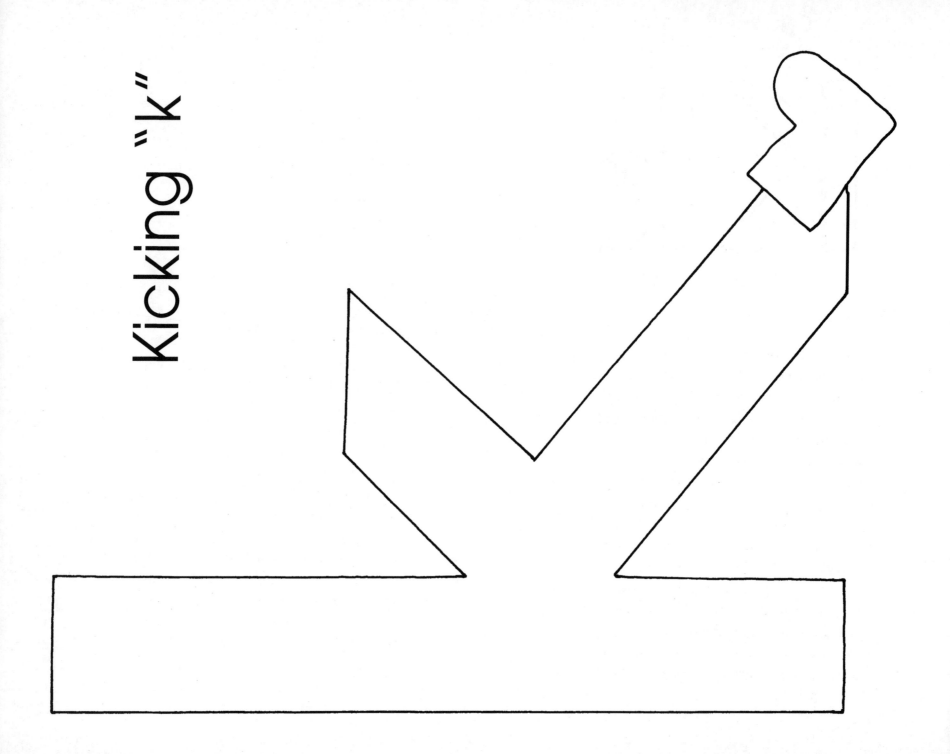

Kicking "k"

See, Say, and Sing

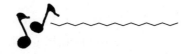

Materials

- ✔ picture dictionary
- ✔ photocopy of the "k" pattern on page 98
- ✔ 8½" x 11" piece of light-colored felt
- ✔ 2" x 2" piece of dark-colored felt
- ✔ scissors
- ✔ glue
- ✔ thin cardboard (such as a cereal box)

Preparation

1. To make the feely letter "k," photocopy and cut out the pattern on page 98 (unless you decide to make this letter freehand, without using the pattern). You may also wish to create a bigger letter by enlarging the photocopy and using larger pieces of felt.

2. Using the pattern as a guide (or cutting free-hand), cut a "k" out of the light-colored felt, then cut the boot out of dark-colored felt.

3. Glue the boot on the "k" as shown in the pattern.

4. Make the entire letter stronger by gluing it onto thin cardboard and cutting around it.

Directions

1. Introduce "k" by making lots of "k-k-k" sounds with the children, showing what it feels like to say "k."

2. Pass around the kicking "k" so the children can see what "k" looks like and can touch the letter while they practice the "k" sound. Exaggerate the "k" sound in the word "k-k-kicking." While I am showing my big feely "k," he will often be incredibly naughty and start to kick with the boot on the end of his kicking leg. Remember to keep the big feely "k" in constant view so the children can make the connection that the activities that follow all relate to "k."

3. Tell the children that "k" has a name just like they do and discuss the difference between the name of the letter "k" and the sound it makes. Sing through the alphabet to find where "k" is hiding.

4. Sing through the alphabet again as you turn the pages of the picture dictionary. Pick out a couple of "k" pictures to show the class more words that start with the "k" sound.

The *BIG* Event

Materials

- ✔ table
- ✔ three dinner plates
- ✔ three stuffed kittens
- ✔ bag of chocolate Kisses
- ✔ crown (see page 101 for instructions for making a crown)
- ✔ 2' x 3' boxes and markers (if you don't have play kitchen equipment)

Feeding Kisses to the kitten.

Preparation

1. Set up the kitchen. Some of you may be lucky enough to have a pretend kitchen in your home area. Otherwise use large boxes and, with markers, draw on cupboard fronts, stove burners, or even a sink.

2. Hide the chocolate Kisses all over the kitchen.

3. Set up the stuffed kittens at a table with dinner plates in front of them.

4. Set the crown on the table. If you decide to make one, do this ahead of time. See the instructions for making a crown on page 101. You won't be able to fit the crown perfectly to each child's head, so make it a little big so it fits everyone.

Directions

1. Introduce the children to the kittens—we shall call them Kelly, Kerry, and Kim—and explain that the kittens are hungry, but they eat only food beginning with "k."

2. Each child takes a turn finding something in the kitchen for the kittens to eat. While in the kitchen, the child gets to wear the crown so that he can be king in his kitchen. While the king searches around the kitchen, the other boys and girls help by saying "k-k-k" to remind him of the sound he is looking for in the kitchen.

3. After he finds some Kisses to feed to the kittens, the next child gets a turn.

4. When everyone has found a Kiss, they can all unwrap and eat them at the end of the session. For a child with chocolate allergies, you will need to plant a small treat wrapped in shiny paper. Maybe that child could go last, after all of the other Kisses have been found. You could secretly put out this special treat just before the child's turn.

More Ideas for "k"
Sensational "k"

Pour a layer of ketchup into a tray (such as a cafeteria tray) and let the children take turns tracing a "k" in the ketchup with their fingers, so they can see and feel the shape. Make sure the feely letter "k" is clearly visible to all children as a model.

Silly Pictures

A silly picture composed of things that start with "k" is one more way to solidify the sound in children's minds. Use a large sheet of paper with colored pens, a dry-erase board, or a chalkboard—anything that enables the children to watch you draw. Start with something that begins with the letter (such as an animal), then ask the children for ideas. (Have the picture dictionary open at the relevant page to help, but let the children feel that you believe they really did think up the ideas on their own.)

Remember that silly pictures are most effective if they seem novel to the children. You don't have to draw for every letter but can try this activity when you haven't done it in a while or when you have a letter that lends itself to lots of ideas. (For more tips on drawing silly pictures with your class, see page 12.)

For "k" you might start your picture with a kangaroo kissing kittens and kicking. After you finish the class picture, have the children draw their own sound pictures.

Let's Pretend

Involving the "k" sound in games of pretend will make the sound even more memorable and fun for the children. Whether you do all or just one of the following ideas, remember to keep the session relatively short to hold the children's attention. Try to keep the novelty factor alive: For example, choose activities that are different from the Let's Pretend activities you've recently done for other letters.

- The song "Let's Go Fly a Kite" from *Mary Poppins* provides loads of miming ideas, from making the kite to flying the kite and having the wind really pull on the handle, to pretending to be the kite or a bird soaring up high in the air.

- The children can be kangaroos jumping over different types of objects. They might have to jump in slow motion or very fast. They might have to jump carefully over lots of little frogs, or over a big valley. They might have to jump in a zigzag shape along the ground, or even backwards! Their baby might be asleep in the pouch so they must jump very quietly.

Let's go fly a kite.

Crafts for "k"
Crown for a King

If you are studying "q" within a couple of weeks of "k," keep the crowns in school to use again at that time. That way, the children won't need to share one crown for the "q" Big Event.

Materials
- ✔ an 18" x 12" sheet of yellow construction paper for each child
- ✔ stapler
- ✔ sequins
- ✔ glitter
- ✔ glue for each child or small group
- ✔ scissors

Preparation

Cut each sheet of paper in half lengthways, then staple these pieces together to make one long strip. Then cut along one edge of each strip with a large zigzag design.

Directions

1. Measure each crown (the zigzag construction-paper strips) around each child's head and staple to the correct position.

2. The children then decorate their crowns with sequins and glitter.

The Kite with the Wondrous Tail

These kites can be displayed beautifully on a blue background for the sky, with white clouds, maybe cut from fluffy white batting. Provide at least three pieces of ribbon and three pieces of lace per child. Some children won't need that much; other children will want to tie many more knots. Some will favor the lace; others will prefer the ribbon.

Materials

- ✔ a sheet of construction paper for each child (12" x 9" recommended, but any rectangular size will work)
- ✔ single hole punch

TiP

To make it easier for children to tie ribbon and lace to the tails of their kites, anchor the tail, using masking tape at the top and bottom, to the table, a tray, or a box.

- ✔ 18" piece of yarn for each child
- ✔ at least three pieces of 4" (or longer) ribbon for each child
- ✔ at least three pieces of 4" (or longer) lace for each child
- ✔ crayons
- ✔ scissors

Preparation

1. Cut a kite shape out of each sheet of construction paper.

2. Punch one hole in the bottom point of each kite.

Directions

1. Have the children decorate their kites with the crayons.

2. Help each child thread a piece of yarn through the hole at the bottom of each kite and tie it to make the tail.

3. The children can then tie scraps of ribbon and lace onto the tails of their kites. This gives the children practice in tying knots. Those who are ready for shoelaces may need longer pieces of ribbon and lace to practice bow tying.

L l

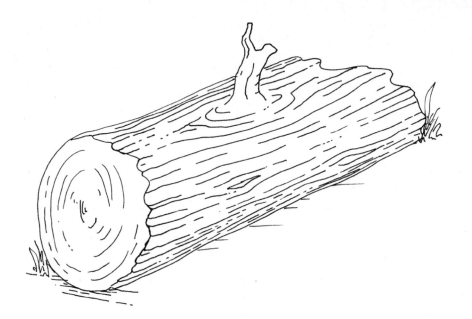

The children pick up "l" so quickly, mainly because as they run their finger from the top of the "ladder" to the bottom, they like to say "l-l-l-l" gradually deepening their voices as they get to the bottom. It is effective to introduce "l" quite soon after a visit to the firestation because there is still such a strong reference to "ladder." It is also convenient to introduce "l" near St. Patrick's Day, when there are lots of leprechaun stories, poems, and pictures around. Near Valentine's Day is another good time because everyone is talking about love!

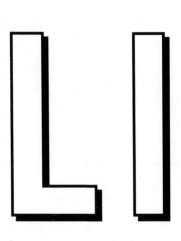

Activities to Introduce "l"

The activities in this section are for the first day you introduce "l" to the children. The first activity—See, Say, and Sing—involves a picture dictionary, a big feely letter "l" made out of felt, and the alphabet song all used together to involve the children in this exciting new sound. The second activity—The Big Event—will involve the children in a physical activity to help reinforce the sound of the letter. The Big Event for "l" has children looking for a leaf at the top of a ladder. *Important note:* The Big Event should follow immediately after the brief introduction of See, Say, and Sing activities to be most effective in solidifying the new letter for the children. Gather materials and prepare for *both* activities before you introduce "l" to your class. (See pages 7–11 for more information on introducing a new sound.)

Ladder "I"

See, Say, and Sing

Materials

- ✔ picture dictionary
- ✔ photocopy of the "l" pattern on page 104
- ✔ 3" x 11" piece of brown felt
- ✔ 3" x 11" piece of light blue felt
- ✔ scissors
- ✔ glue
- ✔ thin cardboard (such as a cereal box)

Preparation

1. To make the feely letter "l," photocopy and cut out the pattern on page 104 (unless you decide to make this letter freehand, without using the pattern). You may also wish to create a bigger letter by enlarging the photocopy and using larger pieces of felt.

2. Cut out the squares in the pattern and use the ladder that remains as a guide for cutting the ladder out of the brown felt (leaving holes in the felt where the squares were on the pattern), unless you decide to cut your ladder pieces freehand.

3. Cut a piece of light blue felt that's the size of the "l" in the pattern. Glue this piece to the back of the brown felt to form the background for the ladder. The blue should peek through the squares but not around the edges.

4. Make the entire letter stronger by gluing it onto thin cardboard and cutting around it.

Directions

1. Introduce "l" by making lots of "l-l-l" sounds with the children, showing what it feels like to say "l."

2. Pass around the feely "l" so the children can see what "l" looks like and can touch the letter while they practice the "l" sound. Exaggerate the "l" sound in the words "l-l-ladder" and "l-l-letter." Remember to keep the big feely "l" in constant view so the children can make the connection that the activities that follow all relate to "l."

3. Tell the children that "l" has a name just like they do and discuss the difference between the name of the letter "l" and the sound it makes. Sing through the alphabet to find where "l" is hiding.

4. Sing through the alphabet again as you turn the pages of the picture dictionary. Pick out a couple of "l" pictures to show the class more words that start with the "l" sound.

The *BIG* Event

Materials

- ✔ one 12" x 18" sheet each of red, orange, and yellow construction paper
- ✔ masking tape
- ✔ marker
- ✔ small stepladder (two steps and a platform seat)

✔ a lantern-type flashlight (with a handle) or a paper lantern (see page 108 for lantern-making instructions)

Preparation

1. Draw a trunk and branches on the chalkboard.
2. Cut out a bunch of leaves (at least as many leaves as there are children in your class) from construction paper and write a big "l" on each one.
3. Using masking tape, tape the leaves to the branches you've drawn on the chalkboard.
4. If you don't have a lantern flashlight, then you'll need to make the paper lantern ahead of time. See the instructions on page 108.
5. Set out the stepladder next to the tree so that the children can reach the leaves from the second step.

TIP

I have a stand-up tree in my classroom. You can make one by sawing two tree shapes approximately three feet tall from quarter-inch plywood. Cut a quarter-inch slot from the top of one piece down the center to halfway down. On the other piece, cut a quarter inch slot from the bottom up the center to halfway up. Slide the two pieces together at right angles. Decorate with green and brown paint, or green and brown felt. This tree will last for many years and has a multitude of uses.

6. Set the lantern on a desk or table next to the stepladder where the children can pick it up and put it back with each turn.

Directions

1. "L" offers a great opportunity to turn out the lights and make the classroom fairly dark because "l" is for "lantern!" A flashlight with a carrying handle makes an ideal lantern. Otherwise, use a pretend paper lantern and don't turn off quite so many lights.
2. With your assistance, each child takes a turn climbing the ladder while holding the lantern. She should look around for the last leaf while calling, "L-l-l-leaf. Where are you?" In the meantime, narrate the action for the class, emphasizing the "l-l-l" sounds whenever you use them as initial consonants.
3. The child should pick a leaf from the tree and, when she gets to the bottom of the ladder, ask the other children, "Is this the last leaf?" to which they will probably say, "No."
4. The child then puts her leaf with the rest of the leaves in a line on the floor and passes the lantern to the next child. It may be diplomatic, when all the children have had a turn, to have a favorite class toy (such as a stuffed lion or leopard) take the lantern, climb the ladder, and find the last leaf!

More Ideas for "l"

Sensational "l"

Empty a packet of leaf-shaped sequins into a tray (such as a cafeteria tray) and have the children trace an "l" with their fingers, so they can see and feel the shape. Make sure the feely letter "l" is clearly visible to all children as a model.

> **TiP**
>
> As an alternative, you could use lots of little leaves, fake or real. In fall, brown crunchy leaves can be crushed to make a very rough leaf "glitter."

Silly Pictures

A silly picture composed of things that start with "l" is one more way to solidify the sound in children's minds. Use a large sheet of paper with colored pens, a dry-erase board, or a chalkboard— anything that enables the children to watch you draw. Start with something that begins with the letter (such as an animal), then ask the children for ideas. (Have the picture dictionary open at the relevant page to help, but let the children feel that you believe they really did think up the ideas on their own.)

Remember that silly pictures are most effective if they seem novel to the children. You don't have to draw for every letter but can try this activity when you haven't done it in a while or when you have a letter that lends itself to lots of ideas. (For more tips on drawing silly pictures with your class, see page 12.)

There are so many possibilities for "l," you and the children should have no trouble building a l-l-lovely silly picture. You might think about a lion, a leopard, a lizard, or a lobster on a ladder.

Let's Pretend

Involving the "l" sound in games of pretend will make the sound even more memorable and fun for the children. Whether you do all or just one of the following ideas, remember to keep the session relatively short to hold the children's attention.

How long are the lines of lace?

> **TiP**
>
> Another idea for "l" is to lay lines of lace on the floor, as shown in the picture at left. Have the children lie down along the length of a piece of lace to determine whether they or the piece of lace is longer. Don't forget to stress the "l-l-l" sound.

Try to keep the novelty factor alive: For example, choose activities that are different from the Let's Pretend activities you've recently done for other letters.

- If you introduce "l" in the fall, you can use the session to act out leaves falling and have fun with the leaves (as described under "f," on page 64).

- If you introduce "l" around St. Patrick's Day, you can have the children mime out a story about a leprechaun.

- If you are working on a unit about people who help us, you can mime the activities of a firefighter with special emphasis on using his ladder.

- "Left and right" is a good theme to work with physically at this time. Divide your movement area into two parts, the children's left and the children's right. Label the two areas with a big "l" and a big "r." This activity is almost like Simon Says but much more active. You give instructions such as, "If you have brown hair, go to the left," or, "If you have a big brother, go to the right."

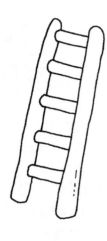

As this is a double instruction, it is best if the children raise their hands first if they believe the first part of the instruction refers to them. Then it will be easier for the children to know who is moving. You, of course, will be pointing to help even more. So even if the children have no idea about left and right, there should be enough other clues that they can still join in the fun.

Crafts for "l"
Lantern

Very young children can make these beautifully as long as the paper is big enough so the manipulative skills needed are not too difficult. The lining up of the paper, the creasing, and the cutting to a certain point are all wonderful skill builders. These big, bold, bright lanterns look great hanging from the ceiling along the length of the room.

Materials

- ✔ 8½" x 11" up to 12" x 18" rectangular paper with color on one side (such as wrapping paper)
- ✔ scissors for each child
- ✔ glue for each child or small group
- ✔ stapler

Preparation

No preparation necessary unless you want to do some of the cutting ahead of time.

Directions

1. First, have each child cut a strip about one inch wide off the length of the paper. This will be the handle.
2. Next, each child folds the main piece of paper in half lengthwise, with the colored side on the outside. Show the children how to make a sharp crease on the fold.

3. Each child then folds it again lengthwise, making a crease, then opening up the last fold so the paper is still folded in half.

4. With the folded side facing him, he should cut up to the crease (in the center) at one-inch intervals all the way along the paper.

5. Have each child open up the paper and pull the two short edges together to make a tube shape. The slits should be pointing outward. Help him glue along one of the two short edges to secure the tube shape.

6. Help each child staple the handle on the top of his lantern in a rainbow shape.

Long Leaf Garlands

These work especially well during fall when you can use a bright mixture of red, yellow, and orange tissue papers; but with other colors, these look wonderful hanging from your classroom ceiling at any time of the year.

Materials

- ✔ tissue paper (as many sheets as possible)
- ✔ scissors
- ✔ 2' piece of plastic-coated thin wire thread (as used for threading beads) for each child
- ✔ a handful of pony beads for each child
- ✔ blunt darning needle for each child

Preparation

1. Cut the tissue paper into five-inch squares.

2. Fold the tissue paper squares twice.

3. Hold the center fold while you cut out a leaf-shaped point on the opposite corner.

4. Open out the tissue. You should have a shape like a flower with four petals. Some children like to make very long garlands, so cut out as many of these flower shapes as you can. To save time, fold several squares of tissue paper together and cut them out at the same time.

TiP

Guess How Much I Love You (McBratney 1996) is a terrific resource during "l" week: lots of l-l-love in this book.

Directions

1. Thread a piece of wire thread onto the needle for each child. Thread through a bead and knot the end.

2. The child should first thread on a tissue flower, pushing his blunt needle in as close to the center of the flower as possible.

3. Next, he should thread on a bead.

4. He should continue threading alternately a bead and a tissue flower until he comes within about five inches of the top of the thread.

5. Tie a loop in the remaining thread and hang the cascading garland of long leaves from the ceiling.

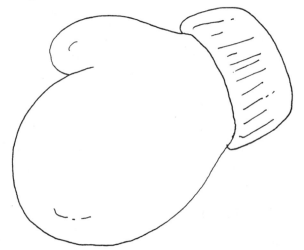

T his letter is so easily recognizable and such fun to say that I always have "m" as one of my very first letters. It is usually the third letter of the alphabet to be introduced after "s" and "t." The children enjoy endlessly reproducing the rainbow shapes, which are in sharp contrast to the squiggly "s" and the straight lines of "t."

Activities to Introduce "m"

The activities in this section are for the first day you introduce "m" to the children. The first activity—See, Say, and Sing—involves a picture dictionary, a big feely letter "m" made out of felt, and the alphabet song all used together to involve the children in this exciting new sound. The second activity—The Big Event—will involve the children in a physical activity to help reinforce the sound of the letter. The Big Event for "m" involves a mailbox full of "m" objects. As mail carriers, the children deliver "m" objects from the mailbox to the moon. *Important note:* The Big Event should follow immediately after the brief introduction of See, Say, and Sing activities to be most effective in solidifying the new letter for the children. Gather materials and prepare for *both* activities before you introduce "m" to your class. (See pages 7–11 for more information on introducing a new sound.)

Mountain "m"

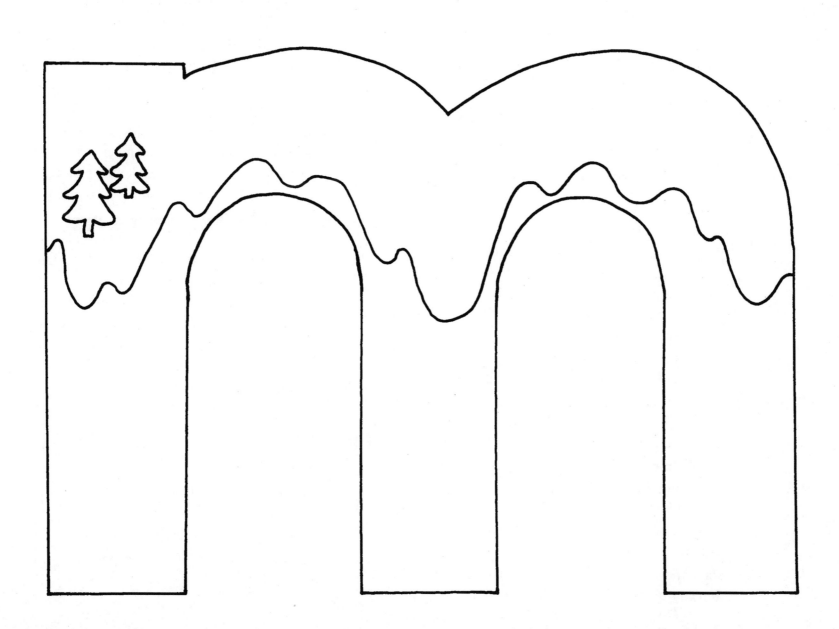

See, Say, and Sing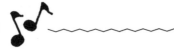

Materials

✔ picture dictionary

✔ photocopy of the "m" pattern on page 111

✔ 3" x 9" piece of white felt

✔ 8½" x 11" piece of gray felt

✔ 4" x 4" (or larger) piece of dark green felt

✔ scissors

✔ glue

✔ thin cardboard (such as a cereal box)

Preparation

1. To make the feely letter "m," photocopy and cut out the pattern on page 111 (unless you decide to make this letter freehand, without using the pattern). You may also wish to create a bigger letter by enlarging the photocopy and using larger pieces of felt.

2. Using the pattern as a guide (or cutting freehand), cut the "m" shape out of the gray felt.

3. Next, you can cut the white snow freehand out of white felt or you can cut the snow using the pattern as a guide.

4. Cut the pine trees out of green felt (freehand or by cutting the pine trees from the pattern to use as a guide).

5. Glue the snow onto the "m" as shown on the pattern, then glue the trees anywhere on the "m."

6. Make the entire letter stronger by gluing it onto thin cardboard and cutting around it.

Directions

1. Introduce "m" by making lots of "m-m-m" sounds with the children, showing what it feels like to say "m."

2. Pass around the big mountain "m" so the children can see what "m" looks like and can touch the letter while they practice the "m" sound. Exaggerate the "m" sound in the word "m-m-mountain." You could also point out that the lowercase "m" looks like two rainbows. Remember to keep the big feely "m" in constant view so the children can make the connection that the activities that follow all relate to "m."

3. Tell the children that "m" has a name just like they do and discuss the difference between the name of the letter "m" and the sound it makes. Sing through the alphabet to find where "m" is hiding.

4. Sing through the alphabet again as you turn the pages of the picture dictionary. Pick out a couple of "m" pictures to show the class more words that start with the "m" sound.

The *BIG* Event

Materials

✔ mailbox (buy or make one with a box and markers)

✔ various small objects that start with "m"

✔ moon poster or poster-size paper and markers

Preparation

1. If you don't use a store-bought mailbox, first you'll want to create one. You can use a box and decorate it with markers, perhaps with a bunch of "m"s all over it. Be sure to leave an opening in the box.

2. Gather all kinds of "m" objects to put in the box, such as toy monkeys, toy monsters, a little mirror, a map, a magazine, a mint, a mitten, a mug, Mickey Mouse (always a favorite), a magnet . . . there's a huge selection for "m."

3. Set out the moon poster on the floor near the mailbox. If you decide to make the poster, simply draw a large circle with lots of craters.

Directions

1. Each child takes a turn as the mail carrier, feeling in the mailbox and bringing out one item. While she is choosing, the other children can be getting ready with their "m-m-m" to say the word when the object is produced.

2. After everyone names the object, the mail carrier then delivers her goodies to the moon to finish her turn.

TiP

To add to the excitement, bring in a children's plastic echo-type microphone so that the child who has just chosen can then say what she has into the microphone.

There's something that starts with "m" in this mailbox.

More Ideas for "m"
Sensational "m"

Fill a tray (such as a cafeteria tray) with a layer of marshmallows or M & Ms and let the children take turns tracing an "m" with their fingers, so they can see and feel the shape. Make sure the feely letter "m" is clearly visible to all children as a model.

Silly Pictures

A silly picture composed of things that start with "m" is one more way to solidify the sound in children's minds. Use a large sheet of paper with colored pens, a dry-erase board, or a chalkboard—anything that enables the children to watch you draw. Start with something that begins with the letter (such as an animal), then ask the children for ideas. (Have the picture dictionary open at the relevant page to help, but let the children feel that you believe they really did think up the ideas on their own.)

113

Remember that silly pictures are most effective if they seem novel to the children. You don't have to draw for every letter but can try this activity when you haven't done it in a while or when you have a letter that lends itself to lots of ideas. (For more tips on drawing silly pictures with your class, see page 12.)

The letter "m" should be a lot of fun for this activity. You could start with a monster, a monkey, a million mosquitoes, a marching mouse, or even a mermaid. After you finish the class picture, have the children draw their own sound pictures.

Let's Pretend

Involving the "m" sound in games of pretend will make the sound even more memorable and fun for the children. This activity involves pretending to go to the moon, which is always a favorite. It will give you the opportunity to use the "m" sound many times while the children are engaged in a fun physical activity.

Have the children put on their space suits, climb into their rockets, and blast off into space. They can steer their rockets down to land on the moon. In slow motion, they climb down the steps onto the moon's surface. They take some big steps and plant the flag. They can go exploring, finding and collecting rocks. They can slide down into a crater and climb back out.

The atmosphere is greatly enhanced if you have some space-type music playing in the background. I like to play music from *2001: A Space Odyssey* or some psychedelic music from the seventies. Music by the group Tangerine Dream fits very well.

Crafts for "m"
Monsters
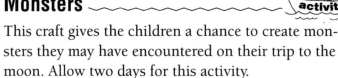

This craft gives the children a chance to create monsters they may have encountered on their trip to the moon. Allow two days for this activity.

Materials
- ✔ collage treasures such as small boxes, egg cartons, cardboard tubes, lids, onion bag netting, cotton reels, craft sticks, and so on (see page 15)
- ✔ glue for each child or small group
- ✔ masking tape
- ✔ liquid tempera paint
- ✔ scissors for each child
- ✔ paintbrushes

Preparation
No preparation necessary except to gather enough collage materials for each child to have plenty to choose from for his monster.

Directions
1. This is something of a free-for-all craft that has children gluing together whatever objects they wish from the collage treasure pile to create a monster. Give a demonstration first as an excuse to show some techniques such as fanning out the end of a cardboard tube before attempting to stick it on to something else, or showing that attaching two objects by the flat sides is the easiest method. Then let the children and their imaginations free!

2. The next day, when the monsters are dry (some of our monsters have been heavily laden with glue), the children can paint them.

Grass Monsters

Children love anything to do with simple comical monsters, and they don't come looking much more plain or amusing than our grass monster—especially when the grass "hair" starts growing! (This activity can also be used for "g" or "h.")

Materials

- ✔ old hose and knee-highs (one leg for each child)
- ✔ sawdust (enough to fill one leg of hose or one knee-high for each child)
- ✔ two rubber bands for each child
- ✔ a small packet of grass seed
- ✔ pair of large wiggle eyes for each child
- ✔ plastic plate for each child

Preparation

Cut the hose just under the knees (so that it's the same length as the knee-highs). If your old hose has big holes in the toes, double up two feet with holes in the toes. If you position them correctly, they should cover up each other's holes.

Directions

1. Have the children put enough sawdust in the foot of the hose to make the monster's nose (about a one-inch ball)

2. Next each child loops a rubber band around tightly to keep the sawdust in the nose.

3. Now have them fill the main bodies of their monsters with sawdust. (About five inches of sawdust works well, but however much the child wants to use is fine as long as the monster is not overfilled to the bursting point.)

4. Have each child sprinkle a tablespoon of grass seed inside each sock, along what will be the monster's back.

5. Then each child should secure the sawdust and seed inside the main body by looping a rubber band tightly around the end of the sock. This should leave a small part of the sock as the tail.

6. They keep their monsters on the plastic plate (where you can write the child's name), watering it regularly.

Watching the grass monsters grow.

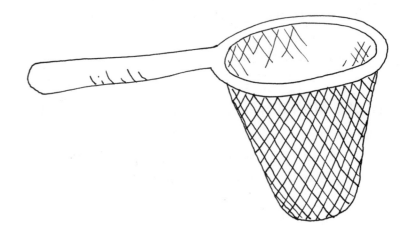

The letter "n" lends itself beautifully to any subject involving the night, especially nocturnal animals. If we are studying the theme of people who help us, we talk about nurses while learning about "n." We usually try to have a nurse come in to the class for a toy hospital day. The children bring in a doll or stuffed toy from home and the nurse puts a bandage on where the toy says it's hurting. (Make it clear to the parents and children that this is not for mending toys!) There are also plenty of opportunities to refer to "n" during the theme of opposites. Night and day or yes and no would be good reference points for the sound of "n."

Activities to Introduce "n"

The activities in this section are for the first day you introduce "n" to the children. The first activity—See, Say, and Sing—involves a picture dictionary, a big feely letter "n" made out of felt and gold stars, and the alphabet song all used together to involve the children in this exciting new sound. The second activity—The Big Event—will involve the children in a physical activity to help reinforce the sound of the letter. The Big Event for "n" is a combination of dressing up in a nightgown and searching for nails and nuts in a nest of noodles. *Important note:* The Big Event should follow immediately after the brief introduction of See, Say, and Sing activities to be most effective in solidifying the new letter for the children. Gather materials and prepare for *both* activities before you introduce "n" to your class. (See pages 7–11 for more information on introducing a new sound.)

Nighttime "n"

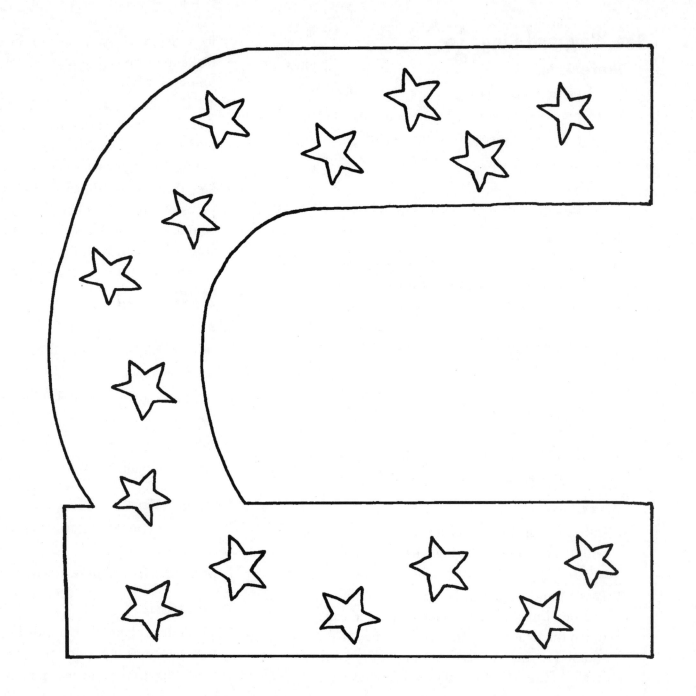

See, Say, and Sing

Materials

✔ picture dictionary

✔ photocopy of the "n" pattern on page 117

✔ 8 ½" x 11" piece of dark blue felt

✔ gold star stickers

✔ scissors

✔ thin cardboard (such as a cereal box)

Preparation

1. To make the feely letter "n," photocopy and cut out the pattern on page 117 (unless you decide to make this letter freehand, without using the pattern). You may also wish to create a bigger letter by enlarging the photocopy and using a larger piece of felt.

2. Using the pattern as a guide (or cutting freehand), cut the "n" shape out of the dark blue felt.

3. Stick the gold stars all over the "n."

4. Make the entire letter stronger by gluing it onto thin cardboard and cutting around it.

Directions

1. Introduce "n" by making lots of "n-n-n" sounds with the children, showing what it feels like to say "n."

2. Pass around the feely nighttime "n" so the children can see what "n" looks like and can touch the letter while they practice the "n" sound. Exaggerate the "n" sound in the word "n-n-nighttime." Remember to keep the big feely "n" in constant view so the children can make the connection that the activities that follow all relate to "n."

3. Tell the children that "n" has a name just like they do and discuss the difference between the name of the letter "n" and the sound it makes. Sing through the alphabet to find where "n" is hiding.

4. Sing through the alphabet again as you turn the pages of the picture dictionary. Pick out a couple of "n" pictures to show the class more words that start with the "n" sound.

The *BIG* Event

Materials

✔ big frilly nightgown (optional)

✔ large bowl

✔ uncooked or precooked noodles

✔ nuts (the kind that go with bolts)

✔ nails

✔ fishing net

Preparation

1. Cook the noodles, or crunch them up raw, and put them in the bowl.

2. Mix the nails and nuts in with the noodles.

Directions

1. The letter "n" provides another opportunity to turn out some lights and pretend it is nighttime. I have an over-the-top nightgown, in my

dress-up box, that is bright pink with big frills around the edge. The children, boys and girls alike, absolutely love it. When I introduce "n," we turn off the lights and take turns putting on the gown. Don't worry if somebody does not want to take a turn to dress up.

2. When it is their turn, the children try to find a nut or nail in the noodles. Remember to have the other children already saying the "n-n-n" sound in anticipation so that as the nut or nail is pulled out, they can all declare what has been found.

3. The child then puts the nut or nail in the net and another child takes a turn.

4. After everybody has had a turn, the children can all pretend to nap on the floor until night-time is over and the lights go on again.

Searching for nails in the noodles.

More Ideas for "n"
Sensational "n"

Fill a tray (such as a cafeteria tray) with a layer of edible nuts and let the children take turns tracing an "n" in the nuts with their fingers, so they can see and feel the shape. Make sure the feely letter "n" is clearly visible to all children as a model. If the nuts you have chosen will roll about, put a layer of sand or soap powder in first, but watch the children closely to make sure they don't eat any of the nuts.

Be sure to check with parents before using nuts for this activity. If any child has a nut allergy of any kind, it's best to choose another "n" item or substance, such as cut-up or cooked noodles.

Silly Pictures

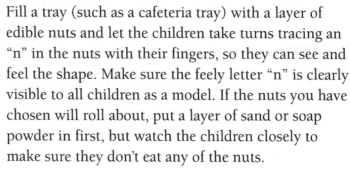

A silly picture composed of things that start with "n" is one more way to solidify the sound in children's minds. Use a large sheet of paper with colored pens, a dry-erase board, or a chalkboard—anything that enables the children to watch you draw. Start with something that begins with the letter (such as an animal), then ask the children for ideas. (Have the picture dictionary open at the relevant page to help, but let the children feel that you believe they really did think up the ideas on their own.)

Remember that silly pictures are most effective if they seem novel to the children. You don't have to draw for every letter but can try this activity when you haven't done it in a while or when you have a

letter that lends itself to lots of ideas. (For more tips on drawing silly pictures with your class, see page 12.)

Instead of starting with an animal for "n," you could draw a nurse napping in a nest. After you finish the class picture, have the children draw their own sound pictures.

Let's Pretend

Involving the "n" sound in games of pretend will make the sound even more memorable and fun for the children. Remember to keep the session relatively short to hold the children's attention. Try to keep the novelty factor alive: For example, choose activities that are different from the Let's Pretend activities you've recently done for other letters.

The nocturnal world is fascinating to young children. Think about all the different animals and people who are up and active during the night and mime what they might be up to. Begin the session by having the children pretend to prepare for bed. That will help put into perspective for them that these things are going on while they are tucked in and asleep. You and the children can pretend to be

- an owl watching, preening, listening, and silently swooping
- a nurse arranging a bed, taking a temperature, looking in on his patients

- a supermarket worker unloading a truck, putting prices on the packs, then stocking the shelves
- a factory worker operating her machinery
- a police officer patrolling the streets to keep them safe

Crafts for "n"

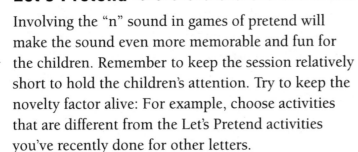

Necklace

This craft is a great activity near Thanksgiving. The children wear their necklaces during our musical program. The necklaces can also be given as gifts, such as for Mother's Day. The craft involves threading various items, including pasta shapes, on yarn or string to create a necklace.

Materials

- ✔ about 2' piece of yarn or string for each child
- ✔ 1" to 2" strips of paper
- ✔ clear tape
- ✔ masking tape
- ✔ pencil for each child
- ✔ markers
- ✔ at least 10 beads and pasta pieces (especially tubes and wheels) for each child

Preparation

Tightly wrap a small piece of masking tape around one end of each child's piece of yarn or string. This will aid the children a great deal with threading.

Directions

1. Have the children make colored stripes on the strips of paper using the markers.

2. Next, they wrap each strip around a pencil and secure it with a piece of clear tape to make a paper bead.

3. Show them how to knot a piece of pasta near one end of the yarn or string to act as an anchor, leaving enough free yarn or string to knot on the other end when the child is finished threading objects onto the necklace.

4. Help them thread the paper beads and other beads and pasta shapes onto the yarn.

Night and Day

This craft is particularly useful when teaching children about the idea of half and for practicing the skill of folding in half. It is also a good craft to do when studying opposites.

Materials

✔ paper plate for each child

✔ a sheet of 8 ½" x 11" black construction paper for each child

✔ dark blue liquid tempera paint

✔ at least eight gold star stickers for each child

✔ light blue liquid tempera paint

✔ 4" x 2" piece of yellow construction paper for each child

✔ scissors

✔ brass paper fasteners

Preparation

1. Cut the yellow construction paper into suns about the size of a quarter and yellow paper crescent moons, one sun and one moon for each child.

2. Cut each sheet of black construction paper into the same shape and size as the paper plate.

3. Fold each black circle in half. Using a white or yellow pencil, on one half, draw a simple landscape that the child will cut out. It could be a hill, or skyscrapers, or waves on the sea. The waves would be just a couple of zigzags.

Directions

1. Have each child cut out the landscape you've drawn on half the black paper. The other half of the black paper stays complete and attached to the cut half.

2. Next have each child fold her paper plate in half.

3. Each child should paint one half of the plate dark blue and stick on the gold stars and the crescent moon and paint the other half light blue and stick on the yellow sun. Be sure they paint their landscapes so that they are oriented top and bottom (rather than with the day on the right and the night on the left or vice versa).

4. Help each child push a brass fastener through the center of the fold line on the black paper and then on through the center of the fold line on the plate. They should be able to turn their landscape to make it either night or day.

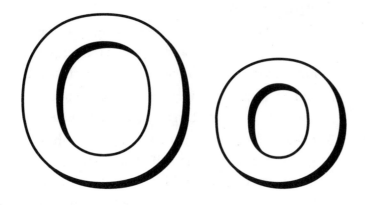

This is such an easy sound for the children, mainly because their mouths make the shape of an "o" when they say "o." Focus on this point and make a big deal of having the children run their fingers around their mouths while they are saying "o" so they are making the round "o" sound and feeling the "o" shape at the same time. After children are writing, I often see them self-checking that the sound they want really is "o" by running their fingers around their mouths.

"O" is also easy because an orange is round, just like an "o." The vowel sounds can be difficult to master because of how similar they sound, so it is a relief to come across "o," which is so clear in every way.

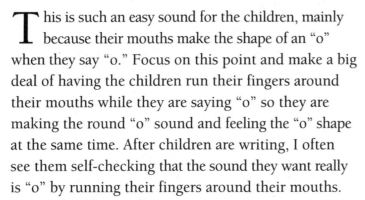

Activities to Introduce "o"

The activities in this section are for the first day you introduce "o" to the children. The first activity—See, Say, and Sing—involves a picture dictionary, a big feely letter "o" made out of felt, and the alphabet song all used together to involve the children in this exciting new sound. The second activity—The Big Event— will involve the children in a physical activity to help reinforce the sound of the letter. The Big Event for "o" is a version of musical chairs, but the emphasis is on the words "orange," "on," and "off." *Important note:* The Big Event should follow immediately after the brief introduction of See, Say, and Sing activities to be most effective in solidifying the new letter for the children. Gather materials and prepare for *both* activities before you introduce "o" to your class. (See pages 7–11 for more information on introducing a new sound.)

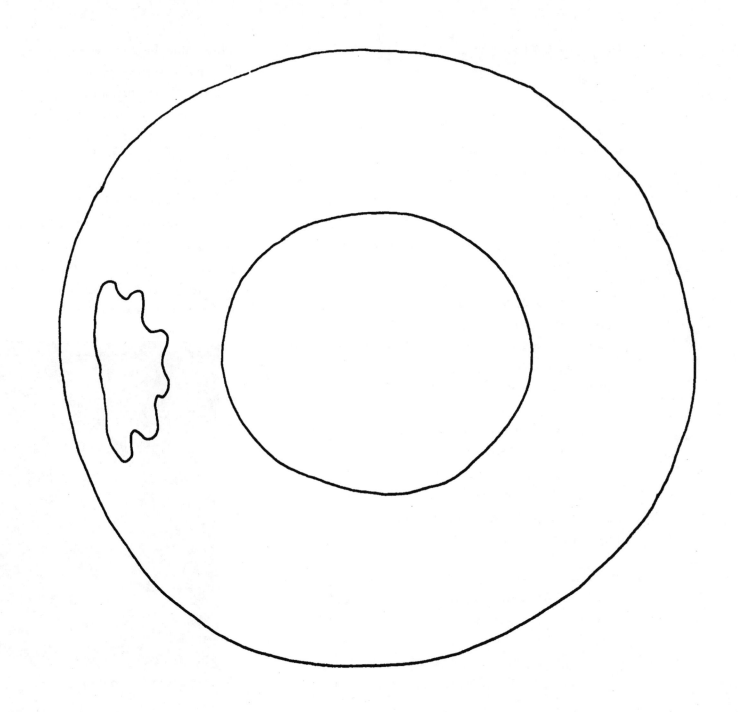

Orange "o"

See, Say, and Sing

Materials

✔ picture dictionary

✔ photocopy of the "o" pattern on page 123

✔ 8" x 8" piece of orange felt

✔ 2" x 1" piece of green felt

✔ scissors

✔ glue

✔ thin cardboard (such as a cereal box)

Preparation

1. To make the feely letter "o," first photocopy and cut out the pattern on page 123 (unless you decide to make this letter freehand, without using the pattern). You may also wish to create a bigger letter by enlarging the photocopy and using larger pieces of felt.

2. Using the pattern as a guide (or cutting freehand), cut the "o" shape out of orange felt.

3. Cut a small leafy part out of the green felt and glue it on the orange as shown on the pattern.

4. Make the entire letter stronger by gluing it onto thin cardboard and cutting around it.

Directions

1. Introduce "o" by making lots of "o-o-o" sounds with the children, showing what it feels like to say "o."

2. Pass around the big orange "o" so the children can see what "o" looks like and can touch the letter while they practice the "o" sounds. Exaggerate the "o" sound in the word "o-o-orange," and the "o" sound in the words "on" and "off." Remember to keep the big feely "o" in constant view so the children can make the connection that the activities that follow all relate to "o."

3. Tell the children that "o" has a name just like they do and discuss the difference between the name of the letter "o" and the sound it makes. Sing through the alphabet to find where "o" is hiding.

4. Pick out a couple of "o" pictures from the picture dictionary to show the class more words that start with the "o" sound.

Making the "o" sound.

The *BIG* Event

Materials

✔ orange construction paper (a few more sheets than there are children in your class)

✔ five to ten sheets of green construction paper

✔ ruler

✔ marker

✔ scissors

✔ glue

✔ masking tape (optional)

✔ radio or audiocassette or CD player for music

Preparation

1. Cut large orange circles out of the orange construction paper so there is one orange circle for each child to sit or stand on.

2. Cut leafy stalks for the orange circles out of the green construction paper and glue them on the circles. Use a marker to dot the circles to make them really look like oranges.

3. Create a large open space in the classroom and lay the circles all around. Depending on your floor surface, you may want to put a loop of masking tape on the back of each orange to keep it from slipping.

4. Cut out two more orange circles (identical in size to each other). Write "off" on one of them and "on" on the other. Glue these together with the ruler in between them to create a lollipop sign.

When the sign says "on," everyone gets on the oranges.

When the sign says "off," everyone gets off the oranges.

Directions

1. Start the music and show the "off" side of the lollipop sign. Tell the children they can dance and skip around whenever you show "off" on the sign.

2. Tell them that when you show the "on" side of the sign and stop the music, they each need to find an orange to sit or stand on.

3. Try a practice run first. Then, each time the "off" is showing, take an orange away so that one child is out. The first time you do this, take two away so one person doesn't have to sit alone. The winner is the last person to be left on an orange when there is only one orange left.

More Ideas for "o"

Sensational "o"

Pour a layer of nontoxic orange paint in a tray (such as a cafeteria tray) and place the tray on newspapers on the floor or on a table. Have the children take turns tracing an "o" in the paint using their fingers, so they can feel and see the shape. The child taking a turn should wear a smock or an old shirt to avoid getting paint on his clothes. Have wipes ready to clean orange fingers.

TiP

You could use orange gelatin instead of paint for a different tactile experience.

Silly Pictures

A silly picture composed of things that start with "o" is one more way to solidify the sound in children's minds. Use a large sheet of paper with colored pens, a dry-erase board, or a chalkboard—anything that enables the children to watch you draw. Start with something that begins with the letter (such as an animal), then ask the children for ideas. (Have the picture dictionary open at the relevant page to help, but let the children feel that you believe they really did think up the ideas on their own.)

Remember that silly pictures are most effective if they seem novel to the children. You don't have to draw for every letter but can try this activity when you haven't done it in a while or when you have a letter that lends itself to lots of ideas. (For more tips on drawing silly pictures with your class, see page 12.)

The letter "o" may be a difficult letter for this activity, but you could try starting with an octopus. She may be juggling oranges, or even playing the organ. After you finish the class picture, have the children draw their own sound pictures.

Let's Pretend

Involving the "o" sound in games of pretend will make the sound even more memorable and fun for the children. Whether you do all or just one of the following ideas, remember to keep the session relatively short to hold the children's attention. Try to keep the novelty factor alive: For example, choose activities that are different from the Let's Pretend activities you've recently done for other letters.

- Have the children imagine they are octopuses under the sea. They can pretend they are swimming about on the floor using all of their bodies to bend and then stretch. Have the children pair up and sit back to back with a friend. Now they have eight arms and legs just like an octopus! Between the two of them, they can do lots of different things at the same time. One could be cooking dinner or fishing while the other is putting on makeup or playing the piano.

- Discuss how the "o" is round. Find lots of different ways of making a circle. You could walk in a circle, spin in a circle, and curl up in a circle.

- Think of different things that are round. For instance, an umbrella is round when it's open. You and the children could mime going outside then feeling a few raindrops on your hand. You reach into your bags for your umbrellas and put them up.

- The sun is round. Have the children imagine they are very hot from the heat of the sun. How do they move? What do they need? How will they cool down?

- A steering wheel is also round. The children can imagine they are driving cars, putting on the indicator to turn the corner, stopping at the traffic light.

- There are many other possibilities. You can rely upon the children to suggest some round things when they get the idea.

Pretending to be an octopus.

Crafts for "o"
Octopuses

This could be part of an under the sea unit. The octopuses look particularly good displayed on a blue background with the children's names written on colored paper cut into fish shapes.

Materials
- ✔ paper plate for each child
- ✔ four pipe cleaners for each child
- ✔ markers for each child
- ✔ single hole punch

Preparation
No preparation necessary except to gather the materials.

Directions

1. Have each child draw an octopus face on the plate using markers.

2. Help each child punch four holes along the bottom of each plate.

3. Next show the children how to fold a pipe cleaner in half and thread the fold through the hole so a loop of pipe cleaner is peeping through the hole.

4. Each child should then thread the two ends of the pipe cleaner through that loop, pulling the ends through firmly to secure. If the child does this four times, the octopus will have eight legs! This threading is a very good exercise to develop fine manipulative skills and coordination. If you have some collage treasures available, you may want the children to decorate their octopuses. (See page 15 for tips on building a collection of collage treasures.)

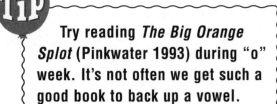

Try reading *The Big Orange Splot* (Pinkwater 1993) during "o" week. It's not often we get such a good book to back up a vowel.

Oranges

We usually make oranges during our shopping unit. We also make simple baskets in which to display the oranges and other salt dough fruit.

Materials

- ✔ 2 cups plain flour for each group of four
- ✔ 1 cup salt for each group of four
- ✔ 1 cup cold water for each group of four
- ✔ 1 tablespoon cooking oil for each group of four
- ✔ mixing bowl for each group of four
- ✔ wooden spoon for each group of four
- ✔ wax paper
- ✔ permanent marker
- ✔ baking sheet
- ✔ orange liquid tempera paint and brushes for each group of four
- ✔ a sheet of green tissue for each group of four
- ✔ glue for each group of four
- ✔ oven

Preparation

1. Tear off a sheet of wax paper that's the size of your baking sheet. Write the children' names on the wax paper at intervals along the bottom and the top. These names will indicate where to place the salt dough oranges so you can keep track of which belongs to whom. (For a large class, you may need to prepare two sheets of wax paper.)

2. Set out the ingredients for making the salt dough, the mixing bowl, and the spoon at the craft table.

Directions

1. The children can make the salt dough, each taking a turn to put in an ingredient, stir, and knead.

2. Give out a piece of salt dough to every child. Let the children knead and play with the dough, then ask them to roll it into balls to make oranges. The dough will be baked, so it should not be too solid.

3. Place the finished dough balls on the wax paper (which should be on the baking sheet) labeled with the children's names. To be doubly sure none of the oranges get mixed up, you can etch each child's initials in her orange while the dough is still soft.

4. Bake in a warm oven at 300°F for a couple of hours. Watch that they do not turn brown; salt dough should stay light.

5. The next day, the children can paint their oranges. When the paint dries, let the children snip off small pieces of green tissue, then scrunch it up before gluing onto the orange as a stalk.

Orange Activity Day

For variety at this late date in the year, when you introduce "o," instead of an activity center, try having an orange day! Everybody wears something orange and you all sit down to eat orange segments and drink orange juice.

I usually try to introduce "p" at about pumpkin time and incorporate it with a trip to a mini-farm to pick pumpkins. Try to introduce "p" not far from "d" and "b." Bouncy "b" and drill-like "d" really contrast with the soft pink "p." The letters look so alike that their differences need to be emphasized. If the children manage to produce any combination of a circle and a stick, be happy; do not be tempted to correct them at this early stage.

Activities to Introduce "p"

The activities in this section are for the first day you introduce "p" to the children. The first activity—See, Say, and Sing—involves a picture dictionary, a big feely letter "p" made out of felt, and the alphabet song all used together to involve the children in this exciting new sound. The second activity—The Big Event—will involve the children in a physical activity to help reinforce the sound of the letter. The Big Event for "p" has children choosing items that start with "p" from a pink pillowcase. *Important note:* The Big Event should follow immediately after the brief introduction of See, Say, and Sing activities to be most effective in solidifying the new letter for the children. Gather materials and prepare for *both* activities before you introduce "p" to your class. (See pages 7–11 for more information on introducing a new sound.)

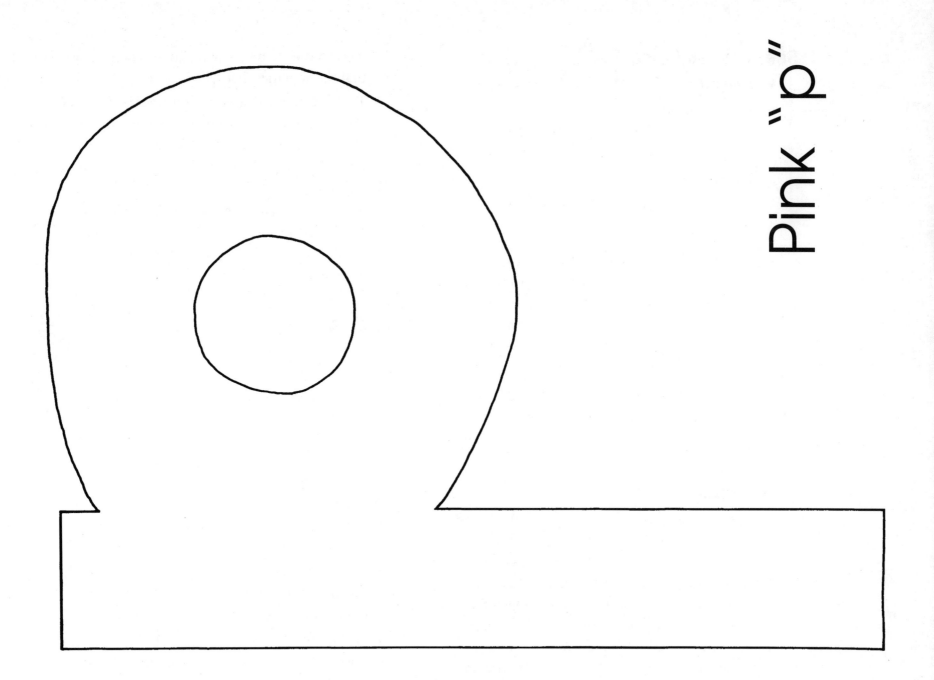

Pink "p"

See, Say, and Sing

Materials

✔ picture dictionary

✔ photocopy of the "p" pattern on page 131

✔ 8 ½" x 11" piece of pink felt

✔ scissors

✔ thin cardboard (such as a cereal box)

Preparation

1. To make the feely letter "p," first photocopy and cut out the pattern on page 131 (unless you decide to make this letter freehand, without using the pattern). You may also wish to create a bigger letter by enlarging the photocopy and using a larger piece of felt.

2. Using the pattern as a guide (or cutting freehand), cut the "p" shape out of pink felt.

3. Make the entire letter stronger by gluing it onto thin cardboard and cutting around it.

Directions

1. Introduce "p" by making lots of "p-p-p" sounds with the children, showing what it feels like to say "p."

2. Pass around the big feely "p" so the children can see what "p" looks like and can touch the letter while they practice the "p" sound. Exaggerate the "p" sound in the word "p-p-pink." Remember to keep the big feely "p" in constant

view so the children can make the connection that the activities that follow all relate to "p."

3. Tell the children that "p" has a name just like they do and discuss the difference between the name of the letter "p" and the sound it makes. Sing through the alphabet to find where "p" is hiding.

4. Pick out a couple of "p" pictures from the picture dictionary to show the class more words that start with the "p" sound. Avoid the words that start with "ph," or the children will be confused.

The *BIG* Event

Materials

✔ pink pillowcase

✔ three sheets of 8 ½" x 11" paper

✔ markers or colored pencils

✔ plastic plum, peach, or pear for each child (available at craft stores)

Preparation

1. Put all the peaches, plums, and pears in the pink pillowcase.

2. Using markers or colored pencils, draw a peach on one sheet of paper, a pear on another, and a plum on the third sheet.

3. Lay out the drawings on the floor.

4. Ensure that the children are familiar with peaches, pears, and plums.

Directions

1. Give each child a turn to come forward and pick out something from the pillowcase.
2. While one is choosing, the other children make the "p-p-p" sound in anticipation.
3. As the child pulls out the fruit, everyone is able to join in saying whether it is a peach, pear, or plum.
4. The child puts his fruit on the matching drawing.

More Ideas for "p"

Sensational "p"

Fill a tray (such as a cafeteria tray) with a layer of nontoxic pink paint, mashed pumpkin, or pudding and let the children take turns tracing a "p" with their fingers, so they can see and feel the shape. Make sure the feely letter "p" is clearly visible to all children as a model.

> **Tip**
>
> Instead of tracing "p," the children could actually make a "p" with pink play dough.

Silly Pictures

A silly picture composed of things that start with "p" is one more way to solidify the sound in children's minds. Use a large sheet of paper with colored pens, a dry-erase board, or a chalkboard—anything that enables the children to watch you draw. Start with something that begins with the letter (such as an animal), then ask the children for ideas. (Have the picture dictionary open at the relevant page to help, but let the children feel that you believe they really did think up the ideas on their own.)

Remember that silly pictures are most effective if they seem novel to the children. You don't have to draw for every letter but can try this activity when you haven't done it in a while or when you have a letter that lends itself to lots of ideas. (For more tips on drawing silly pictures with your class, see page 12.)

A parrot, pig, pelican, porcupine, peacock, or even a group of pets are good starting points for a silly p-p-picture. With the picture dictionary open in front of them, the children should have no trouble shouting out lots of good "p" ideas. After you finish the class picture, have the children draw their own sound pictures.

> **Tip**
>
> You can't go wrong reading *If You Give a Pig a Pancake* (Numeroff 1999) during the week of "p."

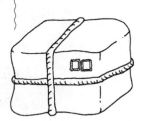

> **Printing Activity Center**
>
> Set up a printing table for the week. Put out some rubber stamps, an ink pad (washable), and some paper. Sponge printing or even potato printing would work just as well.

Let's Pretend

Involving the "p" sound in games of pretend will make the sound even more memorable and fun for the children. Whether you do all or just one of the following ideas, remember to keep the session relatively short to hold the children's attention. Try to keep the novelty factor alive: For example, choose activities that are different from the Let's Pretend activities you've recently done for other letters.

- A very good book for the children to act out individually in a group, not as a play, is *It's Pumpkin Time* (Hall 1999), which shows the development of a pumpkin.
- *The Three Little Pigs* is another miming option.
- *Oh, Were They Ever Happy* (Spier 1989) is such an inspiration for miming about painters.

Decorating my potpourri pot.

Crafts for "p"
Potpourri Pot

This makes a super long-lasting gift for Mom.

Materials

- ✔ baby food jar for each child (lids not necessary)
- ✔ four or five cotton swabs for each child
- ✔ acrylic craft paint
- ✔ A circle cut from fine netting fabric (larger than the top of the jar) for each child
- ✔ ribbon for each child
- ✔ potpourri
- ✔ masking tape and marker
- ✔ rubber band for each child

Preparation

No preparation necessary except to gather materials (and perhaps cut the ribbon to lengths suitable for wrapping around each jar). Put a masking tape label with each child's name on the bottom of each jar.

Directions

1. Using the cotton swabs as brushes, each child decorates his baby food jar with paint. It is nice to use a spotted pattern (to which the cotton swab lends itself), rather than dragging the cotton around.
2. When the paint is dry, help each child fill his jar with potpourri.

3. Then each child puts a netting circle over the top of the jar and secures it with a rubber band.

4. Finally, with help, each child ties a ribbon around the jar, over the rubber band, in a bow. Even if the child is only able to hold the ribbon and netting in place while you tie the bow, she is still actively involved, and therefore keeps ownership of the project.

Pumpkin Pots

This activity requires a different kind of manipulative skill than the children may be used to. The pumpkin will actually end up as a jack-o'-lantern, so this craft is best done around Halloween. I have always used gallon juice containers because of their round pumpkinlike shape. However, they really do use up a lot of paint, so if you can find a suitable smaller clear plastic container that will take the kind of paint you have, it would be better.

Materials

✔ a clear gallon juice jug with a lid for each child (do not use opaque milk jugs; the paint won't show through)

✔ orange liquid tempera paint

✔ a sheet of black construction paper for each child

✔ a sheet of green tissue paper for each child

✔ rubber band for each child

✔ glue

✔ water available to water down paint as desired

✔ a funnel for each child or small group

Preparation

1. Make sure the containers are absolutely clean and dry.

2. Cut at least six triangles out of the black construction paper for each child (one to two inches each, depending on the size of the jug).

3. Cut a six-inch circle out of the green tissue paper for each child.

Directions

1. Using the funnel, the children pour about half a cup of paint into their jugs.

2. Next have each child water down the paint inside the jug slightly, making sure it still clings to the sides of the jug.

3. Then the children should put the lids on their jugs and start to turn the jugs so that the paint moves about inside to gradually coat the inside.

5. The children can add more paint and water with the help of the funnel, as needed. They keep tipping and turning the jug until the inside is virtually covered.

6. Next have each child stick the black triangles on one of the sides of the jug to make the face of a jack-o'-lantern.

7. Finally, each child holds a piece of green tissue over the lid and secures it with a rubber band.

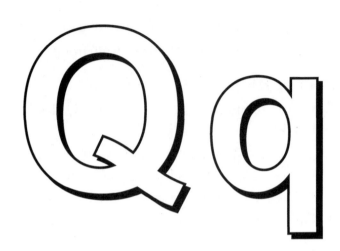

This should be one of the very last consonants you introduce. There are not many common words that begin with "q," so it is not that valuable early on as a tool for teaching a basic understanding of how sounds work. By this time of the year, the children will probably have an idea of how the sounds work and will now be "collecting" new sounds. That is the point when they will really enjoy the quirky fun of "q." Keep the flick on the tail of the lowercase "q" to keep it distinct from the "p." With all the reversal that is naturally happening at this stage, the children can use this help.

Activities to Introduce "q"

The activities in this section are for the first day you introduce "q" to the children. The first activity—See, Say, and Sing—involves a picture dictionary, a big feely letter "q" made out of felt, and the alphabet song all used together to involve the children in this exciting new sound. The second activity—The Big Event—will involve the children in a physical activity to help reinforce the sound of the letter. The Big Event for "q" gives children a chance to be a queen wearing the royal crown and quilt. *Important note:* The Big Event should follow immediately after the brief introduction of See, Say, and Sing activities to be most effective in solidifying the new letter for the children. Gather materials and prepare for *both* activities before you introduce "q" to your class. (See pages 7–11 for more information on introducing a new sound.)

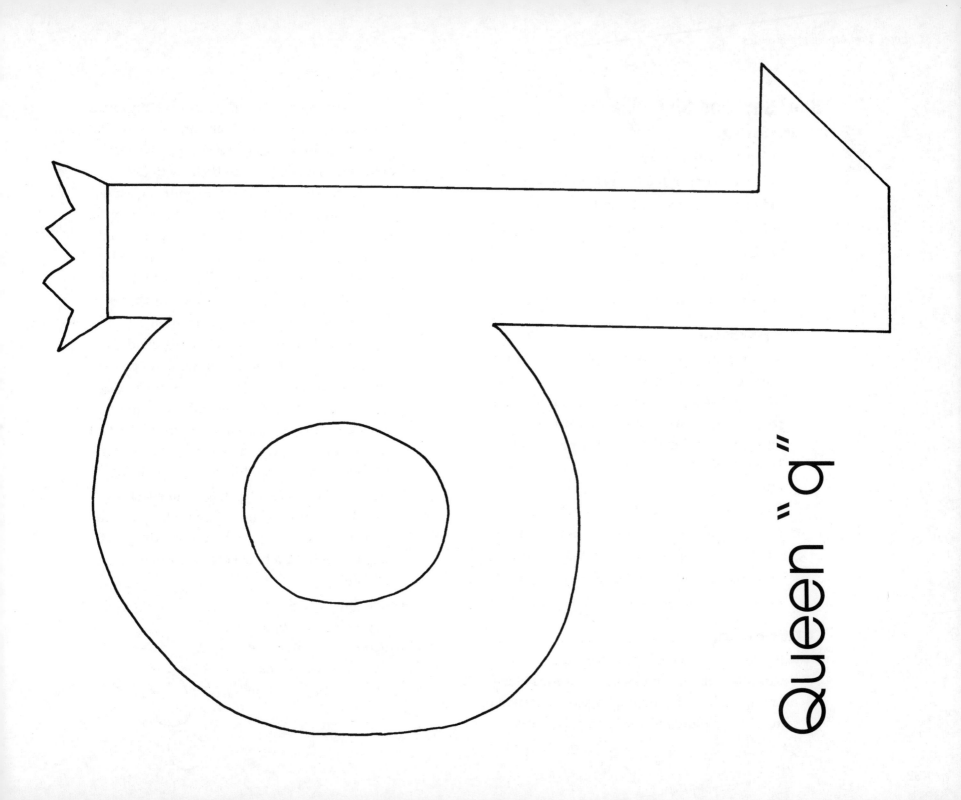

Queen "q"

See, Say, and Sing

Materials

- ✔ picture dictionary
- ✔ photocopy of the "q" pattern on page 137
- ✔ 8 ½" x 11" piece of purple felt
- ✔ 2 ½" x 1" piece of orange felt
- ✔ scissors
- ✔ glue
- ✔ thin cardboard (such as a cereal box)

Preparation

1. To make the feely letter "q," photocopy and cut out the pattern on page 137 (unless you decide to make this letter freehand, without using the pattern). You may also wish to create a bigger letter by enlarging the photocopy and using larger pieces of felt.

2. Using the pattern as a guide (or cutting freehand), cut the "q" shape out of purple felt.

3. Cut the crown shape out of the orange felt and glue it on the "q" as shown on the pattern.

4. Make the entire letter stronger by gluing it onto thin cardboard and cutting around it.

Directions

1. Introduce "q" by making lots of "q-q-q" sounds with the children, showing what it feels like to say "q." Depending on the stage of understanding of the children in your group, you may want to mention that "q" never goes anywhere without her friend "u." Make up a story about the queen not wanting to get her crown wet and always having her umbrella with her, wherever you see her. Consequently, "q" and "u" are always together! Just mention this when you are introducing the letter; you don't want to overload the children. However, there will probably be one bright spark who will spot that "u" with the "q" when he sees it written in a book, so it is always worth a mention.

2. Pass around the big feely "q" so the children can see what "q" looks like and can touch the letter while they practice the "q" sound. Exaggerate the "q" sound in the word "q-q-queen." Remember to keep the big feely "q" in constant view so the children can make the connection that the activities that follow all relate to "q."

3. Tell the children that "q" has a name just like they do and discuss the difference between the name of the letter "q" and the sound it makes. Sing through the alphabet to find where "q" is hiding.

4. Pick out a couple of "q" pictures from the picture dictionary to show the class more words that start with the "q" sound.

The **BIG** Event

Materials

✔ a quilt

✔ a crown

✔ a quarter

Preparation

No preparation unless you decide to make a crown instead of buying one (see instructions for making one on page 101).

Directions

1. Each child takes a turn to be the queen, using the quilt as a cloak. The queen also gets to wear a crown. Everybody else has to be very quiet when the queen walks by.

2. The queen has a quarter in her hand. When she reaches the person she wants to be queen next, she stops and quietly puts the quarter in his

Quilt queens.

hand. Now it is that child's turn to dress up in the quilt and the crown and pretend to be queen.

3. After this activity (or later in the day or week), give the children a chance to just look at the quilt. Children tend to love quilts and especially enjoy examining them when they are laid out flat.

TiP

At this young age, the boys do not mind dressing up as girls. In fact, when I get out the dress-up box in my room, there are often arguments among the boys, who all want to wear the tutus! I relish every moment of their innocence.

More Ideas for "q"

Sensational "q"

Fill a tray (such as a cafeteria tray) with a layer of quarters and let the children take turns tracing a "q" in the quarters with their fingers, so they can see and feel the shape. Make sure the feely letter "q" is clearly visible to all children as a model. The beauty of this letter is the flick on the tail that makes it that much more distinctive.

If you cannot manage a tray of quarters, plastic play ones will do, but the real ones feel so much better and make a super sound. Another option is to use fewer quarters on a background of shaving foam, salt, or sand. The "q" will stand out in this background, but the children will still think of this as drawing a "q" in the quarters.

Silly Pictures

A silly picture composed of things that start with "q" is one more way to solidify the sound in children's minds. Use a large sheet of paper with colored pens, a dry-erase board, or a chalkboard—anything that enables the children to watch you draw. Start with something that begins with the letter (such as an animal), then ask the children for ideas. (Have the picture dictionary open at the relevant page to help, but let the children feel that you believe they really did think up the ideas on their own.)

Remember that silly pictures are most effective if they seem novel to the children. You don't have to draw for every letter but can try this activity when you haven't done it in a while or when you have a letter that lends itself to lots of ideas. (For more tips on drawing silly pictures with your class, see page 12.)

Unless the children know what a quail is (most will probably think of it as just a bird), you might not be able to start with an animal for "q," which is another difficult letter for silly pictures. Still, you could have fun with a quaking quarterback who quacks when he gets queasy.

Let's Pretend

Involving the "q" sound in games of pretend will make the sound even more memorable and fun for the children. Whether you do all or just one of the following ideas, remember to keep the session relatively short to hold the children's attention. Try to keep the novelty factor alive: For example, choose activities that are different from the Let's Pretend activities you've recently done for other letters.

This activity for "q" requires a bit of preparation. It will work particularly well if you are studying opposites. To prepare, cut two eight-inch circles out of construction paper. Write "quick" on one with a thick marker. On the other circle, write "slow." Using loops of masking tape, stick one circle to the top of one side of a ruler and the other backing it, making a big lollipop shape.

Have the children act out any specific tasks. Start off with "slow" showing, so their actions have to be slow. When you turn the lollipop around to "quick," the children have to speed up their actions, still making sure they are miming the same action. After a couple of minutes, change back to "slow." Continue to change the speed a couple more times, then change the activity to be mimed.

Some ideas for tasks to give the children:

- making a cake
- building a wall
- getting washed and dressed
- shopping in the supermarket
- rowing a boat

If you think the children can handle it, make a "quiet/noisy" lollipop. You could have them be all sorts of things that make noise, but they still have to keep pretending, albeit quietly, when the lollipop says "quiet." They could be cars, ducks, dump trucks, lions, fire engines, or even mice.

Crafts for "q"
Quilt for a Queen

These little quilts can all be put together on display to make one very large spectacular quilt, enhancing further the idea about a quilt being made up of lots of little pieces, fitting together to make one big piece.

Materials
- about 12" x 18" sheet of construction paper for each child
- fabric scraps, as many different types as possible
- glue for each child or small group

TiP Burlap works well for the background instead of construction paper, especially to make the quilt all fabric, but you may need to anchor it to the table with masking tape first.

Preparation
Cut the fabric scraps into two-inch squares.

Directions
The children glue the fabric squares onto construction-paper backgrounds to make their quilts. Some children will make patterns with the different types of fabric, and others will need all their concentration to fit the squares together. The result is always very pleasing to the children.

Making a quilt.

Quarter Rubbings Activity Center

Being the largest of the common usage coins, quarters work best for making rubbings. Provide on the activity table this week several sheets of paper about four inches square (not too thick), crayons (dark colors work best), and a bowl containing a few quarters.

The child takes a quarter, positions it underneath a piece of paper, holds it as steady as possible (the advantage of the small pieces of paper), and then rubs over the quarter with his crayon. He should soon be able to see an impression of the pattern on the quarter. Very young children are not usually able to make rubbings of wonderful accuracy, but they always seem happy as long as something shows through, even the circle shape! They will, of course, improve with practice.

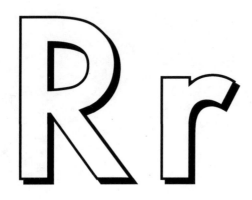

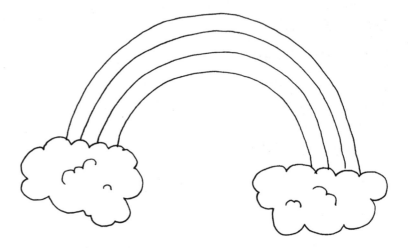

The letter "r" has the good fortune to sound just like the revving of a racing car. Use the idea of a red racing car r-r-revving, and this will be an easy sound to introduce fairly early.

Activities to Introduce "r"

The activities in this section are for the first day you introduce "r" to the children. The first activity—See, Say, and Sing—involves a picture dictionary, a big feely letter "r" made out of felt, and the alphabet song all used together to involve the children in this exciting new sound. The second activity—The Big Event— will involve the children in a physical activity to help reinforce the sound of the letter. The Big Event for "r" gives children a chance to fish for red fish in the river using their red fishing rods. *Important note:* The Big Event should follow immediately after the brief introduction of See, Say, and Sing activities to be most effective in solidifying the new letter for the children. Gather materials and prepare for *both* activities before you introduce "r" to your class. (See pages 7–11 for more information on introducing a new sound.)

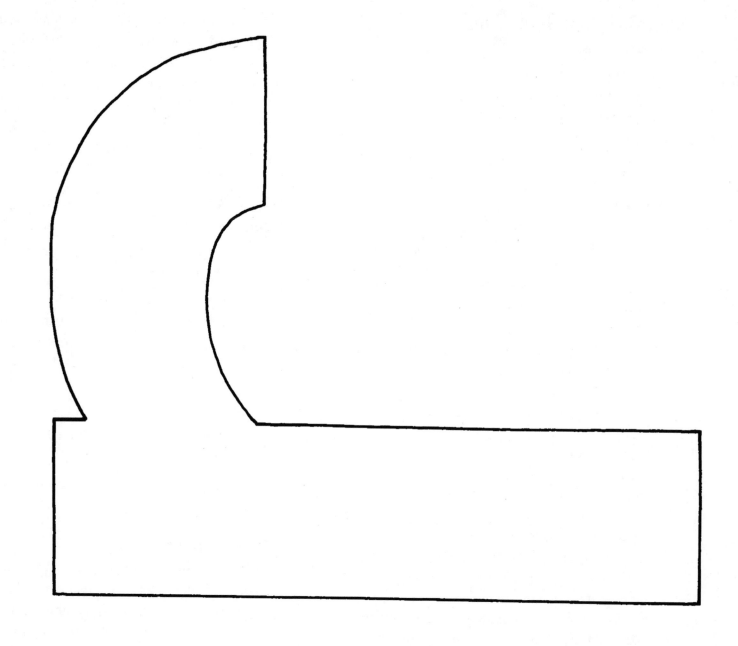

Red "r"

See, Say, and Sing

Materials

✔ picture dictionary

✔ photocopy of the "r" pattern on page 143

✔ 8½" x 11" piece of red felt

✔ scissors

✔ thin cardboard (such as a cereal box)

Preparation

1. To make the feely letter "r," photocopy and cut out the pattern on page 143 (unless you decide to make this letter freehand, without using the pattern). You may also wish to create a bigger letter by enlarging the photocopy and using a larger piece of felt.

2. Using the pattern as a guide (or cutting free-hand), cut the "r" shape out of red felt.

3. Make the entire letter stronger by gluing it onto thin cardboard and cutting around it.

Directions

1. Introduce "r" by making lots of "r-r-r" sounds with the children, showing what it feels like to say "r"—lots of fun!

2. Pass around the big feely "r" so the children can see what "r" looks like and can touch the letter while they practice the "r" sound. Exaggerate the "r" sound in the word "r-r-red." Remember to keep the big feely "r" in constant view so the children can make the connection that the activities that follow all relate to "r."

3. Tell the children that "r" has a name just like they do and discuss the difference between the name of the letter "r" and the sound it makes. Sing through the alphabet to find where "r" is hiding.

4. Pick out a couple of "r" pictures from the picture dictionary to show the class more words that start with the "r" sound.

The *BIG* Event

Materials

✔ 12" dowel (or ruler)

✔ about 18" red ribbon

✔ magnet (horseshoe, doughnut, or rectangular)

✔ several sheets of red construction paper

✔ one picture of something that begins with "r" for each child

✔ glue

✔ hot glue gun (optional)

✔ paper clip for each child

✔ 1 to 3 yards of blue fabric

✔ red bowl (or other red round object)

✔ scissors

Preparation

1. Cut fish shapes (about 3" x 2") out of the red construction paper (one fish per child). You could also try this activity using just the "r" pictures, without the fish shapes, as shown in the photo on page 145.

Directions

1. Each child takes a turn using the rod to fish in the river for a red fish on which there is something beginning with "r." The other children can all make the "r-r-r" sound as he pulls up his catch in anticipation of the "r" word that will appear in the picture.

2. After everyone names the "r" word on the fish, the child puts his catch in the red bowl (or other red round shape).

Fishing with a red rod in a river of "r" pictures.

> **TiP**
>
> **A good source of "r" pictures is a first-grade sound workbook. There you will find plenty of simple line art—reindeer, racing cars, and raccoons—ready to copy or trace.**

2. Gather or cut out pictures of things that begin with "r."

3. Glue one picture to each fish.

4. Attach a paper clip to each fish.

5. To make the fishing pole, tie the ribbon to one end of the dowel, and tie the magnet to the other end of the ribbon. (Use hot glue to attach the magnet if you can't acquire a magnet shape, such as horseshoe, doughnut, or rectangle, that's easy to tie to the ribbon.)

6. The blue fabric will be a river. Set your river on the floor, and put the fish on the river, picture side down.

7. Set the red bowl nearby. The children will put their catch in this. You don't have to use a red bowl, of course. Any red and round object, even a red circle cut from construction paper, will work for this purpose.

More Ideas for "r"

Sensational "r"

Fill a tray (such as a cafeteria tray) with a layer of rice and let the children take turns tracing an "r" in the rice with their fingers, so they can see and feel the shape. Make sure the feely letter "r" is clearly visible to all children as a model.

Silly Pictures

A silly picture composed of things that start with "r" is one more way to solidify the sound in children's minds. Use a large sheet of paper with colored pens, a dry-erase board, or a chalkboard—anything that enables the children to watch you draw. Start with something that begins with the letter (such as an animal), then ask the children for ideas. (Have the picture dictionary open at the relevant page to help, but let the children feel that you believe they really did think up the ideas on their own.)

Remember that silly pictures are most effective if they seem novel to the children. You don't have to draw for every letter but can try this activity when you haven't done it in a while or when you have a letter that lends itself to lots of ideas. (For more tips on drawing silly pictures with your class, see page 12.)

A rhinoceros riding a roller coaster, a rat racing a car, or a rabbit on a rocking chair—these are just a few of the many, many possibilities for "r." Get the children started, and they might even have too many ideas! After you finish the class picture, have the children draw their own sound pictures.

Let's Pretend

Involving the "r" sound in games of pretend will make the sound even more memorable and fun for the children. Racing cars are a very good reference point for the sound of "r-r-r," not just because they begin with "r," but also because the "r" can represent the roaring and revving sound of the racing car's engine. Remember to keep the session relatively short to hold the children's attention, and try to keep the novelty factor alive: For example, choose activities that are different from the Let's Pretend activities you've recently done for other letters.

Set definite safety rules before you all pretend to be racing car drivers, maybe letting a few children have a turn at a time. The children will certainly remember this event, and it will be a time when you positively encourage them to be making that r-r-r-revving, r-r-r-roaring sound.

Begin by having the children polish their racing cars and lift the hoods to check their engines. They can also check the oil and the tires and put in gas. You could even involve all the children in a race while they are sitting down on the floor. They will still be having great fun turning the steering wheel and taking the corners. All the while, you can be waving that red "r" while you are being the commentator on the "race" amid their roaring "r" sounds. After the race, the children need to wheel their cars back into the garage and check them over again.

Revving our engines.

Crafts for "r"
Round Printing

This craft works very well if you are studying shapes in class.

Materials

- ✔ a collection of round items, such as orange halves, pasta wheels, the ends of cardboard tubes, spools, round lids, sponge circles, and so on
- ✔ various colors of liquid tempera paint
- ✔ small plastic trays for each color of paint
- ✔ one sheet of paper for each child

Preparation

No preparation necessary except to gather the round items and pour each color of paint into a separate tray.

Directions

The children use the round items to print colored circles on the paper. Demonstrate how printing is a straight up-and-down movement and does not involve dragging. Show also how it is best to keep the same items in the same color paint (for example, keep the orange half in the orange paint and the spool in the yellow paint). There will be enough mixing on the page! Some children will attempt to create a pattern or a picture while others will just enjoy the physical experience of randomly banging the objects on the paper and seeing what happens.

Round Activity Center

Put out a variety of round objects that can be drawn around, such as different-sized lids and containers, cylindrical blocks, and cardboard tubes. Put out colored pencils and sheets of paper also. The children get practice in the manual dexterity of this activity and produce a colorful design or pattern if they wish. If you have round stencils, where the children draw around the inside of the template, put those out also.

Rainbows

Rainbows are always a favorite with young children, so to find hidden rainbows around us is especially exciting. Experiment with the markers first. There are so many different types on the market now with different qualities; you don't want to risk somebody's rainbow not appearing!

Materials

- ✔ round coffee filter for each child
- ✔ nonwashable markers (dark colors, such as black, work best)
- ✔ pot of water for each child (such as a yogurt or margarine container)
- ✔ prism

TiP

You can use a sun catcher instead of a prism, as long as the sun catcher filters a rainbow of colors through the glass.

TiP

What Makes a Rainbow? (Schwartz 2000) is a unique resource if you are studying rainbows.

Preparation

Prepare the pots of water before starting this activity.

Directions

1. Take the prism out on a sunny day and show how there are lots of secret colors all around us. Children are enchanted by the rainbow a prism can make.

2. In the classroom, help each child make two tears up to the center of her coffee filter to form a flap.

3. At the top of the flap, in the center of the filter, each child should use one colored marker to make a blob of color about one inch round.

4. Next, each child rests the filter on top of a pot of water with the flap hanging in the water, so the water can gradually soak into the paper. Watch in amazement as the water hits the color blob and it spreads into a rainbow of colors.

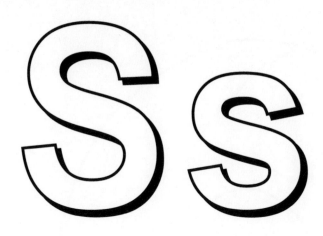

I always introduce "s" first as it is so easily recognizable; it looks and sounds like a snake. Children always love to make the "s-s-s-s" sound, so it is easy to generate lots of enthusiasm for this letter.

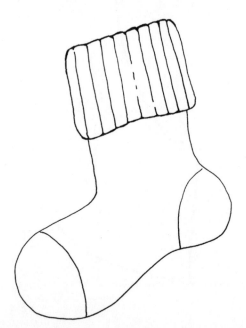

Activities to Introduce "s"

The activities in this section are for the first day you introduce "s" to the children. The first activity—See, Say, and Sing—involves a picture dictionary, a big feely letter "s" made out of cardboard and aluminum foil, and the alphabet song all used together to involve the children in this exciting new sound. The second activity—The Big Event—will involve the children in a physical activity to help reinforce the sound of the letter. The Big Event for "s" has children choosing "s" items from a sack and placing them on a seat. *Important note:* The Big Event should follow immediately after the brief introduction of See, Say, and Sing activities to be most effective in solidifying the new letter for the children. Gather materials and prepare for *both* activities before you introduce "s" to your class. (See pages 7–11 for more information on introducing a new sound.)

Silver "S"

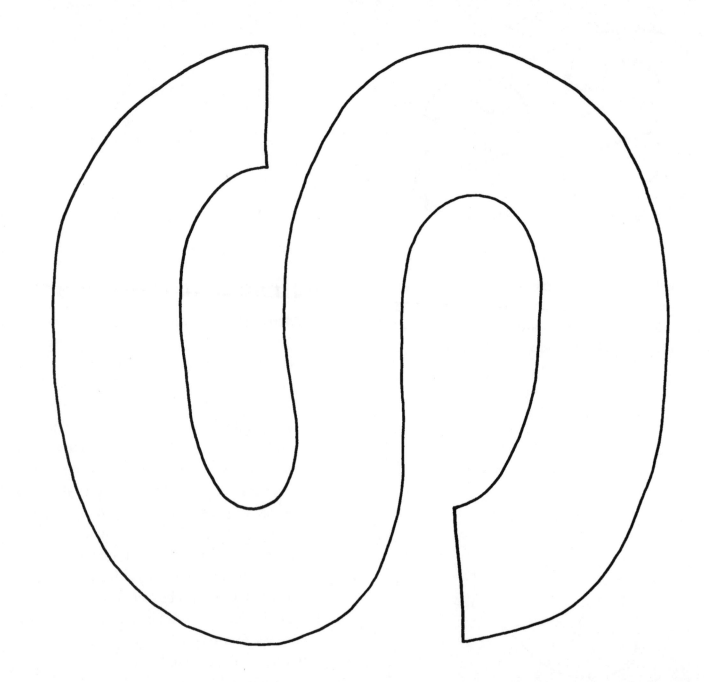

See, Say, and Sing

Materials

- ✔ picture dictionary
- ✔ photocopy of the "s" pattern on page 150
- ✔ 8 ½" x 11" piece of light cardboard
- ✔ glue or tape
- ✔ aluminum foil

Preparation

1. To make the feely letter "s," photocopy and cut out the pattern on page 150 (unless you decide to make this letter freehand, without using the pattern). You may also wish to create a bigger letter by enlarging the photocopy and using a larger piece of cardboard.

2. Using the pattern as a guide (or cutting free-hand), cut the "s" shape out of cardboard.

3. Wrap the "s" in aluminum foil and secure with glue or tape on the back.

Directions

1. Introduce "s" by making lots of "s-s-s" sounds with the children, showing what it feels like to say "s." Show the silver "s" and have everybody make the "s-s-s" sound as you slide your finger down the big feely letter.

2. Pass around the big silver "s" so the children can see what "s" looks like and can touch the letter while they practice the "s" sound. Exaggerate the "s" sound in the word "s-s-silver." Remember to keep the big feely "s" in constant

view so the children can make the connection that the activities that follow all relate to "s."

3. Tell the children that "s" has a name just like they do and discuss the difference between the name of the letter "s" and the sound it makes. Sing through the alphabet to find where "s" is hiding.

4. Pick out a couple of "s" pictures from the picture dictionary to show the class more words that start with the "s" sound. Be sure not to choose any words that begin with "sh," as that would be very confusing!

The *BIG* Event

Materials

- ✔ a sack (paper, cloth, any material will do)
- ✔ one small object that begins with "s" for each child
- ✔ chair

Preparation

Gather enough objects that begin with "s" so that each child can pull one out of the sack. These will need to be small enough so that all of them will fit in the sack at one time. You might try a sock, toy snowman, can of soup, spaghetti, Slinky, scarf, plastic spiders, safety scissors, sunflower seeds, a toy snake, a skirt, a slipper, soap, sunglasses, and so on. Have them in the sack, with the chair (that you will call the "seat") nearby before you introduce "s" to the class.

Directions

1. Pull out the sack full of "s" goodies and let the children come up one at a time to choose something from the s-s-sack. While they are choosing, encourage the other children to be making the "s-s-s" sound, ready to say the name of whatever is pulled out of the sack.

2. Have each child put her item on the seat nearby when she has finished her turn.

More Ideas for "s"

Sensational "s"

Fill a tray (such as a cafeteria tray) with a layer of sand and let the children take turns tracing an "s" in the sand with their fingers, so they can see and feel the shape. Make sure the feely letter "s" is clearly visible to all children as a model.

Silly Pictures

A silly picture composed of things that start with "s" is one more way to solidify the sound in children's minds. Use a large sheet of paper with colored pens, a dry-erase board, or a chalkboard—anything that enables the children to watch you draw. Start with something that begins with the letter (such as an animal), then ask the children for ideas. (Have the picture dictionary open at the relevant page to help, but let the children feel that you believe they really did think up the ideas on their own.)

Remember that silly pictures are most effective if they seem novel to the children. You don't have to draw for every letter but can try this activity when you haven't done it in a while or when you have a letter that lends itself to lots of ideas. (For more tips on drawing silly pictures with your class, see page 12.)

The letter "s" has a slew of possibilities for s-s-silly pictures. You might start with the ever-popular snake, or go for a snail instead. Sally snake might be climbing stairs in a skyscraper or skateboarding and wearing sunglasses to start. After you finish the class picture, have the children draw their own sound pictures.

Surfing!

Let's Pretend

Involving the "s" sound in games of pretend will make the sound even more memorable and fun for the children. Whether you do all or just one of the following ideas, remember to keep the session relatively short to hold the children's attention. Try to keep the novelty factor alive: For example, choose activities that are different from the Let's Pretend activities you've recently done for other letters.

- Children love to pretend to be snakes wriggling around on the floor. They can be swimming snakes, snakes looking up to see if their friends are close by, or snakes curling up for a sleep.

- Another great "s" activity is "sun, sea, and sand." The children can pack their suitcases to go to the beach. They pack their sunscreen, sunglasses, swimsuit, and sandals. They can pretend to be playing in the sand at the beach, building a sandcastle. They can go down for a swim in the sea and splash in the waves. They can put on their lotion and sunglasses. I usually have the sound of waves playing in the background. At the end of the session, the children can be sleepy after their action-packed day and curl up on the floor for a sleep.

Sand play.

Sand Table Activity Center

The sand table is a permanent feature in my room, as I am sure it is for many of you. It is particularly handy that "s" is the first sound because it gives me a chance to turn the introduction of the sand table into a sound reference point also. I can introduce all the toys and rules for the inside sandbox, as well as suggestions for activities for the sandbox in the playground. If you do not have a sandbox, bring in a bowl of sand for the children to play with. They do not need elaborate toys. Laundry detergent scoops, a funnel, a few small containers (such as yogurt containers), and a sieve, if you can get one, will provide hours of enjoyment.

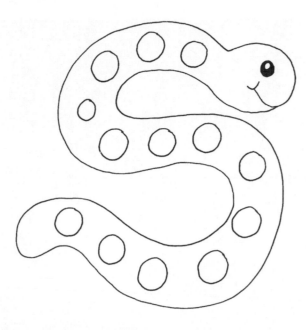

Preparation

1. Cut an "s" for each child out of the construction paper.
2. Cut several two-inch circles for each child out of the different colors of construction paper.
3. Draw a mouth and eyes on each snake so that the "s" will be in the right position, with the face at top right.

Directions

The children glue the spots onto their snakes, creating spotty snakes. If they trace down the "s" with their finger, they know to start at the snake's head.

Crafts for "s"

Spotty Snake

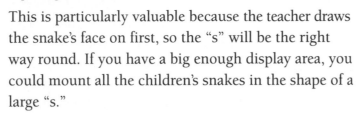

This is particularly valuable because the teacher draws the snake's face on first, so the "s" will be the right way round. If you have a big enough display area, you could mount all the children's snakes in the shape of a large "s."

Materials

✔ a sheet of construction paper for each child
✔ several sheets of different colors of construction paper for cutting out spots
✔ glue for each child or small group
✔ crayons
✔ scissors

Spelling out "sky" with the big feely letters.

154

Salt Dough Snail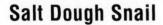

This will be one of the first activities in the school year. For some children, it may be their first experience with salt dough. Give them a chance to really play with the dough before you start encouraging them to roll the sausage shape needed. As long as they end up with some sort of swirly sausage shape, that's fine. Some children will be able to produce a handsome swirl. For this reason, I don't usually paint this item so that we can focus on enjoying the lovely shapes the children make.

Materials

- ✔ 2 cups plain flour for each group of four
- ✔ 1 cup salt for each group of four
- ✔ 1 cup cold water for each group of four
- ✔ 1 tablespoon cooking oil for each group of four
- ✔ mixing bowl for each group of four
- ✔ wooden spoon for each group of four
- ✔ wax paper
- ✔ permanent marker
- ✔ baking sheet
- ✔ oven

Preparation

1. Tear off a sheet of wax paper that's the size of your baking sheet. Write the children's names on the wax paper at intervals along the bottom and the top. These names will indicate where to place the salt dough snails so you can keep track of which belongs to whom. (For a large class, you may need to prepare two sheets of wax paper.)
2. Set out the ingredients for making the salt dough, the mixing bowl, and the spoon at the craft table.

Directions

1. The children can make the salt dough, each taking a turn to put in an ingredient, stir, and knead.
2. Give out a piece of salt dough to every child. Let the children knead and play with the dough, then show them how to roll out long snakes and then spiral those snakes to make a snail. The dough will be baked, so it should not be too solid.
3. Place the finished snails on the wax paper labeled with the children's names (which should be on the baking sheet).
4. Bake at 300°F for a couple of hours. Watch that they do not turn brown; salt dough should stay light.

> **TiP**
>
> *Skyfire* (Asch 1990), *Eensy Weensy Spider* (Hoberman 2000), and *Time to Sleep* (Fleming 1997) are all great books for reinforcing the "s" sound.

155

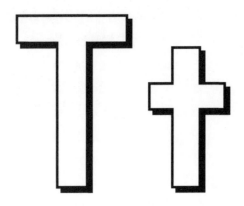

T t

Make "t" the second letter you introduce, after "s." The straight lines contrast well with the swirly "s." Also the short, sharp repetitive "t-t-t" is extremely different from the everlasting sound of "sssssss."

Activities to Introduce "t"

The activities in this section are for the first day you introduce "t" to the children. The first activity—See, Say, and Sing—involves a picture dictionary, a big feely letter "t" made out of felt, and the alphabet song all used together to involve the children in this exciting new sound. The second activity—The Big Event—will involve the children in a physical activity to help reinforce the sound of the letter. The Big Event for "t" has children matching tickets with "t" objects on them to your tickets. When a child matches your ticket, she gets to take a Tootsie Roll from the Tootsie Roll tree. *Important note:* The Big Event should follow immediately after the brief introduction of See, Say, and Sing activities to be most effective in solidifying the new letter for the children. Gather materials and prepare for *both* activities before you introduce "t" to your class. (See pages 7–11 for more information on introducing a new sound.)

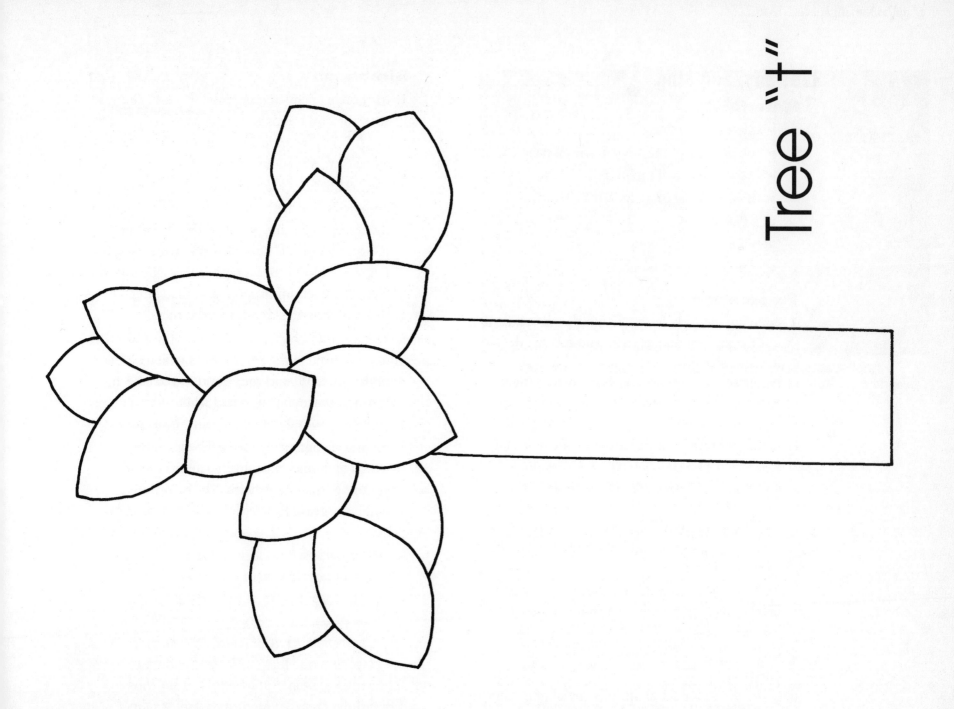

Tree "t"

See, Say, and Sing

Materials

- ✔ picture dictionary
- ✔ photocopy of the "t" pattern on page 157
- ✔ 2" x 7" piece of brown felt
- ✔ 8" x 6" piece of green felt
- ✔ scissors
- ✔ glue
- ✔ thin cardboard (such as a cereal box)

Preparation

1. To make the feely letter "t," photocopy and cut out the pattern on page 157 (unless you decide to make this letter freehand, without using the pattern). You may also wish to create a bigger letter by enlarging the photocopy and using larger pieces of felt.

2. Cut the leaves from the trunk in the pattern if you wish to use the pattern as a template for cutting. Otherwise, you can cut your tree freehand, referring to the pattern as a guide.

3. Use the trunk part of the pattern as a guide to cutting the trunk out of brown felt (or cut the trunk freehand).

4. Use the leaves pattern as a guide to cutting leaves out of green felt, or just cut a bunch of leaves out of the felt without using the pattern.

5. Glue the leaves to the trunk as shown on the pattern.

6. Make the entire letter stronger by gluing it onto thin cardboard and cutting around it.

Directions

1. Introduce "t" by making lots of "t-t-t" sounds with the children, showing what it feels like to say "t." Tell the children that to make a nice "t," we need to show our teeth.

2. Pass around the big feely tree "t" so the children can see what "t" looks like and can touch the letter while they practice the "t" sound. Exaggerate the "t" sound in the word "t-t-tree." Remember to keep the big feely "t" in constant view so the children can make the connection that the activities that follow all relate to "t."

3. Tell the children that "t" has a name just like they do and discuss the difference between the name of the letter "t" and the sound it makes. Sing through the alphabet to find where "t" is hiding.

4. Pick out a couple of "t" pictures from the picture dictionary to show the class more words that start with the "t" sound. Avoid anything that begins with "th" or the children will be confused.

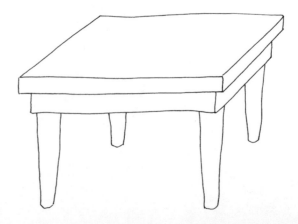

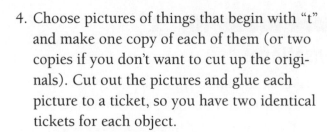

The *BIG* Event

Materials

- ✔ a Tootsie Roll for each child
- ✔ masking tape
- ✔ glue
- ✔ tissue box
- ✔ thin cardboard
- ✔ a picture of something that begins with "t" for each child
- ✔ marker
- ✔ a tin

> **TiP**
>
> A first-grade sound workbook is a great source of simple line drawings of lots of different objects that begin with the same sound.

Preparation

1. Ensure that giving out Tootsie Rolls will be acceptable to parents.
2. Draw a tree on the chalkboard and tape some Tootsie Rolls to it using masking tape. (I use a free-standing tree that my husband made for my classroom. See the instructions for making one on page 106.)
3. Cut the cardboard into tickets so that you have two tickets for each child in your class.

4. Choose pictures of things that begin with "t" and make one copy of each of them (or two copies if you don't want to cut up the originals). Cut out the pictures and glue each picture to a ticket, so you have two identical tickets for each object.
5. Write a "t" on each ticket.
6. Put half the tickets in a tissue box. (Alternatively, you could use a toy truck or anything that begins with "t" to hold the tickets.)
7. Put the other half of the tickets (those that match the tickets in the tissue box) in your tin.

Directions

1. Each child takes a ticket from the tissue box.
2. After everyone has a ticket, pull one ticket at a time out of your tin and ask who has the matching item. For example, "Who has the ticket with the T-T-Teddy?"
3. The child who has that ticket brings it up, puts it back in the tissue box, and takes a Tootsie Roll from the tree. Repeat until all of the children have had a chance to take a Tootsie Roll.

Taking a Tootsie Roll from the tree.

More Ideas for "t"

Sensational "t"

Put a layer of toothpaste in a tray (such as a cafeteria tray) and let the children take turns tracing a "t" in the toothpaste with their fingers, so they can see and feel the shape. Make sure the feely letter "t" is clearly visible to all children as a model.

Silly Pictures

A silly picture composed of things that start with "t" is one more way to solidify the sound in children's minds. Use a large sheet of paper with colored pens, a dry-erase board, or a chalkboard—anything that enables the children t o watch you draw. Start with something that begins with the letter (such as an animal), then ask the children for ideas. (Have the picture dictionary open at the relevant page to help, but let the children feel that you believe they really did think up the ideas on their own.)

Remember that silly pictures are most effective if they seem novel to the children. You don't have to draw for every letter but can try this activity when you haven't done it in a while or when you have a letter that lends itself to lots of ideas. (For more tips on drawing silly pictures with your class, see page 12.)

A lot of things begin with "t," so you should have no trouble getting a silly picture going with your class. Start with a tiger, turkey, toad, or even a turtle. Perhaps a tiger is taking a taxi, or a turtle is in a tree, or a turkey is on a trapeze! After you finish the class picture, have the children draw their own sound pictures.

Let's Pretend

Involving the "t" sound in games of pretend will make the sound even more memorable and fun for the children. Whether you do all or just one of the following ideas, remember to keep the session relatively short to hold the children's attention. Try to keep the novelty factor alive: For example, choose activities that are different from the Let's Pretend activities you've recently done for other letters.

- Most children will be familiar with the tin man from *The Wizard of Oz*. Have the children work in pairs. One child can be the tin man and the other can be Dorothy with the oil can. First the tin man is stiff and stuck. Gradually, as Dorothy oils him piece by piece, the tin man can use his fingers, arms, waist, neck, legs, and feet. When they have finished, the children can swap roles so that they each get the chance to play both Dorothy and the tin man.

- Build a pretend teepee. Make sure the children are familiar with what a teepee looks like. Have them look for a flat piece of ground, flatten it down further, push the sticks into the ground, and tie them at the top. Then have them drape the tent part around the framework, tying it and decorating it further. When it is finished, they climb inside.

- Sing the action song "Teddy Bear, Teddy Bear" and then imagine some of the things the Teddy bear might get up to when everybody in the house is fast asleep. (You may remember this classic folk chant from your own childhood, but if you don't, you can find the lyrics as well as other Teddy bear poems and songs at www.canteach.ca/elementary/songspoems18.html.)

Crafts for "t"

Trees

This has always been a popular craft with a variety of ages. The pattern can be adapted for fall simply by cutting out red, yellow, and orange leaves.

Materials

- ✔ a 6" long cardboard tube for each child
- ✔ a page of newspaper for each child
- ✔ a sheet of newsprint paper for each child
- ✔ brown liquid tempera paint
- ✔ green liquid tempera paint
- ✔ masking tape
- ✔ glue for each child or small group
- ✔ several sheets of green construction paper
- ✔ scissors for each child
- ✔ paintbrush for each child

Preparation

Cut out a bunch of leaves (about 2" x 1") from the green construction paper.

Directions

1. Show the children how to cut a fringe along the bottom of the cardboard tube to about half an inch up from the bottom. When they spread out the flaps, the tree trunk will stand up.

2. Have the children paint the tube brown.

3. Next, the children scrunch up newspaper to make a ball about the size of an adult fist and wrap plain newsprint paper around it, gathering up the excess in a "stalk," which should be securely closed with masking tape.

4. The stalk sits inside the trunk while the ball is the crown of the tree. Before setting it in the trunk, each child should paint her crown green.

5. When the green paint is dry, each child glues on green leaves to give a more realistic effect before sticking the stalk in the trunk.

TiP *Turtle Time* (Stoddard 1997) is ideal for introducing "t" because the words "turtle time" repeat several times throughout the book.

Telephone

This is hugely popular because the telephones really do work! When the children are using them, they should keep the yarn as taut as possible. The most difficult aspect for the children is figuring out who should be speaking and who should be listening!

Talking on our homemade telephones.

**Hello?
Who's calling?**

Materials

✔ two paper cups for each child

✔ a 5' piece of yarn for each child

✔ skewer or knitting needle

✔ masking tape

Preparation

1. Pierce a hole in the bottom of each cup with a skewer or knitting needle, large enough to thread the yarn through.

2. Wrap a piece of masking tape tightly around each end of each piece of yarn to make threading easier.

Directions

1. Give each child two paper cups and a piece of yarn. Have each child thread the yarn through the hole in one cup and tie a knot so the knot is on the inside of the cup and the remainder of the yarn is dangling out from the bottom.

2. Next each child threads the other end through the other cup and again ties a knot inside the cup. With the yarn pulled tight, the children can use these as telephones, taking turns to speak and listen.

Toothbrush Pictures

Give moms and dads the chance they need to clear out the toothbrush holder and send any old toothbrushes into school for their child to completely finish off. Toothbrushes are a lovely size for children to work with.

Materials

✔ fingerpaint (or thicken up tempera with liquid soap)

✔ a piece of thick paper or cardboard for each child

✔ toothbrush for each child

✔ paintbrush for each child

Preparation

No preparation necessary except to gather and set out materials. If you like, you can have the children bring in old toothbrushes from home.

Directions

Have the children paint on their paper or cardboard and, while the paint is still wet, make patterns and trails in it with their toothbrushes.

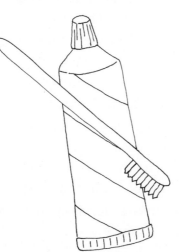

TiP

Another fun way to reinforce "t" is to make a class train. As you all travel around the room, call out "tata-tata" in a train sound and "toot-toot" for the train whistle.

Toy Train Activity Center

Put out a toy train set for the week. The simpler the train set, the better for the very little ones. My son lets me bring in his precious wooden train set to school, but only for one week!

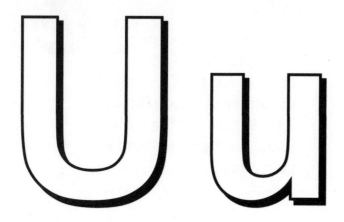

Introduce this sound several months into the school year, when some children are ready for consonant-vowel-consonant word building. "U" is very easily confused with "a," so really do emphasize "u-u-up" and "u-u-umbrella," because the children will need those strong reference points to hear the difference as words present themselves in the future.

Activities to Introduce "u"

The activities in this section are for the first day you introduce "u" to the children. The first activity—See, Say, and Sing—involves a picture dictionary, a big feely letter "u" made out of felt, and the alphabet song all used together to involve the children in this exciting new sound. The second activity—The Big Event— will involve the children in a physical activity to help reinforce the sound of the letter. The Big Event for "u" has children climbing up to an umbrella. *Important note:* The Big Event should follow immediately after the brief introduction of See, Say, and Sing activities to be most effective in solidifying the new letter for the children. Gather materials and prepare for *both* activities before you introduce "u" to your class. (See pages 7–11 for more information on introducing a new sound.)

Umbrella "u"

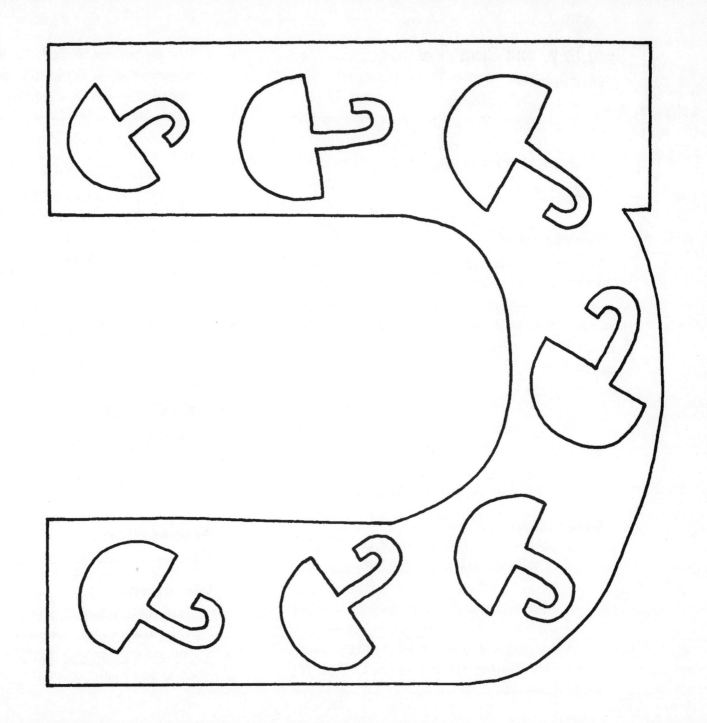

See, Say, and Sing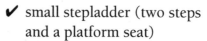

Materials

- ✔ picture dictionary
- ✔ photocopy of the "u" pattern on page 165
- ✔ 8" x 8" piece of dark-colored felt
- ✔ scraps of felt in bright colors
- ✔ scissors
- ✔ glue

Preparation

1. To make the feely letter "u," photocopy and cut out the pattern on page 165 (unless you decide to make this letter freehand, without using the pattern). You may also wish to create a bigger letter by enlarging the photocopy and using larger pieces of felt.

2. Using the pattern as a guide, cut the "u" shape out of dark felt.

3. Cut little umbrellas out of the felt scraps.

4. Glue the umbrellas onto the "u."

5. Make the entire letter stronger by gluing it onto thin cardboard and cutting around it.

Directions

1. Introduce "u" by making lots of short "u-u-u" sounds with the children, showing what it feels like to say "u." Point out how the top of your mouth and head really do go up when you say this sound. When you say "u-u-up," raise your voice higher and higher, even gradually standing from a sitting position, so you really are going u-u-up!

2. Pass around the big feely "u" so the children can see what "u" looks like and can touch the letter while they practice the "u" sound. Exaggerate the "u" sound in the word "u-u-umbrella." Remember to keep the big feely "u" in constant view so the children can make the connection that the activities that follow all relate to "u."

3. Tell the children that "u" has a name just like they do and discuss the difference between the name of the letter "u" and the sound it makes. Sing through the alphabet to find where "u" is hiding.

4. Pick out a couple of "u" pictures from the picture dictionary to show the class more words that start with the "u" sound. There will not be many words here, and to really confuse the issue, one of the main pictures will probably be a unicorn!

The *BIG* Event

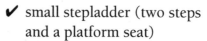

Materials

- ✔ small stepladder (two steps and a platform seat)
- ✔ colorful child's umbrella

Preparation

Place the umbrella at the top of the stepladder.

Directions

1. Have the children climb the ladder one at a time. As they climb, the other children chant "up, up, up," raising their voices higher as the child gets higher up on the ladder.

2. When they reach the top, they can hold the umbrella up and everyone can say, "u-u-umbrella." If you're not too superstitious about opening umbrellas indoors, the children can even push the umbrella open a little way.

TIP

The last time I did this Big Event was the week we were studying firefighters as part of our people who help us project. I had a big picture of a firefighter at the top of the steps, and the children had to wear a firefighter's hat before they climbed the ladder. It was so simple, but the children absolutely adored it, and the experience was a wonderful reference point.

More Ideas for "u"
Sensational "u"

This activity usually involves the children tracing a "u" in a substance that begins with "u." I have never been able to think of anything suitable beginning with "u," so I usually drape a sheet over two chairs and put a tray of sand or foam underneath. The children have to go u-u-underneath the "bridge" to make the "u" with their fingers. Make sure the feely letter "u" is clearly visible underneath the sheet as a model.

Silly Pictures

A silly picture composed of things that start with "u" is one more way to solidify the sound in children's minds. Use a large sheet of paper with colored pens, a dry-erase board, or a chalkboard—anything that enables the children to watch you draw. Start with something that begins with the letter (such as an animal), then ask the children for ideas. (Have the picture dictionary open at the relevant page to help, but let the children feel that you believe they really did think up the ideas on their own.)

Remember that silly pictures are most effective if they seem novel to the children. You don't have to draw for every letter but can try this activity when you haven't done it in a while or when you have a letter that lends itself to lots of ideas. (For more tips on drawing silly pictures with your class, see page 12.)

The letter "u" is a difficult letter for this activity, especially when you try to stick to the "uh" sound. You can't really start with an animal, but you could draw an uncle instead, who perhaps is uncomfortable because he's upside down (just draw him and turn your picture around!). After you finish the class picture, you could have the children draw their own sound pictures, although there really are so few "u" words, you might skip this step or just draw upside down pictures.

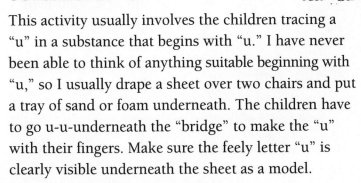

TIP

The Monster Under My Bed (Gruber 1985) is a great resource to reinforce the "u" sound in "under."

Let's Pretend

Involving the "u" sound in games of pretend will make the sound even more memorable and fun for the children. Whether you do all or just one of the following ideas, remember to keep the session relatively short to hold the children's attention. Try to keep the novelty factor alive: For example, choose activities that are different from the Let's Pretend activities you've recently done for other letters.

- Have the children pretend that it has started to rain very hard while they are playing outside and that they cannot get to their umbrella. They start to feel the rain on their hands and look up to see if there are any rain clouds. They rush under a tree for shelter, then try to edge their way along the side of the building so they do not have to go out in the rain. Eventually, they manage to run and grab their umbrellas from the porch. They put up their umbrellas, then go out to play in the puddles.

- Think of all the different things you could climb up and have the children pretend to climb them one by one. The children will be good at making suggestions once they get the idea. You could climb up a ladder, up a mountainside, up into a big truck, up into a crane, up the stairs to the top floor, or even up a tree!

Crafts for "u"
Umbrella Stand

These umbrella stands really are quite practical.

Materials

- ✔ sturdy tubing, such as the roll from the inside of a carpet—enough from which you can cut tubes about 2' long for each child
- ✔ liquid tempera paint
- ✔ saw (such as a simple handsaw)
- ✔ paintbrush for each child

I made this umbrella stand!

TiP

Carpet stores will usually be happy to donate sturdy tubing. Department-store gift-wrapping departments also have sturdy tubes left over from their gift wrap, which otherwise they would throw away.

Preparation

Saw the tubing into two-foot tubes.

Directions

Have the children decorate their umbrella stands with the paint.

TiP The children could decorate their tubes with fabric and lace, or even decoupage, instead of paint.

activity

Under the Sea Bottle

When the children shake their bottles, they can watch as the glitter and sequins stay suspended in the water, moving much more slowly than they normally would without the cooking oil.

Materials

- ✔ clear plastic bottle with lid for each child
- ✔ light-colored cooking oil (glycerin can be used but is much more expensive)
- ✔ small pitcher of water
- ✔ blue food coloring with dropper
- ✔ funnel for each child
- ✔ a teaspoon of glitter for each child
- ✔ fish sequins
- ✔ masking tape
- ✔ 12" piece of ribbon for each child
- ✔ single hole punch
- ✔ fish-shaped label (or sheet of construction paper and scissors) for each child

Preparation

Punch one hole in each fish label through which to thread the ribbon. If you can't find fish labels, cut fish shapes out of construction paper.

Directions

1. Have each child write or trace over his name on the fish.
2. Using the funnel, each child fills up one-third of the bottle with oil.

Sprinkling glitter in the Under the Sea Bottle.

3. Next he pours water through the funnel to bring the level up to just below the neck of the bottle.
4. Then each child adds a couple of drops of food coloring to make the water turn blue.
5. He adds a teaspoon of glitter and some fish sequins.
6. Then he closes the lid and seals it with masking tape.
7. Finally, each child threads the ribbon through the hole on the fish and ties it around the neck of the bottle.

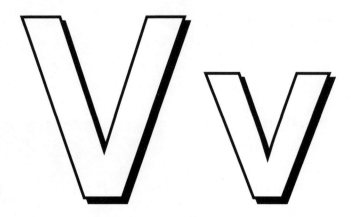

It is very convenient that the "v" looks so much like a heart, so we can make the valentine connection again and again. I love the way children use Valentine's Day as a celebration of friendship.

Activities to Introduce "v"

The activities in this section are for the first day you introduce "v" to the children. The first activity—See, Say, and Sing—involves a picture dictionary, a big feely letter "v" made out of felt, and the alphabet song all used together to involve the children in this exciting new sound. The second activity—The Big Event— will involve the children in a physical activity to help reinforce the sound of the letter. The Big Event for "v" lets children choose a special valentine from the valentine van. *Important note:* The Big Event should follow immediately after the brief introduction of See, Say, and Sing activities to be most effective in solidifying the new letter for the children. Gather materials and prepare for *both* activities before you introduce "v" to your class. (See pages 7–11 for more information on introducing a new sound.)

Valentine "v"

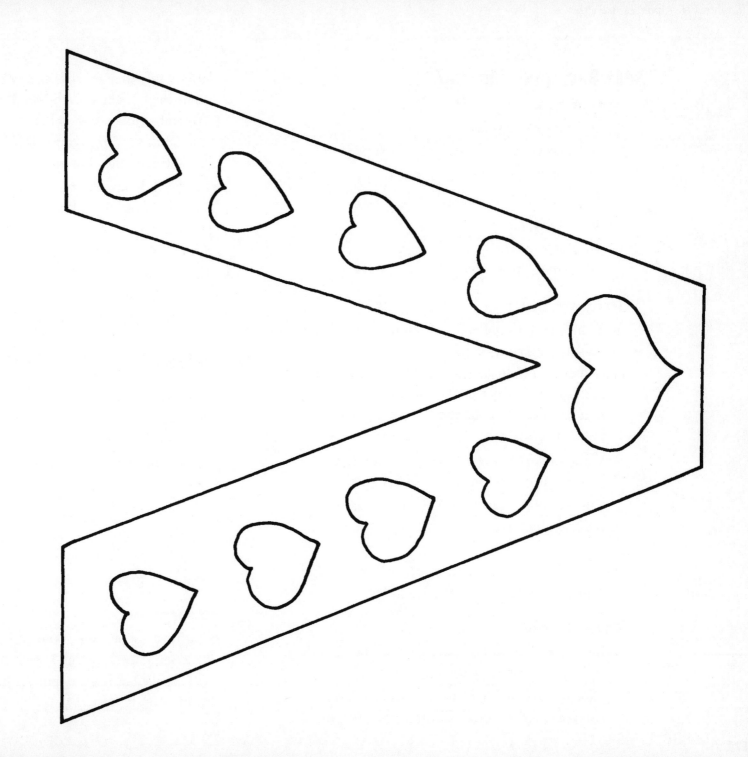

See, Say, and Sing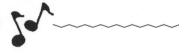

Materials

- ✔ picture dictionary
- ✔ photocopy of the "v" pattern on page 171
- ✔ 7" x 9" piece of light pink felt
- ✔ scraps of dark pink felt
- ✔ scissors
- ✔ glue
- ✔ thin cardboard (such as a cereal box)

Preparation

1. To make the feely letter "v," photocopy and cut out the pattern on page 171 (unless you decide to make this letter freehand, without using the pattern). You may also wish to create a bigger letter by enlarging the photocopy and using larger pieces of felt.

2. Using the pattern as a guide (or cutting freehand), cut the "v" shape out of light pink felt.

3. Cut the small heart shapes out of the dark pink felt and glue them on the "v" as shown on the pattern.

4. Make the entire letter stronger by gluing it onto thin cardboard and cutting around it.

Directions

1. Introduce "v" by making lots of "v-v-v" sounds with the children, showing what it feels like to say "v."

2. Pass around the big feely "v" so the children can see what "v" looks like and can touch the letter while they practice the "v" sound. Exaggerate the "v" sound in the word "v-v-valentine." Remember to keep the big feely "v" in constant view so the children can make the connection that the activities that follow all relate to "v."

3. Tell the children that "v" has a name just like they do and discuss the difference between the name of the letter "v" and the sound it makes. Sing through the alphabet to find where "v" is hiding.

4. Pick out a couple of "v" pictures from the picture dictionary to show the class more words that start with the "v" sound.

The *BIG* Event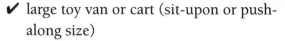

Materials

- ✔ large toy van or cart (sit-upon or push-along size)
- ✔ several sheets of red and pink construction paper
- ✔ marker
- ✔ vest
- ✔ safety pins (optional)
- ✔ masking tape

Preparation

1. Cut heart shapes out of the pink and red construction paper, enough for a heart for each child as well as several leftover hearts for decorating the van.

2. Write a "v" and a child's name on a heart for each child in your class.

3. Put the valentines for the children in the van.

4. Tape leftover hearts all over the van.

5. If you have a vest with hearts on it already, you're all set. Otherwise, you can tape or pin several hearts on a vest (or sew fabric hearts on a vest, if you're really ambitious).

TiP

If you don't have a toy van, you can use any toy vehicle and draw a van with hearts on it on a thin piece of pink cardboard. Simply tape it to the side of your vehicle and voilà!—valentine van.

Directions

1. Bring in the valentine van and have the first child come up and put on the valentine vest.

2. That child picks a valentine from the van and drives over to deliver the valentine to the child whose name is on the heart.

3. That child then puts on the valentine vest, picks out the next name, and drives the valentine van. So it goes on until everyone has a valentine.

More Ideas for "v"
Sensational "v"

Have some whole vegetables available to show the children, preferably vegetables that can be eaten raw, such as broccoli, carrots, celery, and corn. Talk about them all belonging to the vegetable family.

Cut up enough of these vegetables into one-inch or smaller pieces to cover a tray, such as a cafeteria tray. (To make life easier, you could substitute drained canned corn at this point.) Let the children take turns tracing a "v" in the vegetables with their fingers. Make sure that the feely letter "v" is clearly visible to all the children as a model. If you cut up some extra vegetables in advance, the children can even enjoy eating vegetables also!

Silly Pictures

A silly picture composed of things that start with "v" is one more way to solidify the sound in children's minds. Use a large sheet of paper with colored pens, a dry-erase board, or a chalkboard—anything that enables the children to watch you draw. Start with something that begins with the letter (such as an animal), then ask the children for ideas. (Have the picture dictionary open at the relevant page to help, but let the children feel that you believe they really did think up the ideas on their own.)

Remember that silly pictures are most effective if they seem novel to the children. You don't have to draw for every letter but can try this activity when you haven't done it in a while or when you have a letter that lends itself to lots of ideas. (For more tips on drawing silly pictures with your class, see page 12.)

A vulture might be eating and carrying all sorts of vegetables. She could be vacuuming or watching videos on top of a volcano. After you finish the class picture, have the children draw their own sound pictures.

Let's Pretend

Involving the "v" sound in games of pretend will make the sound even more memorable and fun for the children. Whether you do all or just one of the following ideas, remember to keep the session relatively short to hold the children's attention. Also try to keep the novelty factor alive: For example, choose activities that are different from the Let's Pretend activities you've recently done for other letters.

My valentine card.

- Valentines give lots of opportunities for play-acting. First the children pretend to make a card, then put it in the envelope and put on a stamp for mailing. They walk down to the mailbox to mail the card. On Valentine's Day, they can look out for the mail carrier, then rush outside to look in the box. When each child finds her valentine card, she opens the envelope and acts so thrilled to have a secret admirer.

- Keeping with the theme, *Clifford's First Valentine's Day* (Bridwell 1997) is a good story to mime.

- Introduce the role and title of a veterinarian. The children start with grooming and generally checking a pet cat: first of all his ears, followed by his paws, his shiny coat, and his tail. Then move on to a puppy that will not keep still. A snake could be the next patient; the children need to think carefully about the way they will get her out of the box! Then tell the children they have fixed the wing of a bird and now it's time to check that he is ready and set him free. They can imagine how they would deal with a camel. They may need steps to climb up to be able to check his humps!

- Introduce the violin to the children, sharing what it looks and sounds like. Demonstrate the movements of how to play. Now put on some string music and let the children play their imaginary violins.

Crafts for "v"
Valentine Bag

We make these every year in time for Valentine's Day. As our classroom valentine mailbox is emptied, the children sit in a circle and collect their cards in their own bags as the cards are delivered to them.

Materials

- ✔ a paper gift bag with string handles for each child (some bath stores use these as little shopping bags)
- ✔ several sheets of pink, red, and purple construction paper
- ✔ decoupage glue
- ✔ paintbrush for each child
- ✔ a sheet of pink, red, or purple tissue paper for each child
- ✔ newspaper
- ✔ a few inches of thin ribbon for each child
- ✔ single hole punch
- ✔ marker

Preparation

1. Cut hearts out of the pink, red, and purple construction paper.
2. Stuff each bag with newspaper to hold it open, so the children don't glue over a fold.
3. Write each child's name on a heart and punch a hole in the top.

Directions

1. The children glue the hearts onto the bags, using the decoupage glue to varnish the hearts in place. Make sure the gusset of the bag is open so that the children do not glue over a fold.
2. Help each child tie on his heart-shaped name label using ribbon.
3. When the bags are dry and ready to be displayed, have the children put a piece of red, pink, or purple tissue paper just inside the top so the edges flare out. Very chic!

Vortex Activity Center

Purchase a vortex-maker at your local parent-teacher/educational supply store. They are just a couple inches long, inexpensive, and hold two plastic bottles together when attached to both bottle openings. You can even add a little glitter as well as the required water. Leave a couple of prepared vortex bottles on the activity table during the week, and just let the children tip, turn, shake, and observe the vortex. Sometimes you can purchase different kinds of vortex tubes, which give a different effect in the water.

Vegetable Printing

Explain to the children about the vegetable food family before embarking on this craft.

Materials

- ✔ a green or red pepper for each small group
- ✔ a Brussels sprout for each small group
- ✔ a sprig of broccoli for each small group
- ✔ one whole corn cob without the leaves for each small group
- ✔ a sheet of construction paper (black or white would work well) for each child
- ✔ three trays of liquid tempera paint in vegetable colors: green, yellow, and red for each small group

Preparation

Cut each of the vegetables, except the corn, in half, revealing an interesting cross-section.

Directions

1. Using the yellow paint, each child covers the corn in as much paint as possible, then rolls it up and down the page.
2. For the next vegetables, review the rules for printing to encourage the children to bounce their print makers up and down rather than drag the paint across the paper.

3. Using the green paint for the Brussels sprout and broccoli, the children cover the vegetables and print with them on the page. If using black construction paper, use a light, bright green.
4. The children use the red paint for the pepper.

TiP

A great book to read during this week is Annie Rockwell's *Valentine's Day* (2002).

You can introduce this sound early on. The children particularly enjoy and understand the w-w-water connection, and the up-and-down shape is very easy for them to reproduce successfully. You could introduce "w" before "b," then use the weaving craft (page 181) to enhance the hot air balloon (page 35).

Activities to Introduce "w"

The activities in this section are for the first day you introduce "w" to the children. The first activity—See, Say, and Sing—involves a picture dictionary, a big feely letter "w" made out of cardboard and yarn or cotton balls, and the alphabet song all used together to involve the children in this exciting new sound. The second activity—The Big Event—will involve the children in a physical activity to help reinforce the sound of the letter. The Big Event for "w" has children wiggling toy whales in water to wash them, followed by making wishes with a magic wand. *Important note:* The Big Event should follow immediately after the brief introduction of See, Say, and Sing activities to be most effective in solidifying the new letter for the children. Gather materials and prepare for *both* activities before you introduce "w" to your class. (See pages 7–11 for more information on introducing a new sound.)

White woolly "w"

See, Say, and Sing

Materials

✔ picture dictionary

✔ photocopy of the "w" pattern on page 178

✔ 8 ½" x 11" piece of white cardboard

✔ a handful of cotton balls

✔ scissors

✔ glue

TiP

You could use white yarn instead of cotton balls for a different woolly texture on the big feely "w."

Preparation

1. To make the feely letter "w," photocopy and cut out the pattern on page 178 (unless you decide to make this letter freehand, without using the pattern). You may also wish to create a bigger letter by enlarging the photocopy and using a larger piece of cardboard.

2. Using the pattern as a guide (or cutting freehand), cut the "w" shape out of the white cardboard.

3. Glue the cotton balls to the card "w."

Directions

1. Introduce "w" by making lots of "w-w-w" sounds with the children, showing what it feels like to say "w."

2. Pass around the big woolly "w" so the children can see what "w" looks like and can touch the letter while they practice the "w" sound. Exaggerate the "w" sound in the word "w-w-woolly." Remember to keep the big woolly "w" in constant view so the children can make the connection that the activities that follow all relate to "w."

3. Tell the children that "w" has a name just like they do and discuss the difference between the name of the letter "w" and the sound it makes. Sing through the alphabet to find where "w" is hiding.

4. Pick out a couple of "w" pictures from the picture dictionary to show the class more words that start with the "w" sound.

Weighing Activity Center

Set up a weighing table during this week. Put out some balance scales along with containers of dried beans, small blocks, buttons, little plastic animals, and anything else you have of a suitable size in your classroom.

The *BIG* Event

Materials

✔ toy whale for each child

✔ big bowl of water

✔ plastic undersea landscape (optional)

✔ a few sheets of construction paper

✔ hand towels

✔ magic wand, purchased or made with the following materials:

- 12" dowel or ruler
- yellow paper star
- tape
- glitter

Wiggling whales in the water.

Preparation

1. Make the magic wand, if you don't purchase one, by taping a yellow paper star to the top of the dowel or ruler. Sprinkle glitter on the star.

2. Cut a "w" out of the construction paper for each child.

3. Set out the plastic landscape (if you use one) and place the bowl of water on it. Don't fill the bowl too full or the water will splash out of it too easily. Keep towels on hand for drying wet hands.

Directions

1. Each child gets a turn to choose a whale and wiggle him to the water, where he gives him a wash.

2. When the child is finished, he takes the magic wand and waves it to wish for something.

3. As he does this, he takes a construction-paper "w" to help him remember his wish.

More Ideas for "w"

Sensational "w"

Fill a tray (such as a cafeteria tray) with nontoxic white paint and let the children take turns tracing a "w" with their fingers, so they can see and feel the shape. Make sure the feely letter "w" is clearly visible to all children as a model. Keep wipes handy for white fingers.

Silly Pictures

A silly picture composed of things that start with "w" is one more way to solidify the sound in children's minds. Use a large sheet of paper with colored pens, a dry-erase board, or a chalkboard—anything that enables the children to watch you draw. Start with something that begins with the letter (such as an animal), then ask the children for ideas. (Have the picture dictionary open at the relevant page to help, but let the children feel that you believe they really did think up the ideas on their own.)

Remember that silly pictures are most effective if they seem novel to the children. You don't have to draw for every letter but can try this activity when you haven't done it in a while or when you have a letter that lends itself to lots of ideas. (For more tips on drawing silly pictures with your class, see page 12.)

A walrus or whale could be wearing a wig or even eating waffles while riding in a wheelbarrow. After you finish the class picture, have the children draw their own sound pictures.

Let's Pretend

Involving the "w" sound in games of pretend will make the sound even more memorable and fun for the children. Whether you do all or just one of the following ideas, remember to keep the session relatively short to hold the children's attention. Try to keep the novelty factor alive: For example, choose activities that are different from the Let's Pretend activities you've recently done for other letters.

- All children just love *Where the Wild Things Are* (Sendak 1992). It is great for miming, especially if you can get some rhythmic music for when the monsters are dancing.

- Another fun activity for "w" is pretending to walk and wade. Start the children with a walk in the woods. It is easy to walk through at first, but then the vegetation gets thicker and thicker, making it so much more difficult to walk. Eventually, they come to a waterfall that they have to carefully climb down. At the bottom, is a pool of water. Have them wade through the water. At first, it is not too deep, but gradually it becomes deeper until it is up to their waists! The water now becomes a flowing river. It is time to be in a small boat on the water, battling their way down the fast running water with their oars. Finally, the river flows out to the sea. Now it is time to play in the waves!

Crafts for "w"
Weaving

One of these strips of weaving can be used to wrap around the basket of the hot air balloon, a "b" craft (page 35). It is easy to introduce "b" and "w" close to each other, as they are both excellent for use early in the school year. Let the children choose their own color combinations for all three strips. They particularly enjoy looking at the back and seeing the pattern they unintentionally create.

Materials

✔ two 12" x 1" strips of paper in various colors
✔ one 12" x 3" strip of paper for each child
✔ stapler

Preparation

1. Let the children choose their own color combinations from among the strips.
2. Fold the larger pieces of paper in half lengthwise and draw lines on them for the children to cut on, from the fold toward the long edge. The lines should be at least an inch apart and go up just under an inch.
3. When you open up the bigger piece of paper, staple two small strips to the end, in line with the slits, ready for weaving. Do this for each sheet of paper for each child.

Directions

With the paper prepared, the children should be able to manage weaving the smaller strips through the slits in the larger piece of paper.

TiP *Wemberly Worried* (Henkes 2001) is terrific reading during "w" week.

Window

This craft makes a particularly effective calendar display.

TiP The children can further decorate their windows with other cut-out pictures, such as a cat or a flower box sitting on the window ledge.

Materials

✔ a piece of construction paper for each child
✔ pictures from vacation brochures or travel magazines
✔ two pieces of 2" x 6" fabric for each child
✔ two 1/2" strips of construction paper for each child
✔ glue for each child or small group

Preparation

Cut out pictures in rectangular or square shapes from vacation brochures or travel magazines so that each child has one. Views work best.

Directions

1. Have each child choose a picture and glue the picture on a piece of construction paper.
2. Next, each child should glue two strips of construction paper to make a horizontal and vertical stripe on the "window."
3. The child then uses the fabric to make curtains, gluing them on both sides of the picture. You may need to help her gather the curtain fabric in folds at the top.

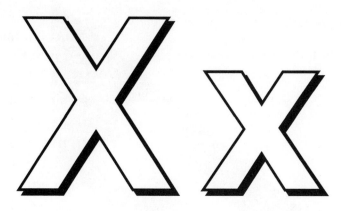

This is usually an easy letter for the children because of its dramatic look and unusual sound. It is best to introduce "x" some months into the year so that the children who are ready can benefit from its use as a final consonant.

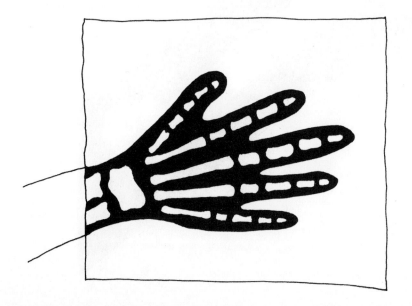

Activities to Introduce "x"

The activities in this section are for the first day you introduce "x" to the children. The first activity—See, Say, and Sing—involves a picture dictionary, a big feely letter "x" made out of felt, and the alphabet song all used together to involve the children in this exciting new sound. The second activity—The Big Event— will involve the children in a physical activity to help reinforce the sound of the letter. The Big Event for "x" involves a treasure map, on which the children take turns putting an "x" to show where they think a treasure is buried. *Important note:* The Big Event should follow immediately after the brief introduction of See, Say, and Sing activities to be most effective in solidifying the new letter for the children. Gather materials and prepare for *both* activities before you introduce "x" to your class. (See pages 7–11 for more information on introducing a new sound.)

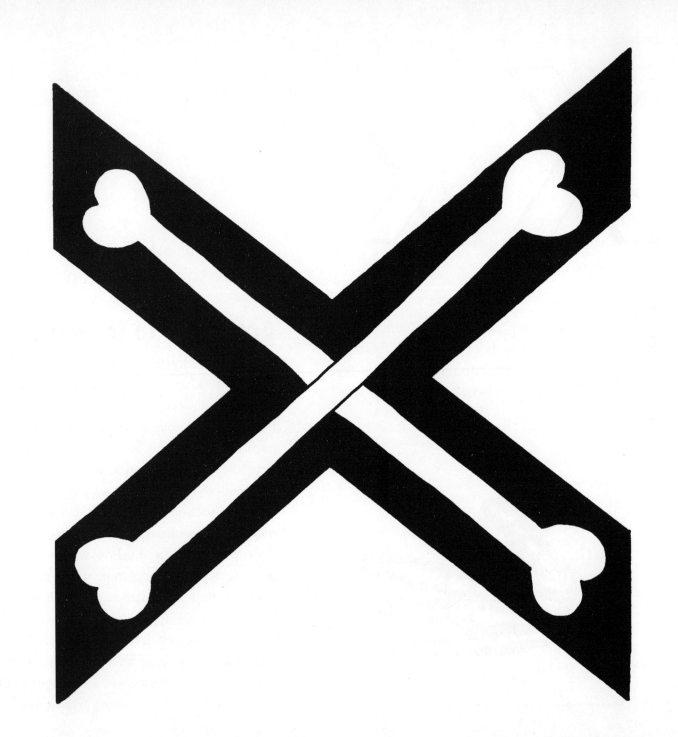

X-ray "X"

See, Say, and Sing

Materials

- ✔ picture dictionary
- ✔ photocopy of the "x" pattern on page 184
- ✔ 7" x 7" piece of black felt
- ✔ 4" x 7" piece of white felt
- ✔ scissors
- ✔ glue
- ✔ thin cardboard (such as a cereal box)

Preparation

1. To make the feely letter "x," photocopy and cut out the pattern on page 184 (unless you decide to make this letter freehand, without using the pattern). You may also wish to create a bigger letter by enlarging the photocopy and using larger pieces of felt.

2. Using the pattern as a guide (or cutting freehand), cut the "x" out of black felt.

3. Using the pattern as a guide (or cutting freehand), cut the bones out of white felt.

4. Glue the bones to the "x" as shown.

5. Make the entire letter stronger by gluing it onto thin cardboard and cutting around it.

Directions

1. Introduce "x" by making lots of "x-x-x" sounds with the children, showing what it feels like to say "x."

2. Pass around the big feely "x" so the children can see what "x" looks like and can touch the letter while they practice the "x" sound. Exaggerate the "x" sound in the word "x-x-x-ray." Remember to keep the big feely "x" in constant view so the children can make the connection that the activities that follow all relate to "x."

3. Sing through the alphabet to find where "x" is hiding.

4. Pick out a couple of "x" pictures from the picture dictionary to show the class more words that start with the "x" sound.

Tic tac toe is full of x's and o's!

The *BIG* Event

Materials

- ✔ cream construction paper (as large as you wish)
- ✔ markers
- ✔ ribbon
- ✔ brown crayon
- ✔ pirate hat (optional)
- ✔ pirate music (optional)

Preparation

1. Make a treasure map (unless you can find a premade one). Use cream paper to make the map look old. Make the edges look shabby and even darken with a brown crayon. With the markers, draw a bird's eye view of an island. Include such things as a river, a lake, mountains, a volcano, a forest, a beach, a waterfall, two palm trees, a cave, and maybe even a deserted city, plus any other features you would like to include. Roll the map up like a scroll and tie with a ribbon.

2. Find a story about digging for treasure, such as *Elliot Digs for Treasure* (Beck 2001) or *Pirate Pete* (Kennedy 2002).

3. Find pirate music, if possible. The song from the Disney ride "Pirates of the Caribbean" would work beautifully playing in the background.

Directions

1. Read a story about digging for treasure.

2. Have each child take a turn to wear the pirate hat (if you have one) and put an "x" on the map where she thinks the treasure is buried.

TiP

If you would like to save your map, you could use cut-out x's with a loop of masking tape on the back. Otherwise, you could cover your map with clear adhesive-backed plastic.

More Ideas for "x"

Sensational "x"

Talk about how "x" stands for a kiss. Fill a tray with wrapped Hershey Kisses candies and let the children take turns tracing an "x" in the Kisses with their fingers, so they can see and feel the shape. Make sure the feely letter "x" is clearly visible to all children as a model.

TiP

It is also interesting to have the children make the shape of an "x" with five Kisses—a surprisingly difficult task for the very young.

Silly Pictures

A silly picture composed of things that start with "x" is one more way to solidify the sound in children's minds. Use a large sheet of paper with colored pens, a dry-erase board, or a chalkboard—anything that enables the children to watch you draw. Start with something that begins with the letter (such as an animal), then ask the children for ideas. (Have the picture dictionary open at the relevant page to help, but let the children feel that you believe they really did think up the ideas on their own.)

Remember that silly pictures are most effective if they seem novel to the children. You don't have to draw for every letter but can try this activity when you haven't done it in a while or when you have a letter that lends itself to lots of ideas. (For more tips on drawing silly pictures with your class, see page 12.)

The letter "x" is probably too difficult for this activity because the children will find only a couple pictures in the picture dictionary. Still, you could draw a series of simple silly pictures showing x-rays of the children's favorite animals.

Let's Pretend

Involving the "x" sound in games of pretend will make the sound even more memorable and fun for the children. Remember to keep the session relatively short to hold the children's attention. Try to keep the novelty factor alive: For example, choose activities that are different from the Let's Pretend activities you've recently done for other letters.

I love the series of Funnybones books, such as *Funnybones* (Ahlberg and Ahlberg 1990) and *The Pet Shop* (Ahlberg and Amstutz 1990). To work with these books about a family of skeletons after talking about x-rays would be a logical link. The stories are great fun to mime.

Examining an x-ray.

Crafts for "x"
Skeletons

Although the initial aim of this craft is to make skeletons, young children will probably not produce anything remotely resembling a skeleton. That is fine. Remember, the process is much more important than the product.

Materials
- ✔ a sheet of black construction paper for each child
- ✔ cotton swabs
- ✔ glue for each child or small group
- ✔ scissors for each child
- ✔ pictures of skeletons

Preparation

No preparation necessary except to find pictures or books with pictures to show children what a skeleton looks like. The pattern of ribs, for instance, is particularly fascinating.

Directions

Have each child glue cotton swabs on the black construction paper where the bones would be in a skeleton. You could cut the swabs to different lengths to give the children more variety.

Treasure Maps

The children can make their own treasure maps with "x" marking the spot.

Materials

✔ 12" x 18" sheet of dark blue construction paper for each child

✔ cheap or free unwanted map for each child (If you do not have enough, just photocopy an interesting land region from a map you do have.)

✔ glue for each child or small group

✔ crayons

✔ scissors

✔ a sheet of red construction paper for every few children

✔ 8" piece of ribbon for each child (optional)

Preparation

1. Cut each map to about the same size as the blue construction paper.

2. Cut an "x" for each child out of the red construction paper.

Directions

1. Let the children cut out their maps into an interesting shape. Encourage them to keep it as large as possible.

2. Next they color their maps with crayons, adding special features, if desired.

3. Then they glue the maps onto the construction paper.

4. Finally, they glue the red "x" where the treasure is buried! If they wish, the children can transform their maps into scrolls by rolling them up, then tying them with ribbon.

Tic Tac Toe Activity Center

Bring out tic tac toe in whatever form it is accessible and leave it on or near the activity table. Review the rules and objectives of the game.

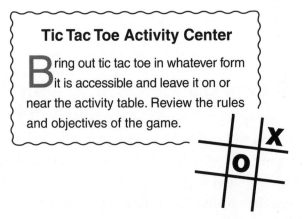

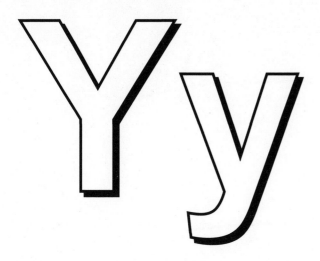

Yy

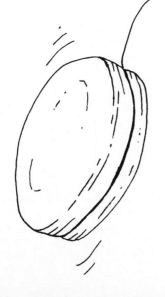

There are so few words relevant to the children that begin with "y" that I usually keep most of the emphasis on "yellow" and "yes." "Y" is a good letter to introduce in the fall when there are lots of yellow leaves.

Activities to Introduce "y"

The activities in this section are for the first day you introduce "y" to the children. The first activity—See, Say, and Sing—involves a picture dictionary, a big feely letter "y" made out of felt, and the alphabet song all used together to involve the children in this exciting new sound. The second activity—The Big Event— will involve the children in a physical activity to help reinforce the sound of the letter. The Big Event for "y" has children pulling on yellow yarn to reveal yellow objects that are tied along the length of the yarn and placed in a yellow bag. *Important note:* The Big Event should follow immediately after the brief introduction of See, Say, and Sing activities to be most effective in solidifying the new letter for the children. Gather materials and prepare for *both* activities before you introduce "y" to your class. (See pages 7–11 for more information on introducing a new sound.)

189

Yellow "y"

See, Say, and Sing

Materials

✔ picture dictionary
✔ photocopy of the "y" pattern on page 190
✔ 8½" x 11" piece of yellow felt
✔ scissors
✔ thin cardboard (such as a cereal box)
✔ glue

Preparation

1. To make the feely letter "y," photocopy and cut out the pattern on page 190 (unless you decide to make this letter freehand, without using the pattern). You may also wish to create a bigger letter by enlarging the photocopy and using a larger piece of felt.

2. Using the pattern as a guide (or cutting freehand), cut the "y" shape out of yellow felt

3. Make the entire letter stronger by gluing it onto thin cardboard and cutting around it.

Directions

1. Introduce "y" by making lots of "y-y-y" sounds with the children, showing what it feels like to say "y."

2. Pass around the big feely "y" so the children can see what "y" looks like and can touch the letter while they practice the "y" sound. Exaggerate the "y" sound in the word "y-y-yellow." Remember to keep the big feely "y" in constant view so the children can make the connection that the activities that follow all relate to "y."

3. Tell the children that "y" has a name just like they do and discuss the difference between the name of the letter "y" and the sound it makes. Sing through the alphabet to find where "y" is hiding.

4. Pick out a couple of "y" pictures from the picture dictionary to show the class more words that start with the "y" sound.

The *BIG* Event

Materials

✔ yellow bag
✔ a small yellow object for each child
✔ yellow yarn (enough for 18" between each object)

Preparation

1. Gather enough small yellow objects for each child to have one. You might choose a banana, stuffed yellow chick, yellow envelope, yellow ribbon, yellow napkin, and a yellow plastic spoon.

2. Tie the objects to one long piece of yellow yarn, allowing about 18 inches between each object. Put all of the objects and yarn into your yellow bag.

Directions

Have the children come up one at a time to pull out the next section of yellow yarn to see what it holds. While the child is carefully pulling, the other children can be preparing with their "y-y-y" sound, ready to join in with the word "yellow" when the item appears out of the bag.

More Ideas for "y"
Sensational "y"

Pour a layer of nontoxic yellow paint into a tray (such as a cafeteria tray) and let the children take turns tracing a "y" in the yellow paint with their fingers, so they can see and feel the shape. Make sure the feely letter "y" is clearly visible to all children as a model. Have wipes ready to clean yucky yellow fingers!

Making a "y" in yellow paint.

Silly Pictures

A silly picture composed of things that start with "y" is one more way to solidify the sound in children's minds. Use a large sheet of paper with colored pens, a dry-erase board, or a chalkboard—anything that enables the children to watch you draw. Start with something that begins with the letter (such as an animal), then ask the children for ideas. (Have the picture dictionary open at the relevant page to help, but let the children feel that you believe they really did think up the ideas on their own.)

Remember that silly pictures are most effective if they seem novel to the children. You don't have to draw for every letter but can try this activity when you haven't done it in a while or when you have a letter that lends itself to lots of ideas. (For more tips on drawing silly pictures with your class, see page 12.)

There aren't a lot of words that being with "y," but you could certainly pull enough elements together for a silly picture, such as a yellow yak on a yacht playing with a yo-yo. After you finish the class picture, have the children draw their own sound pictures, if you haven't used up all the "y" words already!

Let's Pretend

Involving the "y" sound in games of pretend will make the sound even more memorable and fun for the children. Remember to keep the session relatively short to hold the children's attention. Try to keep the novelty factor alive: For example, choose activities that are different from the Let's Pretend activities you've recently done for other letters.

Play "The Yellow Brick Road" from *The Wizard of Oz* in the background while the children pretend to be various characters following the road to see the wizard. Think of the different ways each character would move and pretend along with the children. It's great fun to follow each other around the room in a train while you are doing this. Start with the stiff tin man, the floppy scarecrow, and the timid lion before thinking up some others.

Crafts for "y"
Yarn Pictures

These simple pictures can make some wondrously creative symmetrical designs.

Materials

- ✔ four 18" pieces of yarn for each child
- ✔ a sheet of paper for each child
- ✔ four colors of liquid tempera paint
- ✔ four plastic bowls (cereal-bowl size) for each group of four children

Preparation

No preparation except to pour the paint into bowls.

Directions

1. Have the children fold their pieces of paper in half.

2. Next they dip a piece of the yarn generously into some paint, leaving a small tail to hold so that their fingers do not get too messy.

3. Have them open the folded paper and curl the paint-laden yarn onto one side of the paper, leaving the clean tail sticking out at the bottom, then close down the other half and press hard with their hands.

4. Then they hold onto the tail with one hand while pressing down with the other hand, pulling out the yarn. The process can, of course, be repeated with another color after the first color dries, using a fresh piece of yarn.

TiP

Red Leaf, Yellow Leaf (Ehlert 1999) is great reading during "y" week because of the direct reference to the yellow color of the fall leaves.

More Yarn Pictures

Another fun craft for "y" involves using yarn and clear, quick-drying glue. The children simply dip the yarn in the glue, then form shapes or abstract images or whatever they like by placing the yarn on construction paper and letting it dry. The pieces of yarn can vary in texture, thickness, length, and color. The children could then be free to select the pieces they want to make anything from long swirly random designs to more ordered patterns using short straight pieces of yarn.

You could also integrate this craft with a particular theme. When we are working on "Little Boy Blue" as part of our nursery rhymes unit, the children draw a picture of Boy Blue sleeping, cut it out, and glue it near the bottom of the page. They then make the haystack by sticking on lots of small pieces (about two inches) of colored yarn. You can just imagine—some haystacks are very well planned. Some children are able to build blocks of hay. Other haystacks are just a heap, with Boy Blue just managing to peep out!

Zz

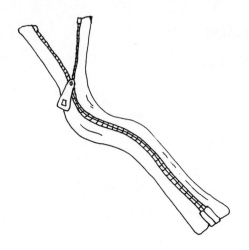

I usually introduce "z" last of all. The children know it comes last in the alphabet and so it emphasizes our achievement of learning all the letters in the alphabet, even though we haven't done the others in alphabetical order.

Activities to Introduce "z"

The activities in this section are for the first day you introduce "z" to the children. The first activity—See, Say, and Sing—involves a picture dictionary, a big feely letter "z" made out of felt, and the alphabet song all used together to involve the children in this exciting new sound. The second activity—The Big Event—will involve the children in a physical activity to help reinforce the sound of the letter. The Big Event for "z" involves the zebra zoo, where children put animals in pens with zebras and where all animals lie down for a few z-z-z's. *Important note:* The Big Event should follow immediately after the brief introduction of See, Say, and Sing activities to be most effective in solidifying the new letter for the children. Gather materials and prepare for *both* activities before you introduce "z" to your class. (See pages 7–11 for more information on introducing a new sound.)

Zebra "z"

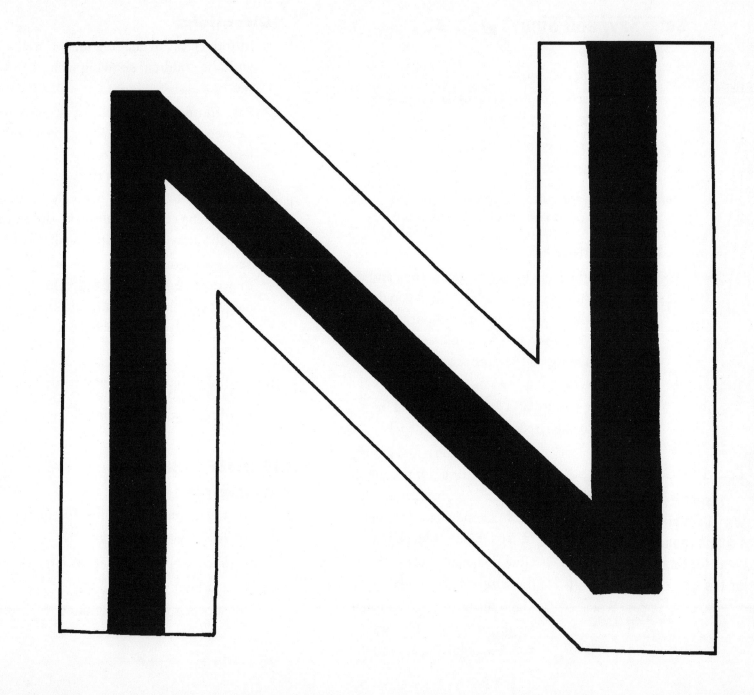

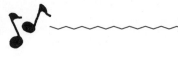

See, Say, and Sing

Materials

✔ picture dictionary

✔ photocopy of the "z" pattern on page 195

✔ 7" x 7" piece of white felt

✔ 6" x 6" piece of black felt

✔ scissors

✔ glue

✔ thin cardboard (such as a cereal box)

Preparation

1. To make the feely letter "z," photocopy and cut out the pattern on page 195 (unless you decide to make this letter freehand, without using the pattern). You may also wish to create a bigger letter by enlarging the photocopy and using larger pieces of felt.

2. Using the pattern as a guide (or cutting free-hand), cut the larger "z" out of white felt.

3. Using the pattern as a guide by first cutting out the smaller black "z" (or by cutting the felt freehand), cut the smaller "z" stripe out of black felt.

4. Glue the smaller black "z" to the white "z" as shown.

5. Make the entire letter stronger by gluing it onto thin cardboard and cutting around it.

TiP

Inside a Zoo in the City (Capucilli 2000) is a rebus readalong story, ideal for this age and for the week of "z."

Directions

1. Introduce "z" by making lots of "z-z-z" sounds with the children, showing what it feels like to say "z."

2. Pass around the big feely "z" so the children can see what "z" looks like and can touch the letter while they practice the "z" sound. Exaggerate the "z" sound in the word "z-z-zebra." Remember to keep the big feely "z" in constant view so the children can make the connection that the activities that follow all relate to "z."

3. Tell the children that "z" has a name just like they do and discuss the difference between the name of the letter "z" and the sound it makes. Sing through the alphabet to find where "z" is hiding.

4. Pick out a couple of "z" pictures from the picture dictionary to show the class more words that start with the "z" sound.

The *BIG* Event

Materials

✔ toy animals, including several toy zebras

✔ toy fences and bricks

✔ sheet of poster paper (as large as you wish)

✔ markers

✔ shoebox or other container for animals

Preparation

1. When I introduce "z," I bring in my son's plastic toy animals and a landscape sheet. You can also create your own landscape using a large sheet of poster paper and markers. Just draw grass and trees and other country features.

2. Use the little fences and classroom bricks to form various areas in the "zebra zoo." Make sure you have enough zebras so that one can go in each area you choose to create. Put all the animals together in the "zoo office," such as a shoebox.

Directions

1. Each child has a turn to come up and choose an animal to go in the zebra zoo. The only rule is that there must be a zebra in each area. Any child can open a new area by putting in a zebra.

2. As the child puts the animal in its new home, it becomes very sleepy and has to lie down for a nap. As it lies down, the children go "z-z-z-z-z" as if they are snoring. Then at the end of the session, they too can snuggle down on the floor going "z-z-z-z-z." This provides an opportunity to turn off the lights, which makes it a memorable occasion for the children.

More Ideas for "z"
Sensational "z"

Fill a tray (such as a cafeteria tray) with a layer of white shaving foam. Try to use a black tray to echo the black-and-white zebra theme. Let the children take turns tracing a "z" with their fingers, so they can see and feel the shape. Make sure the feely letter "z" is clearly visible to all children as a model.

Silly Pictures

A silly picture composed of things that start with "z" is one more way to solidify the sound in children's minds. Use a large sheet of paper with colored pens, a dry-erase board, or a chalkboard—anything that enables the children to watch you draw. Start with something that begins with the letter (such as an animal), then ask the children for ideas. (Have the picture dictionary open at the relevant page to help, but let the children feel that you believe they really did think up the ideas on their own.)

Remember that silly pictures are most effective if they seem novel to the children. You don't have to draw for every letter but can try this activity when you haven't done it in a while or when you have a letter that lends itself to lots of ideas. (For more tips on drawing silly pictures with your class, see page 12.)

"Z" is for "zebra."

A zebra is the logical animal to start with for a "z" silly picture, although this is another difficult letter for silly pictures. Whatever you can draw using a zebra, a zero, zigzags, and a zipper should do the trick if you decide to do a silly picture for "z."

Let's Pretend

Involving the "z" sound in games of pretend will make the sound even more memorable and fun for the children. Remember to keep the session relatively short to hold the children's attention. Try to keep the novelty factor alive: For example, choose activities that are different from the Let's Pretend activities you've recently done for other letters.

The children can pretend they are the various animals in the zoo. You can be the zookeeper, and when you walk up to each animal, she falls asleep, saying "z-z-z-z." The children can mime waking up and performing a typical action of their day as whatever animal they chose.

Crafts for "z"
Zebra

The skill here is to place, then leave a gap, place, then leave a gap. This is valuable positive-negative sequencing. Don't worry if the lines aren't straight—the children are not machines. Therein lies the beauty!

Materials
- ✔ a sheet of black construction paper for each group of four
- ✔ a sheet of white construction paper for each group of four
- ✔ a sheet of blue construction paper for each group of four
- ✔ glue for each child or small group
- ✔ die-cut machine (optional)
- ✔ scissors for each child

Preparation
1. Cut a 5" x 4" rectangle out of each sheet of blue paper.
2. Cut a 5" x 4" rectangle out of each sheet of white paper.
3. Cut half-inch strips from the black paper.
4. Cut out on a die-cut machine or with scissors either a zebra or the letter "z" from the blue paper. You just need the outline for this project, not the shape you're cutting out from the center of the paper.

Directions

1. First, the children glue the black strips onto the white paper, making black and white vertical stripes.
2. Next they glue the blue paper outline over the striped paper, so that the stripes show through where the zebra or the "z" was cut out. The children love this special effect.

> **TiP**
>
> A zoo is a wonderfully creative project in any number of media. The children could make a collage zoo, a play dough zoo, or junk-model animals for the zoo made out of collage treasures (see page 15 for more information about collage treasures).

activity

Zigzag Fingerpainting

This simple painting exercise reinforces the tactile sensation of drawing a "z."

Materials

✔ fingerpaint (or thicken up tempera with liquid soap)
✔ a sheet of construction paper for each child
✔ a tray (such as a cafeteria tray)
✔ lightweight paper that is similar in size to the tray but not bigger
✔ wipes to clean painty fingers

Preparation

Spread out a decent amount of fresh paint on the tray.

Directions

1. The child makes zigzags with her finger in the paint.
2. The child gently lays her paper on top of the paint so that the impression of the zigzags goes onto the paper.

> **TiP**
>
> The children can also have fun fingerpainting zigzags directly on paper, as shown in the picture below.

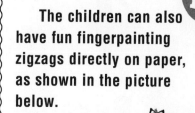

Zigzag "z."

> ### Zigzag Activity Center
>
> On an area of floor, stick down a masking tape zigzag "train track" for the children to walk along. Make each piece of tape at least eight or nine inches long, so that the children will be able to travel up and down comfortably.

4

Parallel Extension Activities

M ost of this book is about the all-important introduction of sounds in a way that will be meaningful to young children. This chapter includes additional activities that introduce letters and words as part of a whole piece of writing, which will enhance the abilities of the children in your class and their enjoyment of language. The chapter ends with advice on two additional activities, emergent writing and drawing, that will enhance children's physical experience with writing as well as their enjoyment. Start these activities at the beginning of the year and work on them in parallel with the letter activities in chapter 3.

The first set of activities are sight-recognition vocabulary (SRV) activities, meaning they focus on introducing words and letters visually. These activities are as follows:

1. Fill in the Word
2. Teddy's Word Review
3. Twister Word Review
4. Word Wall
5. Personal Flash Cards
6. Fill in the Initial Consonant
7. Word Book

The second set of activities are ideas to use throughout the year to encourage the children to physically enjoy the act of writing and to encourage personal identification with this act.

1. Emergent Writing
2. Drawing

The Activity Process

In our room, we rotate activities. After circle time spent as a class, which on sound day includes the Big Event (see page 10), we split into three groups. One group comes to the teacher at the writing table, one group goes to the adult at the craft table, and the third group can choose any of the open centers, such as the home area, painting, sand table, construction, toys, or the independent sound-related creative activity center, suggestions for which are included with each sound in chapter 3.

As the morning progresses, each child rotates around the room so that everybody has a turn to write, create a craft, and have time for free play. There are usually six to eight children at the craft table, at the writing table, or in the choosing area at any one time. Our days cover different areas, but the structure of rotation remains the same. (The children do not always start in the same group each day.)

1. **Journals:** On one day, we focus on journals and a craft. The children all relate their news at circle time, then tell it individually to me when it is their turn to come to the writing table. As described throughout this chapter, I help the child write her sentence. Every child has her own journal, so it is just like a personal diary. For this reason, I like to use a sturdy purchased bound book so that the children can look back at some of their earlier adventures. A book with no lines is preferable to lined, because the child's drawing is such an important part of the news she writes. While I work with one particular child, the other children at the table are drawing their pictures and maybe tracing over their names.

2. **Theme:** On another day, we work on our topic or theme. For instance, if our unit is nursery rhymes, we may spend circle time on this day introducing "Twinkle, Twinkle Little Star." The

children will then split up to go to their first tables. The children at the craft table may be making a sparkly star. At the writing table, each child relates her own individual sentence about the topic covered that morning. I help the child write the sentence using SRV and initial consonants, as described in this chapter, where relevant for that child. The writing and drawing are later mounted on construction paper, and each child's work is then collated in her own book about the whole theme. For instance, at the end of six weeks, each child will be able to take home her very own book full of her very own work on nursery rhymes.

3. **Sound work:** On a third day, we work on the sound of the week plus a related craft, as described fully in chapter 3 (see page 20).

4. **Number work:** On a fourth day, we work on numbers plus a related craft.

5. **Flexible day:** I try to leave one day each week, preferably Friday, flexible for field trips, special science sessions, book making, and catching up. In this way, I try to make sure that all the different areas covered reinforce each other, while ensuring that every day, all the children are practicing a valuable variety of skills.

Sight-Recognition Vocabulary (SRV) Activities

Children successfully discover and learn about the written word in different ways. Some favor phonics, some favor a whole-language reading approach, and some need a mixture. We have to make sure we provide for every need. For this reason, every week I introduce one sight-recognition word to help the children build up a sight-recognition vocabulary (SRV). I highly recommend that you read through this section before beginning any of these activities with your class because many of them are best done almost simultaneously, rather than one after the other.

Fill in the Word
Materials
- ✔ blank flash cards
- ✔ pocket chart with at least 20 pockets (available at educational supply stores)
- ✔ marker
- ✔ pencil for each child
- ✔ each child's journal (as described on page 201)

Preparation
1. Using a marker, prepare flash cards for the first words you will introduce to the class. These words should include I, a, to, am, is, it, in, the, my, went, and, on, me, he, she, we, was, saw, at, of, look, have, came, had, Mom, and Dad.

2. As you introduce words, display the words in the pocket chart, so they are available and accessible when needed.

Directions

1. Introduce one sight word each journal day during circle time, so that you introduce one new word each week. The first word to introduce is "I."

2. At the writing table, ask each child about his individual news. The children in the group will listen to each other's news as they take turns around the table.

3. As each child finishes, write his sentence, while repeating it aloud, leaving blanks for that child to fill in. (This is the time to adapt the sentence to fit on the page, shortening it as necessary for children who talk at length.) If a child went swimming, for example, lightly write with pencil or highlighter, "___ went swimming," putting a dash where the SRV word (in this case "I") should go.

4. When every child at the table has related his news, hand out the journals and coloring pencils so the group can draw their pictures and also trace over the words written in highlighter, while you work with one child at a time.

5. Read the sentence, pointing to each individual word, and tell the child that the word "I" is missing.

6. Have the needed SRV card (the card with "I" on it) on hand. It may be necessary to show it to the child; or you could just leave it lying nearby on the table for the child to find, setting up another achievement.

7. Work on how comfortable the child is with the word. Never risk his not knowing what goes in the gap.

8. After two or three weeks, when you have introduced two or three words, offer a choice of two word cards to fill the gap in the news. One of the cards will be the word the child needs, and the other will be a word that has been introduced that looks very different from the word he is seeking. If the child hesitates too long or looks worried, give clues, maybe even moving the correct card a little.

Helping children fill in words and consonants is fun for both teacher and child.

Making the Most of the Fill-in-the-Word Activity

You and the children can continue inserting SRV words into individual news throughout the year. Some children may only be comfortable within a limited vocabulary. Be aware of how much each child can take in. The words a child doesn't master can be offered as the alternatives when two word cards are offered. Keep on gently trying to introduce the next target word. Following are some more tips for making the most of this activity.

- **Reading and writing are different skills.** There will be a difference in the words a child can read and the words a child can write. Expect children to write words only within their fine-motor-skills capability. Some three-year-olds may only be able to write a six-inch-tall "I" or "to" after six months. That's fine. They can probably read many more words, but you should always head for a successful experience at this tender age, so don't push a child to write too many words too soon.

  For example, the word "my" is relatively easy for a child to recognize and will be one of the first words covered on the SRV list; however, the letter "y" is notoriously difficult to reproduce for a child who is just getting the feel of making a deliberate shape with his pencil. The "m" is fun to write. Just be content to ask for the initial consonant sound (see the Fill-in-the-Initial-Consonant activity on page 209) until the child's pencil control and ability to concentrate are developed enough for him to cope successfully. Do not expect every child to progress at the same rate. Feel your way.

- **The sentence belongs to the child.** Constantly review the whole sentence, pointing to every word, but go at the child's pace. He has dictated the sentence to you. It is his sentence and the aim is for him to keep ownership. Try not to interrupt him while he is reading the sentence; go with his flow and read along so he does not feel as if he is being corrected. We do not want to take his sentence away and make it our own. That would be a definite way for the child to lose interest.

- **Try to keep the sentence short.** A short sentence will be much easier for the child to remember and consequently easier to build and to read back. If she rambles on at great length, use the size of the page as an excuse to shorten what she says. Suggest that she write the rest of what she has to say later when she draws her picture. (Working on half-lined, half-blank paper is ideal because it helps keep the sentence short and the child's picture of the story and her written version of the story on the same page.) This will be an opportunity for the children who prefer emergent writing (the act of free-writing without consciously creating words) to shine as they can write whatever they want when drawing the picture.

- **Review frequently.** Try to review the words already introduced at frequent intervals. I always go over our SRV words on Monday morning, just before I introduce the new word for that week. We have our main journal-writing session on Monday morning also, so after our review, we move straight into an activity where we can use our words in their full and glorious meaning.

   I also go over the list one more time on Fridays before the children go home for the weekend. This is the time I issue the explicit instructions to *tell somebody!* if they see any of these words at any time over the weekend.

- **Try to make the review times as much fun as possible.** There are so many games you can play without preparation, apart from having your word cards on hand. Try Teddy's Word Review and the Twister Word Review (both below) as starting points.

Teddy's Word Review

For this review game, all you need are your SRV flash cards, a Teddy bear (or puppet), and a bag (or other container for the cards). This game is simple,

but the children love it. It's nice to use this at lining-up time. As the child puts his last word card in the bag (or even back on the pocket chart), he can go and join the line.

1. First, have the Teddy (or puppet) distribute the cards to the children, saying the words as they are given out. Be sure to give cards that you expect the child to be able to read; this game is all about feeling good about reading.

2. Teddy can then whisper to you that he needs a certain word to go in his bag. Ask the class who has that word. Whoever has that word puts it in Teddy's bag. This continues until all cards are reviewed and put away.

Twister Word Review

Another quick and easy way to review the SRV vocabulary and get in a little physical exercise is this Twister-inspired game. This is a great activity to help with left and right.

1. Scatter a selection of word cards that you've already introduced on the floor (none too far from others). You may want to tape the word cards to the floor to prevent slipping.

2. Pick out children one at a time to come out and follow your instructions. For example, "Put your left leg on 'and.' Put your right arm on 'to.' Put your nose on 'went.'"

Word Wall

As a child masters a word, record it on her word wall. (Photocopy or re-create the word wall pattern on page 207 for each child in your class.) Try to write each word in a different color or have the child write her own word. The word wall is an invaluable reference point and the first step toward creating an individual word book. (See page 212 for more information about the word book.) Record only one word at a time so the child has a chance to really familiarize herself with her own word bank. She should feel totally in control of all the words on her word wall.

Ultimately, the word wall will take the place of offering cards for SRV words, because the children will be able to find those particular words all by themselves on their word walls. All they will need is your guidance to remind them where they are in their sentences.

The children keep their word walls in their journals. Once they progress to a word book, they will keep their word walls there.

Personal Flash Cards

In addition to the class SRV cards you keep in the pocket chart, individual flash cards will provide further opportunity for practice, review, and mastery of new words.

Materials

✔ 2" x 3" flash cards

✔ pen or marker

✔ sealable bag or small box for each child

Preparation

Prepare a bag or small box for each child by writing each child's name on it with marker. Alternatively, you could make this into an art project, with each child decorating his bag or box.

Directions

1. **Introduce a word:** When you introduce a word, give each child to whom it will be meaningful a flash card with that word written on it. Write the word on the card with each individual child sitting next to you. Then you can chat about the word. The children can collect these personal flash cards in their own bags or boxes. You can also create and hand out a flash card when a new, frequently used word is introduced in a child's reading book, or it can go along with a new word on a child's word wall.

> **TiP**
>
> Be sensitive to how many new words you are giving to each individual child. The children should be trying to master only a couple of new words at most at any one time. Always keep the new words with the child's mastered words in the bag or box; to the child, this is a physical recognition of achievement.

_____ can spell
all these words

2. **Practice new words:** Parents can go through the flash cards every night if they have time. Many of our frequently used words have to be learned by rote, and getting the parents involved is very effective. Flash cards can be used inventively, especially at home where there is a little more one-on-one time. Suggest to parents that they try any of the following ideas:

- Play word bingo, with cards that use the SRV vocabulary words.
- See who can collect the biggest pile of correctly read word cards (a little bit of pretending is in order for this one so that the child feels she can compete with the parent for number of cards).
- Make funny sentence strips on the floor using the cards and other words. The parent can put out cards with other words on the floor, leaving it up to the child to fill in the gaps with her SRV cards. The sentences don't have to make sense!

3. **Work with troublesome words:** There will be some words that a child will struggle with, no matter how many times you flash that card around. To overcome this, ask the child to think of a sentence or phrase containing that word. Write it on the back of the card with the flash-card word underlined. Then draw a little picture to go with the phrase. (The child may like to draw her own picture.) Next time that card comes around and you see that blank look in those eyes, give a quick flash of the back of the card. You will be amazed at how the connections are made in the brain. Most times the child will recall the phrase she composed. The meaning has been returned to the word and it will be just a matter of time before the child does not need the prompt of the back of the card and can even recognize the word in other settings.

When to Stop Using the Flash Cards

The use of personal flash cards will gradually diminish as the child's prowess at reading improves. There is a point when a child becomes adept at building consonant-vowel-consonant words and has built a pleasing sight-recognition vocabulary. He can understand how to work out new words from context or other cues, and suddenly the mastery is there. He will have all the tools and confidence that he needs to move on to other word patterns, a wider vocabulary, and stories with a real plot. The need to make flash cards will be a thing of the past. Let the child keep his personal flash cards. They are an important building block for him, and I find that the children do become attached to their own cards.

Fill in the Initial Consonant

Learning how to fill in initial consonants is an important step in learning to write entire words and complete sentences.

This activity requires similar materials and preparation as Fill in the Word, on page 202, and can be done in parallel to that activity. As the children are filling in words in their individual news, they can also fill in initial consonants in that same news, using the letters they will be learning throughout the year (through the activities described in chapter 3).

Materials

- ✔ 2" x 3" flash cards
- ✔ marker
- ✔ pencil for each child
- ✔ each child's journal (as described on page 201)

Preparation

Using a marker, prepare flash cards for each letter. Alternatively, you could use premade letters. I have a set of Montessori sandpaper letters on little boards in my room. Do not use the feely phonic letters for this activity because they are associated with learning the sound of each letter, as described in chapter 3. Never stop the children from using the feely letters for clues, however, as they may still be relating the sound to the experience, and that is great.

Directions

1. When writing a child's news or a thematic sentence, as well as when leaving gaps for known SRV words, leave gaps, as the child is ready, for known initial consonants (those you are introducing throughout the year using the activities in chapter 3). For example, write "I went _wimming" after the children have learned "s." Write the remainder of the sentence with light pencil or highlighter for each child to write over.

2. Offer flash cards of two letters you have already introduced, which look as different as possible, as a choice. This is why I usually introduce "s" and "t" first; they look so different.

TiP

Some words do not have very clear initial consonants but do have clearer final consonants. Maybe the initial consonant is a sound not yet covered and the final consonant is a wonderfully clear "t." If the child is comfortable with the idea of filling in missing sounds, you can use final consonants. Just work the same way except with the emphasis on the ending sound. Wait on this activity until the child demonstrates an understanding of how the symbols represent sounds.

comfortable with her use of sounds, start offering two similar letters such as "b" and "d" or "n" and "m." Only offer letters to which the child has been introduced; otherwise, you will have a very confused face looking back at you, and it's not our intention to confuse the child.

5. As the children get increasingly confident with the recognition and use of the letters, they may not need the prop of the cards, and they will tell you. They can continue the Fill-in-the-Initial-Consonant activity without the aid of the cards.

3. Always have the child say the word aloud when she is looking for an initial sound. For example:

> **Teacher:** "I went swimming. Say swimming to me."
> **Child:** "Swimming."
> **Teacher:** "Swimming. What sound comes first? S-s-s-swimming."
> **Child:** "S-s-s-swimming. S-s-s-s-s!"
> **Teacher** (offering two letters): "S-s-s-s. Which is s-s-s-s?"
> The child chooses.
> **Teacher** (pointing to the words as she reads): "I . . . went . . . s-s-s-swimming. Can you put in the s-s-s on swimming?"

4. Once the child can choose correctly between two very different letters and is generally

Helping Children Write Their Names

Every child wants to write her own name, but first a child must recognize her own name, see it in various contexts, become actively involved in recognizing it among other names, associate her name with work she's proud of, and ultimately practice tracing and writing her name daily.

- **Name Labels:** There are opportunities all over the classroom for children to see their names displayed in blazing glory so that they can proudly pick out their own name in a quiet moment. Books can give you many ideas for creating attractive seasonal bulletin boards with a place for every child's name and even her photograph. Coat pegs, cubbies, cots, and lunch seats should all be clearly labeled with attractive name tags. These all help with name recognition.

- **Name Tags:** Labels are generally in the same place every day, so the child is learning a routine and may not be paying much attention to the name after a short amount of time. For this reason, it is a good idea to introduce name tags that the children need to find so that they actively must recognize their own names among the distraction of many other names.

  I have a stand-up plywood tree in my classroom that is covered with a brown felt trunk and green felt leaves. At the bottom of the tree is a basket containing red foam cut-out apples. Each apple carries the name of one child. On the back of the apple is a piece of rough Velcro. Each morning when the child enters the classroom, she finds her apple in the basket and puts it on the tree. You can use a variation of this idea for anything that a child has completed during the school day. When she has finished her snack, for instance, she can find the Teddy with her name on it and stick it to the picnic tablecloth board. The possibilities are endless, and these are, of course, physical activities that back up a cognitive learning experience.

- **Names on Display:** The best way for a child to see her name around the room is when it is displayed with her work pinned on the wall for the world to see. So many children will drag their moms and dads into the classroom to see their pictures on the wall. I remember the feeling of worthiness and pride even now whenever my work was displayed. Resist the temptation to send the children's creations home each day. Too many are crushed during the hustle of the carpool. Keep some back so that the children can enjoy looking at them in the classroom. Flaunt these precious pieces by displaying them, and make sure that the artists' names are there for all to admire. Remember to be diplomatic and have at least one creation from each child very clearly labeled. It will help you, and it will help the children.

- **Tracing Practice:** Have each child write her own name in some form every single day. For instance, when she is writing news, her name needs to be on the page. Initially, you will need to write it in highlighter or in faint pencil for the child to write over. To start with, the children will produce squiggles and spidery lines. As writing one's name is almost a Pavlovian process, you can help move the child's arm to help her form the letters. The tracing-over stage usually lasts a long time, but it is better to be overprepared.

  You can encourage progress by leaving out certain sounds in the name for the child to fill in, if she is at that stage. You may even want to take turns with the child, writing one letter each, especially if it is a long name.

- **Writing Practice:** When tracing over her name is becoming too easy, suggest that she take a turn on her own. Just happen to have her name card lying on the desk nearby, just in case, until the child gradually takes complete ownership. Following are some more ideas for helping children practice writing their names:

  - Have laminated individual name cards with erasable marker pens so that the child can practice writing her name repeatedly.

  - Have individual busy books of blank pages purely for the purpose of writing the child's own name. The child can write her name in any way she chooses—upside down, in beautiful colors, in big writing, or in small writing.

  - Have craft activities during which the child has to "produce" her own name. Celebrate those names in the fingerpaint tray, with glitter glued on paper, and created from collage materials—it all works, it is all multisensory, and it does make a fun time out of what can be a basic yet sometimes difficult activity, especially if your name is Esmerelda Ernestine!

Word Book

A word book is a personal dictionary, with a page for each letter of the alphabet, in which each child writes in the words he learns. In our class, it has become a big deal to get a word book. I never intended it to be that way. The children themselves recognize the excitement and value of being able to read and write.

You should give children a word book when they know their sounds and have mastered several words in their sight-recognition vocabulary. You can tell when a child is comfortable with the structure of a sentence. You will probably have already just put out his word wall when he needed to find an SRV word and left him to it, knowing that he can run his finger over the wall and find the word he needs. Give children a word book only if they are comfortable with the use of initial consonant sounds. This, after all, is how they are going to use the book.

I use the word "comfortable" deliberately. The gradual introduction of each progressive step on the road to reading and writing should be enjoyable, stress free, and very, very comfortable. The comfort can be provided by overpreparation in the stage before. Just because a child has picked out a couple of initial consonant sounds correctly does not necessarily mean he has mastered that stage comfortably enough to move on. Let him really enjoy his achievement. Let him be thoroughly successful and feel the confidence that follows the realization, "I can do that." Think of how the brain works and the process of myelination to understand why we need to consolidate a child's newly acquired skills (see page 4 for more information on this process) before moving into new areas. We know from our own experience that when we feel we are good at a particular task, we are more likely to want to practice, and we will shy away from the tasks at which we feel inadequate. Let the early reading skills be overpracticed so that when you introduce the next step, the child is more than ready.

The biggest obstacle to taking things slowly is parental pressure. Once particular parents see that certain children in the room have word books and their child does not, they want to know the criteria for having a word book. If they can see that their child has apparently covered everything on the "checklist," they may feel their child is being denied. It is difficult to describe overpreparation to a competitive parent, but a reference to Piaget may be helpful (see the chart on page 3). Children need to master each stage of development before going on to the next stage; otherwise there will be gaps. These gaps can later be filled with uncertainty and fear. It is our job to ensure that there are no gaps in a child's understanding of reading and writing.

The idea of introducing the word book when the child is at the next stage of readiness is that it plays a very large role in the introduction of totally independent writing. Up until now, even though the child has dictated the sentence, and it is his sentence, the teacher has been providing the skeleton for the writing.

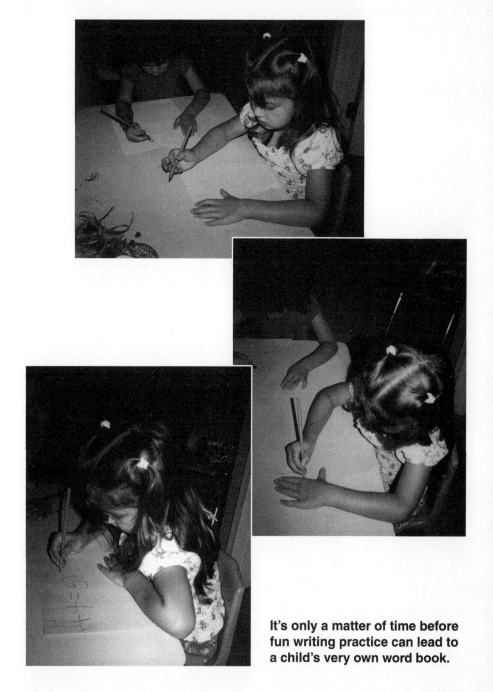

It's only a matter of time before fun writing practice can lead to a child's very own word book.

213

For instance, a child at the stage of word-book readiness who wants to write, "I went to see my grandma," will have this framework written in his book by the teacher: "_ _____ __ _ee __ _randma" (I went to s__ my g_____). The child would feel happy about finding the SRVs on his word wall with hardly any help, and could also happily put in the initial consonant sounds for "see" and "grandma."

When a child uses a word book, he may choose not to have you put in those lines, spaces, and words. You will set him up with everything he needs before he starts writing. But his writing will be independent, straight into the book with no lines or words from you, and no copying. How does he accomplish that? As he is overprepared, he can use a variety of strategies learned from previous SRV activities as well as from the activities in chapter 3.

Materials

- ✔ a notebook for each child with at least 26 pages
- ✔ markers
- ✔ pencil for each child

TiP

Instead of buying a notebook, you could make each child's word book by binding together 26 pieces of plain paper or construction paper.

Preparation

1. Prepare each word book by making a page for each letter, writing the lowercase letter at the top. Each page should have only one letter as a header, and the letters should be in alphabetical order.

2. If you have time, draw a picture on each page, such as an apple for "a" and a balloon for "b." You could also use stamps or stickers of something beginning with each letter instead of drawings. This is not essential, because by the time the child reaches the stage of having a word book, she should know all her sounds. It just adds to the fun of the book.

Directions

1. First, as with Fill in the Word and Fill in the Initial Consonant, have the child dictate her news to you. Say the sentence aloud and then figure out which words the child cannot spell, which are "new words today." In the example above, our words are "see" and "grandma."

2. Starting with one word, such as "see," ask the child to say the word, putting emphasis on the first sound.

3. Ask the child what sound the word begins with. She should say "s-s-s-s."

4. Ask, "Where can you find 's-s-s-s' in your word book?" This is where the alphabet song comes into its own. Sing the alphabet song, pointing to each page as you sing the corresponding letter.

5. When you arrive at the right sound, you may want to give the child a couple of clues as to how the word is built up after the first sound. You can often use this as an excellent opportunity to describe the formation of different letter patterns. For "see," I would let the child write "s" and then describe how "ee" works, drawing pictures of bees and trees. Ultimately, try to have the child write as much of the word as possible; it will be more meaningful that way.

6. "Grandma" can be built up by gently leading a child, using what she knows, and using whatever cues she needs, such as going back to offer a choice between two word cards or sound cards. Emphasis on sound will help the child build up "g" and "r." Ask the child about the little word she can hear tucked in the middle of the big word: "and."

7. If you follow a child's rate of progress, being careful to keep her confidence level high, the transition to independent writing should be painless. You will be amazed at how the child takes the lead. Many children will still want you to be sitting right next to them as they build a sentence independently, but they will tell you every move they are making, probably glancing toward you for your confirmation that what they are doing is correct. The child will tell you that she can get started on her own.

TiP

Sometimes, if the child has worked really hard already or is having a tired day, if the word is devoid of any regular patterns, or if we just need to get that news written, you can write the word in the word book for the child. If you are able to draw the simplest stick person sketch next to it, the child will be more likely to find the word the next time he needs it. Remember, we are fostering confidence and are not out to trick these children or put any pressure on them. If they are reluctant to join you at this stage of writing, ease back on what you are asking them to figure out. Give them a little surge of success to make them feel wonderful about what they can do at journal time by asking them to do something you know they already know how to do.

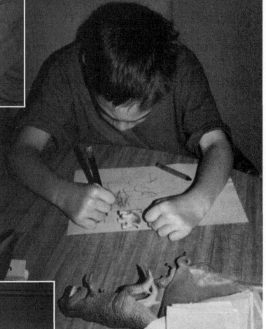

Emergent Writing

Most people know emergent writing as the squiggles and zigzags usually produced as a result of role-play games when the children are pretending to be adults, copying not only their clothes and mannerisms, but also their writing. This can be a most valuable step in the child's understanding of what writing is all about in this world of communication, and it is more important to some children than to others.

It is important to enable every child to have the chance to practice emergent writing if he wishes to do so. In every classroom, there should be some sort of free-writing table where children can scribble, loop, and zigzag, writing in the "grown-up" way to their hearts' content. It should be equipped with pencils, paper, envelopes, and forms just waiting to be filled in. If you are able to make this area into a post office or a bank with "stamps," toy eyeglasses, and an ink stamp, so much the better. Likewise, if there is a pretend hospital station in your room, make sure there is a clipboard and pencil for "writing" prescriptions and taking notes. It will all add to the joy of writing.

As children understand more and more about writing, watch their emergent writing change and develop as they begin to include more real letters and even words! The words are usually more luck than judgment, but what a display of motivation to write for fun. Let's encourage such enthusiasm by providing a variety of novel centers where children can, without inhibitions, enjoy writing just for fun.

The physical act of writing, in and of itself, can be enjoyable and enriching for children.

Two Learning Personalities

I have found that some students who are ready to progress early steam straight on ahead and will be the first to attempt independent writing. Before you know it, they present you with a finished piece of writing. There will probably be many spelling mistakes, but now is not the time for correction. Now is the time for enjoying the recording of an adventure in writing.

One of my favorite spellings, created by five-year-old Benjamin, was "camow" for "camel." Say it aloud and you will hear "camow." There was no sense in correcting that; the only "achievement" would have been to make Benjamin feel a little more cautious and hesitant next time we had a writing session. Our whole purpose is to make sure a child feels happy and motivated where writing is concerned. Benjamin had used the limited skills he had mastered and he had used them very effectively.

Other students will favor accuracy over speed. They tend to want to check that their work is absolutely correct. This works well when you ensure first that the child either knows or can easily find all the sounds and words that she needs before she starts writing. Then she has the resources she needs to check her work to her heart's content.

Drawing

There are two cardinal rules for helping a child with her drawing: First, never interfere with or draw on a child's picture or craft. This is because it will no longer be the child's creation, and art and craft at any stage should be a personal expression. Even if the child paints a red blob day after day, it is her red blob. It means something to her, because that is what she wanted to do. Helping with a class craft project is fine—maybe helping with scissor control, for example—but taking over and doing for the child is not. The parents know that the adults in the room can cut and glue, and they do not want to display the teacher's work on their refrigerators. They want to display what their child did, even if she managed only one scrap of pink tissue in the corner. There is no value in teacher-made projects.

The second rule is to never say, "What is it?" This shows the child that you don't recognize what he is drawing, which can be very hurtful. (You may not initially recognize what he has drawn, but that is beside the point.) We, of course, want the child to be proud of himself and to feel good about what he is doing. On a similar note, don't risk upsetting the child by saying, "I love your picture of the big red boat," only to have him reply, "It's my mommy."

If you want to comment, play it safe by making enthusiastic noises and then asking the child to tell you about his picture. If he looks at you as if you've dropped out of the sky, with a glance that tells you that there is absolutely no reason why he should have to tell you about his purple blob because surely it is obvious to the whole world what it is, then home in on one particular section. Ask exactly what is going on in that bright red section that looks so exciting.

If all else fails, ask the child what he is going to call his picture. We do a lot of junk modeling in our class (that is, creating art out of whatever collage treasures we have on hand, such as small boxes, fabric and paper scraps, onion bag netting, cardboard tubes, and so forth). The children are usually asked to name their creations so they can be labeled for display.

By helping and encouraging a child with her drawing, you also indirectly help that child with learning to write.

We have some wonderful names. One very elaborate toilet-paper-tube and egg-box construction was called the "Zondra."

Remember that children may not know what they are going to draw when they begin drawing. They may just be drawing for the physical sensation. They may be watching how the colors work and mix. Don't always expect the child to have some topic to tell you about. If he is just experiencing the medium he is using, this is a wonderful gift. Celebrate the fun and beauty of what that child is doing without expecting him to create a form.

The picture that goes with a journal entry can be a more accurate representation. Drawing, like writing, is another method of relating a story or reliving an event. By helping and encouraging a child with her drawing, you also indirectly help that child with learning to write. If a child is able to add a few more details to her drawing through a casual conversation about what is happening, she is usually thrilled with the result.

In their journals, the children will almost always want to draw what they have written about. Surround the experience with positive anticipation, making comments like "I can't wait to see the picture of you swimming in the pool." Then, when the child presents you with a blob or a squiggle, you can ask some pointed questions: "What color was your swimming suit?" "Where was Mom?" "Was the sun shining?" "Did your hair get wet?"

If your questions flow as if you are having a casual conversation, it will then seem as if it is the child's idea to add any extra features, which is far preferable to being prompted by the teacher. You'll be amazed by how much this helps with picture construction and pencil control. Having somebody show so much positive interest in his picture without being judgmental has to raise a child's confidence also.

Generally, try to be sensitive as to whether the child's drawing is for the experience or for the record, as in a journal. Remember that, as always, it is the process rather than the product that is of utmost importance. 🍎

Bibliography

Ahlberg, J., and A. Ahlberg. 1980. *Funnybones*. New York: Mulberry Books

Ahlberg, A., and A. Amstutz. 1990. *The Pet Shop*. Funnybones series. New York: Greenwillow Books.

Arnold, T. 1997. *Huggly Gets Dressed*. New York: Scholastic.

Asch, F. 1990. *Skyfire*. New York: Scholastic.

Beck, A. 2001. *Elliot Digs for Treasure*. Tonawanda, N.Y.: Kids Can Press.

Benjamin, C. 1999. *Footprints in the Sand*. New York: Scholastic.

Brett, J. 1997. *The Hat*. New York: Scholastic.

Bridwell, N. 1985. *Clifford: The Big Red Dog*. New York: Scholastic.

———. 1997. *Clifford's First Valentine's Day*. New York: Scholastic.

Brown, M. W. 1991. *Goodnight Moon*. New York: HarperCollins.

Brumbeau, J., and G. de Marcken. 2000. *The Quiltmaker's Gift*. Duluth, Minn.: Pfeiffer-Hamilton.

Cannon, J. 1993. *Stellaluna*. New York: Scholastic.

Capucilli, A. S. 2000. *Inside a Zoo in the City*. New York: Scholastic.

Carle, E. 2001. *Today Is Monday*. New York: Philomel Books.

———. 1994. *The Very Hungry Caterpillar*. New York: Philomel Books.

———. 1999. *The Very Lonely Firefly*. New York: Philomel Books.

———. 1990. *The Very Quiet Cricket*. New York: Scholastic.

Child, D. 1993. *Psychology and the Teacher*. London; New York: Cassell.

Chugani, H. T. 1991. "Imaging Human Brain Development with Positron Emission Tomography." *Journal of Nuclear Medicine* 32, 1:23–26.

Craig, J. 1998. *Little Groundhog's Shadow*. Mahwah, N. J.: Troll.

Csikszentmihalyi, M. 1990. *Flow: The Psychology of Optimal Experience*. New York: Harper & Row.

Dussling, J. 1995. *In a Dark, Dark House*. New York: Scholastic.

Edwards, R. 1999. *Copy Me, Copycat*. New York: Scholastic.

Ehlert, L. 1999. *Red Leaf, Yellow Leaf*. New York: Scholastic.

Fleming, D. 1999. *Mama Cat Has Three Kittens*. New York: Scholastic.

———. 1997. *Time to Sleep*. New York: Scholastic.

Graham-Barber, L. 1998. *Say Boo!* New York: Scholastic.

Gruber, S. 1985. *The Monster Under My Bed*. Mahwah, N.J.: Troll.

Hall, Z. 1999. *It's Pumpkin Time!* New York: Scholastic.

Henkes, K. 2001. *Wemberly Worried*. New York: Scholastic.

Hoberman, M. A. 2000. *Eensy Weensy Spider*. New York: Scholastic.

Hubbard, P. 1996. *My Crayons Talk*. New York: Scholastic.

Jensen, E. 1998. *Teaching with the Brain in Mind*. Alexandria, Va.: ASCD.

Jeram, A. 2000. *Bunny, My Honey*. New York: Scholastic.

Kennedy, K. 2002. *Pirate Pete*. New York: Harry N. Abrams.

Kotulak, R. 1996. *Inside the Brain*. Kansas City, Mo.: Andrews and McMeel.

McBratney, S. 1996. *Guess How Much I Love You.* Cambridge, Mass.: Candlewick Press.

McGeorge, C. W. 1997. *Boomer's Big Day.* New York: Scholastic.

———. 1996. *Boomer Goes to School.* New York: Scholastic.

Marzollo, J. 1997. *I Am an Apple.* New York: Scholastic.

Morris, A. 1989. *Bread, Bread, Bread.* New York: Mulberry Books.

Murphy, J. 1997. *A Piece of Cake.* Cambridge, Mass.: Candlewick Press.

———. 1993. *A Quiet Night In.* Cambridge, Mass: Candlewick Press.

Nicoll, H., and J. Pieńkowski. 1975. *Mog's Lunch Box.* London: Puffin.

Numeroff, L. J. 1992. *If You Give a Moose a Muffin.* New York: Scholastic.

———. 1999. *If You Give a Pig a Pancake.* New York: Scholastic.

Parker, V. 1996. *Bearobics.* New York: Scholastic.

Penn, A. 1998. *The Kissing Hand.* New York: Scholastic.

Pinkwater, D. M. 1993. *The Big Orange Splot.* New York: Scholastic.

Piper, W. 1998. *The Little Engine That Could.* New York: Dutton.

Rauscher, F. H., G. L. Shaw, L. J. Levine, K. N. Ky, and E. L. Wright. 1993. "Music and Spatial Task Performance." *Nature* 365:611.

Rockwell, A. 2002. *Valentine's Day.* New York: Scholastic.

Schwartz, B. A. 2000. *What Makes a Rainbow?* Santa Monica, Calif.: Intervisual Books.

Sendak, M. 1992. *Where the Wild Things Are.* New York: Harper Festival.

Senisi, E. B. 2001. *Fall Changes.* New York: Scholastic.

Siomades, L. 2000. *Three Little Kittens.* New York: Scholastic.

Spier, P. 1989. *Oh, Were They Ever Happy.* New York: Doubleday.

Stoddard, S. 1997. *Turtle Time.* New York: Houghton Mifflin.

Ward, C. 1988. *Cookie's Week.* New York: Scholastic.

Weeks, S. 1998. *Mrs. McNosh Hangs Up Her Wash.* New York: Scholastic.

Wells, R. 1997. *Max's Dragon Shirt.* New York: Scholastic.

Williams, N. 1969. *Child Development.* London: Heinemann.

About the Author

For the last 20 years, Janet Chambers has taught reading and writing to children of all ages first in the United Kingdom and more recently in Alabama.

One of Janet's first jobs as a newly qualified teacher was working with at-risk adolescents who already had many years of negative literacy experiences behind them. Determined to turn this around, Janet devised innovative hands-on learning experiences to get the students engaged in reading and writing. Her success with these students quickly convinced Janet of the value of teaching literacy through the senses. Using the same approach, Janet has developed a rich program for introducing the tools of literacy to young children *before* they learn that reading is "hard," "boring," or "for other people." Currently using her multi-sensory technique in a preschool, Janet is delighted to report that most of her students enter kindergarten already able to read and write and bubbling with enthusiasm for their next adventures in learning.

Index